LITERARY INFLUENCES IN COLONIAL NEWSPAPERS, 1704-1750:

LITERARY INFLUENCES IN COLONIAL NEWSPAPERS, 1704-1750:

Elizabeth Christine Cook

www.General-Books.net

Publication Data:

Title: Literary influences in colonial newspapers, 1704-1750
Author: Elizabeth Christine Cook
General Books publication date: 2010
Original publication date: 1912
Original Publisher: Columbia University Press
Subject:
American newspapers
American literature
History / General
Language Arts Disciplines / Journalism
Law / General
Law / International
Literary Criticism / American / General

CONTENTS

1

SECTION 1

   PREFACE
   The following study aims to give a fairly comprehensive survey of the literary
contributions in colonial newspapers from 1704 to 1750. Aside from the well-known
essays of Benjamin Franklin in *The New England Courant* and in *The Pennsylvania
Gazette,* the literary material in the colonial weeklies has been hitherto neglected.

Especially is this true of the Southern papers. Quotations of some length from the essays and verse published in colonial journals have therefore been considered advisable in the present work. In most instances the originals of these extracts are accessible only in the collections of Historical Societies, or in the files of some especially favored library. The student who wishes to examine *The South Carolina Gazette,* for example, must go to the Charleston Library Society for the only file known to be extant.

All quotations in the present volume follow literally the punctuation, spelling, and capitalization of the originals, no matter how inconsistent these may seem to the modern reader. The only exceptions to this rule are a few corrections of obvious printers' errors, the retention of which would add needless confusion.

It is a pleasure to acknowledge the help received during the progress of this work. To the librarians of the Massachusetts Historical Society, of the Pennsylvania Historical Society, of the Maryland Historical Society, and of the Charleston Library Society, I am indebted for the permission to use rare files of colonial papers and documents. To Mr. Wilberforce Eames of the New York Public Library I am indebted for much bibliographical information. My hearty thanks are especially due to Mr. William G. Stanard, of the Virginia Historical Society, who has generously allowed me to draw upon his rare knowledge of colonial Virginia. I desire also to express my gratitude to my friend, Miss Anne Selleck, for her valuable aid in the research in the South.

To Professor Ashley H. Thorndike I am indebted for much helpful criticism. To Professor Charles S. Baldwin and to Professor John Erskine I am indebted for kindly advice. It is to Professor William P. Trent, however, that I am especially grateful for the criticism and encouragement by which the present work has advanced from its earliest stages.

April, 1912.

2

SECTION 2

LITERARY INFLUENCES IN COLONIAL NEWSPAPERS 1704-1750
  INTRODUCTION

Literature in the American colonies in the earlier half of the eighteenth century was produced chiefly by ecclesiastics and by extremely practical men of affairs. The New England divines were voluminous writers. Any catalogue or bibliography of ante-revolutionary publications shows a large proportion of sermons and theological treatises. Wherever such works have possessed literary or historical value, they have been fully analyzed by the literary historian. On the other hand, men of affairs like Benjamin Franklin and Colonel William Byrd, whose writings represent the overflow from varied activities, have also been studied. And these two classes of men produced all the well- known literature of the period. Men of letters did not exist.

Furthermore, the leaders of thought in the colonies were not anxious to promote the reading of secular literature. In the North they regarded it as a negligible matter compared with theological and religious instruction. In the South they were often friendly to the cause of pure letters, but their lives were occupied with the multitudinous details

of life on their estates. Only in some hour of relaxation could they think of literature. Benjamin Franklin was the only prominent man of the v period who deliberately attempted to spread the knowledge and love of literature among his countrymen. Even in his case, the attempt was rather his favorite avocation than his serious business.

Under such circumstances, ordinary families would know little or nothing of English secular literature. They would not hear of it in literary clubs. They would not see it on the shelves of public libraries, nor in the windows of book shops. Only from some remote, unlooked-for channel could it reach the majority of the people. Peddlers sometimes carried an odd volume of the *Spectator* or *Tom Jones* in their packs. A few secular books could now and then be bought for a song at an auction. Booksellers offered strange, miscellaneous collections for sale with increasing frequency after 1730. But a vastly more important channel of literary influence than all these was the weekly newspaper. And it will be our purpose to investigate the literature tucked away in the odd little papers from 1704 to 1750.

At first sight the ordinary news sheet of the earlier half of the eighteenth century would seem an unpromising vehicle for literature or literary influence of any kind. Small, ill-printed, often half illegible, a newspaper had a precarious existence at best. The printing press itself was regarded as a doiibtful investment, and the issue of a paper was beset with difficulty from first to last. Just be-

i

cause of certain complexities in the situation, however, the small colonial weekly was often forced to become literary or cease to exist.

It was a newspaper, and yet it had no news. Intercolonial communication was irregular and unsystematized during all the earlier years of our period. As to European news, the colonies received a few chance items usually about six months late. No ships from London arrived in colonial ports during the winter months. In fact, navigation was nearly at a standstill during January and February. Again and again occurs the item: " Custom-house, N. York. Inward Entries, None.'" A few vessels from North Carolina, Maryland, or at most, Jamaica, plied the coast even in winter. But it was usually spring before any considerable number even of these coasting craft set sail. By April, we find, in one New York paper,2 ships "entered inward" from Gibraltar, Lisbon, Boston, Rhode Island, St. Augustine, South Carolina, Bar- badoes, Curacoa, and Dover. It is clear that only a third of these could have brought foreign mails. A still more serious difficulty had to be met by the early colonial editor if he tried to write political editorials. Criticism of the government was not in order. Even a casual remark on some petty detail of the administration's policy meant an official inquiry usually followed by the discontinuance of the paper, while any open opposition to the governor soon led to a trial for libel. "As toanything like free discussion of the government, 'r says John Esten Cooke, in his history of Virginia,8 "that was not the fashion of the times, in newspapers." Thus the unfortunate editor could not fall back on political discussion if the week's news failed him. The Governor, his council and his assembly could not be safely mentioned, except in terms of formal and obsequious compliment. Whenever the Governor was in difficulties with his legislature, the newspapers gravely printed all the speeches, without editorial comment. Some papers habitually padded their columns with the complimentary addresses of the various Governors, on the convening of the provincial legislatures. This practice withstood for many years the ridicule of Franklin and other enterprising editors, before it was laughed out of existence.

1 See *The Neiv York Gazette,* No. 480, January 7, 1734-35, and No. 481, January 14,] 734-35. ' Ibid., No. 493, April 7, 1735.

Cut off, then, from news and politics, what was the editor to do? He might write homilies, and he sometimes did. But he knew that his readers were not suffering from any lack of religious and ethical instruction. His subscription list could hardly be kept up if he made his newspaper a mere auxiliary to the pulpit. The people must have something new and entertaining that they would pay for. Thus at length the first bold experiment of writing essays and verse on English models was tried. The result was a definite type of literary weekly which flourished in the colonies for twenty- five years or more.

The Addisonian essay is one of the easiest literary forms to imitate with a measure of success. Even school children can often compose tolerable additions to the *Spectator.* The model may be made to cover a wide variety of subjects, ranging from philosophical speculations, through anecdote and personal reminiscence to connected narrative. The opportunity for satire in character studies is also unlimited. When the colonial editor began to understand these possibilities, he saw that he had a mine of wealth from which he could draw at a moment's notice. If he had clever writers on his staff, who could sustain character and dialogue, so much the better. In any case there were always the traditional subjects of the essay to fall back upon.

Virginia. A History of the People. By John Esten Cooke. P.

If the local wits were momentarily at a loss, they searched their own book shelves for selections to reprint in the colonial press. Entire numbers of the *Spectator* were taken bodily into both Northern and Southern papers, and the editors had the pleasing assurance that Addison would be new to most of their readers. Other essays from later periodicals soon followed. Even plays were reprinted as serials. *The London Merchant, or The History of George Barnwell* appeared serially in *The New . England Weekly Journal* very shortly after its production in London. Dodsley's *Toy Shop, A Dramatick Satire* appeared in both *The Virginia Gazette* and *The South Carolina Gazette.* Scenes from Addison's *Cato* were always in order. Pope's *Essay on Man* and *The Dunciad,* Butler's *Hudibras,* and Dryden's satires were quoted extensively.

And all this reprinting led in turn to more imitation. The Southern papers often contained excellent original couplets. Charleston versifiers wrote prologues and epilogues to the well-known plays presented in Charleston theaters.

Thus in one way or another the colonial weekly became literary. The first page of any paper from 1721 to 1740 is likely to contain essays and verse. Sometimes the literary material fills an entire number. Over and over again "the present scarcity of news" is pleaded as the excuse for publishing "what . . . may be useful to Mankind in general."4 Benjamin Franklin deliberately entertained his readers with his own literary efforts, in preference to stale news from Hungary or Poland.

It would be strange if such literary efforts, becoming normal and constant, produced nothing memorable. In point of fact, not only was a considerable portion of Franklin's best work done for his newspaper, but it is quite probable that all the *J* secular literature of the period, with one or two exceptions, may be found in these early newspapers.

Certainly the newspapers were the centers of all the literary influences in the colonies before 1740. Of course the circumstances under which newspaper literature must be written offer great temptation to the hack writer. And there is a great deal of hack work in the colonial weeklies. But when all due allowances are made, there remains a body of writing worthy of investigation.

4 See *The South Carolina Gazette,* No. 112, March 20, 1735-36.

The present study is an attempt to describe the most typical literary efforts, and to analyze the most typical literary influences, in the weekly journals from 1704 to 1750. It will be impossible to include all the newspapers containing literary essays, since every news sheet in the colonies was occasionally literary. Wherever the essays tend to approach the stereotyped form of moral treatise, they will receive less emphasis. For example, the essays of Jeremiah Gridley in *The Weekly Rehearsal5* will not be treated individually. Nor will the development of any paper be traced after it became a news journal or a purely political journal.

One fact is already clear. Whatever the merit of these literary attempts in the colonial papers, they prove that the English literature of the period was known and imitated on this side of the Atlantic much earlier than has often been supposed.

"Vide infra, Bibliography, p. 271.

3

SECTION 3

CHAPTER I

The New England Coubant

The Boston News-Letter of Monday, April 24, 1704, is indeed, a pitiful enough affair.1 Half a sheet of "pot" paper, the first page filled with stale news about the Pretender and his Popish emissaries in Scotland, extracted from back numbers of the London *Flying Post,* and *The London Gazette,2* the second with a few marine notices and Boston scrap- gatherings – that is all.

In the next seventeen years, two more news-sheets3 were successfully established in the British Colonies, yet the little *Boston News-Letter* of 1704 is typical enough of every issue of any one of them up to 1721. A little more news crept in, it is true, as time went on; more advertisements filled out the last page, or, when these were lacking, the Addressesof the Governors of Massachusetts or Carolina to their Legislatures made a respectable padding.

1An attempt made in Boston, 1690, to set up a newspaper, *Publiok Occurrences,* will not be discussed here, since the authorities regarded it as a pamphlet, and suppressed it after the first number. A copy is extant in the London State Paper office, and has been reproduced several times, notably in *The New England Historical and Genealogical Register,* April, 1876, in Hudson's *Journalism in the United States,* p. 44, and in *Ten Fac-SimUe Reproductions, relating to Old Boston and its Neighborhood,* by Dr. S. A. Green.

'*The Flying Post,* Dec. 4, 1703. *The London Gazette,* Dee. 20, 1703.

'*The Boston Gazette,* Boston, Mass., first issue Monday, Dec. 21, 1719, and *The American Weekly Mercury,* Philadelphia, Penn., first issue, Tuesday, Dec. 22, 1719.

European news failed entirely during the long ice-bound winters.4 When at last, the belated ships arrived in port, they brought ill-assorted bundles of London papers with them for the colonial press, and we presently hear the news of three or four months before, "Taken from the Gazetts and other Pub- lick Prints8 of London, per Captain Barlow," or "per Captain Bourn,"6 "Captain Janverin,"7 "Captain Breed of Dublin," and many more, throughout the early colonial period. The result was a garbled mass of items. "They write from Rorne" of an earthquake or a coronation, follows a fire in Connecticut, with no rhyme nor reason to be discovered anywhere. But this very barrenness and utter dearth of timely news at length forced the editorial mind to turn inward, to become inventive; in brief, to attempt literature.

For fifteen years *The News-Letter* held an undisputed monopoly of dulness. John Campbell, the publisher, with true Scotch persistence, kept the paper going, no one knows quite how. Subscribers seldom paid, and many are the polite but urgent duns to be found in its pages. The fact probably was that his office of postmaster to the province and his trade of bookseller made *The News-Letter* apleasant little speculation of no vital importance to his fortunes. The postmaster naturally got the news at first hand, such as it was. Hence the combination postmaster-editor is seen over and over again in the colonies, and, indeed, the first outcome of a new post-office appointment was likely to be a new weekly. Such was the precise origin of *The Boston Gazette,* in 1719. Scarcely had William Brooker superseded Campbell in the post-office when the new paper appeared, ushered in by a warm dispute between the rivals as to whether Campbell had been removed from office or had resigned voluntarily ; Brooker, of course, insisting that Campbell's retirement had been forced upon him by the Deputy-Postmaster General.8 Even a quarrel like this, however, in which each gentleman politely calls the other a liar, is undeniably tedious. There is nothing to presage the literary development which soon took place.

1" If he does not Print a Sheet every other Week this Winter Time, he designs to make it up in the Spring, when Ships do arrive from Great Britain." *The Boston News-Letter,* No. 821, January 11, 1721. Editorial Notice.

8See *The Boston News-Letter,* December 5, 1720.

Ibid., April 13 and 17, 1721.

' Ibid., October 30, 1721.

James Franklin printed Brooker's new *Gazette.* But Brooker abandoned the enterprise, after forty numbers, to Philip Musgrave, who succeeded him as postmaster and promptly employed another printer, Samuel Kneeland. Kneeland will appear again in these pages. The point to be noted at present is that James Franklin, the young printer with recent London experience, was left without employment. Being an adventurous and rather versatile Yankee, he seized upon the idea of publishing a weekly himself. This was entirely unprecedented. Franklin had no especial access to the news, had no influence

" See Nos. 4 and 6 of *The Boston Gazette,* January 11 and 25, 1719- 20, and *The Boston News-Letter of* January 18, 1719-20.

whatever, and yet, as Isaiah Thomas says, "Encouraged by a number of respectable characters, who were desirous of having a paper of a different cast from those then published, he began the publication, at his own risk, of a third newspaper, entitled *The New England C our ant. "9* It is delightful to be assured by the first President and founder of the American Antiquarian Society, that the founders of *The New England Courant* were respectable char- ' acters. They have been otherwise known to fame as the Hell-Fire Club.10

Competition with the *News-Letter* or the *Gazette* in the matter of news would have been hopeless. Moreover, James Franklin saw clearly enough how absurd the two existing papers were as news journals. He not only made no attempt to rival them j on this ground; he ridiculed their stupid news by every possible device. And for the success of his own paper he had to rely on a totally different appeal to his public.

He had recently returned from England, where he had been apprenticed to a printer. The dates of his London apprenticeship are uncertain. He began business in Boston by March, 1717 j11 hence we can scarcely suppose that he went over to London much later than 1714. In any case, he must have heard the *Spectator and the Guardian* familiarly mentionedeveryvwhere. He could hardly escape hearing talk of books, too, at the printing-house. We know that (he became a "free-thinker," or, to speak accurately, I a Deist. And we know that *The New England I Courant* had in its office a library to draw from, which in the number and variety of its secular books, could have challenged comparison with the few notable colonial libraries of that date. From such materials undoubtedly, James Franklin drew his idea of publishing a forum of wit rather than a newspaper.

See *History of Printing in America.* In *Transactions and Collections of the American Antiquarian Society,* Vol. V, p. 110.

10 See *Transactions of the American Antiquarian Society,* Vol. VI, p. 32, also *The New England Courant,* No. *25,* January 22, 1722.

"See *Memorial History of Boston,* Vol. II, chap. XV, p. 394. Article by Delano Goddard, on *The Press and Literature of The Provincial Period.* The date is here given as 1716, Old Style.

It was a happy moment for such an undertaking. Whoever has looked through the titles of colonial publications,12 and reflected on the *Perpetual Almanacs of Spiritual Meditation,13* sermons such as *The Day of a Godly Man's Death better than the Day of his Birth,1* or Cotton Mather's *Tremenda. The dreadful Sound with which the wicked are to be thunderstruck: Sermon at the Execution of a murderer,15* will readily perceive that the provincial '; mind, starved except for its theological diet, must ' have secretly craved amusement. No doubt the profane reader of to-day would derive some entertainment from a *Tract on Anabaptist Plunging, TM* but the ordinary New Englander of 1720 would have expected to hear immediately "the dreadful sound with which the wicked are to be thunderstruck," if , he had laughed directly at a tract. Even good seri-ous literature was astonishingly scarce. The President of the Massachusetts Historical Society, Mr. Charles Francis Adams, at the tercentenary celebration of the birth of Milton, held in Boston, December 9, 1908, challenged his hearers to produce evidence of a single copy of Milton's *Paradise Lost* in Massachusetts within a century of its first publication.17 Evidence has since been found of several copies, and we shall draw attention to the copy in the possession of the *Courant,* and to an early, hitherto unnoted reference to Milton in the *Courant.* The very fact that these are exceptional, however, tells the story.

u *Ante-Revolutionary Publications,* in *Transactions of the American Antiquarian Society,* Vol. "VT, pp. 309-666. *a* Ibid., p. 400. "Ibid., p. 393. " Ibid., p. 390. " Ibid., p. 382.

English books are never noted for sale in the book " advertisements of the newspapers before 1730 at the earliest. Colonial reprints of English secular literature18 are few and scattering, and do not begin until a later period. Owners of private libraries19

"His later researches are given in a paper on *Milton's Impress on the Provincial Literature of New England,* published by the Massachusetts Historical Society. Various references to Milton in early Massachusetts literature are here gathered together, and a Harvard copy of *Paradise Lost,* 1720, is noted, as well as John Adams's copy which he read at Worcester, Mass., in 1756.

a The only piece of English literature reprinted in full in America before 1720 is *Pilgrim's Progress,* printed for Samuel Sewall, by Samuel Green, the Cambridge printer, in 1681. A copy was secured by the Boston Public Library in 1903. A book for children called *The Temple of Wisdom* was printed by William Bradford, Philadelphia, 1688. It appears to have included George Wither's *Abuses Stript and Whipt,* as well as *Divine Poems* from Francis Quarles, and some Essays of Francis Bacon.

1 Such as the Samuel Lee, Mather, and Prince collections in Massachusetts, and the Colonel Byrd library in Virginia. None of these would have been even remotely accessible to the Franklins or to ordinary citizens of the lower order, unless willed to the city as the Princecollection was, about 1750. Thomas Prince was a Pastor of Old South Church, however, and his library was naturally theological and historical, – "my books that are in Latin, Greek and the Oriental languages" as he described them in his will. Not a trace of secular literature in English. There seems to have been a Boston public library from 1674, – not, of course, a circulating library, and apparently of very little influence for many years. Benjamin Franklin never mentions it. See article on *Llbraries in Boston,* by Justin Winsor, in *Memorial History of Boston,* Vol. IV, p. 279 S.

of any extent throughout all the colonies before 1730 could be counted on the fingers of one hand. The nature of these libraries we shall speak of later. At present, it will be sufficient to recall Benjamin Franklin's delight when, as a boy, he gained access to any collection of books. In fact, the man on the street would simply know nothing of the mere commonplaces of English literature and literary history, when James Franklin and the Hell-Fire Club put together the essays and letters for *The New England Courant.* What these essays in the first seventeen numbers of the *Courant* may have been, we do not know, for unfortunately the only extant file, that in the Massachusetts Historical Society's library, begins with number 18, December 4, 1721. But we have first-hand evidence about the missing numbers in the irate *News-Letters* of August, 1721. ' John Campbell at last flashes into good, picturesque English, as he comments on the young upstart who has given a "very, very frothy, fulsome account of himself" in his first *Courant,* of August 7, "reflecting too, too much that my performances are now and then very, very Dull."

f Let us reflect a moment on what John Campbell would have been likely to call frothy and fulsome injournalism. He very truly maintained that he had faithfully furnished news for seventeen years. No ' opinions, ideas or arguments had ever appeared in his paper. He had never swerved-from his severe ideal. Is it possible that he would have called the first number of the *Spectator* frothy? Be that as it may, we have here a clear indication that Franklin had launched a different sort of paper from any before known in Boston.

As to the literary influence behind the new undertaking, the evidence is overwhelming. The Hell- Fire Club was trying to write like the *Spectator.* The very look of an ordinary first page of the *Courant* is like that of a *Spectator* page. Short, formal essays usually strike the eye first, followed by letters from various fictitious characters whose odd names have a humorous significance. The introductory essay in the *Courant* has caught the very phrases of the *Spectator,* such as "It has often been observed," "Archbishop Tillotson very justly observes," "nothing is more certain than that," "I was not a little pleased," " there is scarce any part of a Man's Life," "an ingenious writer has said." Participial phrases and "since "or "as "clauses frequently introduce paragraphs as in the *Spectator.* The essay is referred to as a *Speculation.* A Latin motto always introduces the more serious papers. The very tricks and manners of Addison and Steele are all here.

After the more formal introductory paper, often on some general topic, such as zeal or hypocrisy or learning or honor, the facetious letters of imaginary

correspondents commonly fill the remainder of the */ C our ant's* first page. Timothy Turnstone addresses flippant jibes to Justice Nicholas Clodpate in the first extant number of the *Courant.* Tom Pen- Shallow quickly follows, with his mischievous little postscript: "Pray inform me whether in your Province Criminals have the Priviledge of a Jury." Tom Tram writes from the Moon about a certain "villainous Postmaster" he has heard rumors of. Ichabod Henroost complains of a gadding wife.20 Abigail Afterwit would like to know when the editor of the *Gazette* "intends to have done printing the Carolina Addresses to their Governour, and give his Readers Something in the Room of them, that will be more entertaining."21 Betty Frugal complains to Mr. Turnstone of the embarrassing addresses of her ardent "journeyman gentleman."22 Fanny Mournful dilates on a stepmother's cruelty.23 Homespun Jack deplores the fashions in general, and small waists in particular.24 Tabitha Talkative and Dorothy Love discuss gossiping.25

Not only is the general treatment of these homely characters like the treatment of corresponding characters in the *Spectator,* but the very names of the fictitious personages in the *Courant* often suggest those of the *Spectator.* Ichabod Henroost, complaining of his gadding wife, is probably a reflection ofNathaniel Henroost of the *Spectator.*26 The similarity of Nathaniel's grievance makes the borrowing almost a certainty. He is a henpecked husband. " There is not such a slave in Turkey as I am to my dear," says he. Biddy Loveless,27 George Gosling,28 Martha Housewife,29 Eve Afterday,30 Alice Thread- needle,31 are all lowly correspondents of Mr. Spectator. Sometimes, it is true, the homeliness of the *Courant's* characters suggests what Defoe was doing about 1718 in Mist's *Weekly Journal.* We know that an occasional copy of Mist's *Journal* reached the office of the *Courant.* Most of the external evidence, however, favors the probability that the Hell-Fire Club was using the *Spectator* directly. / Classical names enter the *Courant* as well. Philanthropos urges the wealthy to help struggling young men along in business.32 Hypercarpus discourses on pride of heart.33 Philomusus writes halting, silly doggerel as a travesty on New England elegiac poetry.34 Hypercriticus also pokes fun at the elegies of the day.35 No one will need to be reminded that just such satire abounds in the pages of the *Spectator.* Above all, when Proteus or Old Janus enters in the forty-sixth *Courant,* for June

" See *The New England Courant,* No. 24, January 15, 1721-22.

21 Ibid., No. 26, January 29, 1721-22.

22 Ibid., No. 29. "Ibid., No. 31. " Ibid., No. 67. Ibid.

26 See *Spectator,* No. 176.

Ibid., No. 196. 28 Ibid., No. 191. "Ibid., No. 178. "Ibid., No. 190. "Ibid., No. 188.

See *The New England Courant,* No. 45, June 11, 1722. "Ibid., No. 46, June 18, 1722.

"Ibid.

Ibid., No. 67.

18, 1722, describing himself as an observer of "all men, and all things at will," and becoming soon the very personification and symbol of the *Courant's* existence, there can be no doubt that we have a reflection of Mr. Spectator himself. Old Janus can be all things to all men; in fact, he can even be a ladies' man if he chooses.

So much for the internal evidence. It might be multiplied, especially if we considered the Dogood papers of Benjamin Franklin, published early in 1722 in the *Courant;* we shall defer any discussion of these, however, until the external and direct evidence for the *Spectator* and the *Guardian,* as models for the *Courant,* has been put forward.

Internal evidence alone is always a bit dubious. The peculiarities of diction and the general essay method which we have seen in the *Courant* might be found in other writings of the period, although nowhere except in Addison and Steele in such fulness. The natural assumption is that a body of essays of this general type follows the most conspicuous example of that type. In this case a solid buttress of fact supports the assumption. Number 166 of the *Guardian* appears in number 141 of the *Courant;* and in number 44 of the *Courant,* we are told that John Harvard, "as cunning a Lad as any we have at our College," charges the *Courant* with copying from other authors, and mentions the *Guardian.* "That Discourse of Honour was in the *Guardian.*" Franklin denies it, yet familiarity with the *Guardian* is evident. John Harvard, by the way, as the *Courant* says, "looks into Books" and "writes Indexes."He is the embodiment of learned, ecclesiastical education, of the Mather type.

Number 190 of the *Courant,* March 22, 1725 (long after Benjamin Franklin left Boston, be it noted), has an editorial essay complaining of bitter letters received from husbands on the idleness of their wives, "whether from the growing custom of Tea-Drinking is best known to the Purses of their Husbands." The editor's advice is that the fair partners be persuaded to keep a journal of their lives and send it to the *Courant.* For an encouragement, he will present them with such a journal of five days, "drawn up by a Maiden Lady, and sent to the *Spectator.*" Then follows, of course, the famous *Spectator* paper,36 *given verbatim,* containing the journal of a London lady of fashion. The very ease and familiarity with which the *Spectator* and *Guardian* are referred to, tell the story. It is not, " a London periodical called the *Spectator.*" It is "the *Spectator.*"

Sometimes (though rarely in the *Courant)* a London weekly which is itself more or less imitative of the *Spectator* is quoted. For instance, the *Courant* of December 16, 1723, number 124, transfers entire a very readable piece of fun from Mist's weekly Journal of Sept. 2,1723. It purports to be criticism and begins quite in the dignified *Spectator* manner: "Meeting the other Day with the excellent Ballad of *Moor of Moore Hall and the Dragon of Wantley* and reading it over attentively, I wonder'd the *Spectator* had never oblig'd the World with a Criticism

"*Spectator,* No. 323.

of it, as well as of *Chevy-Chase;* for in my Opinion, it may boast of as ancient Song, nor is the Hero of it at all inferiour to Percy or Douglass." Then follows a racy satire on the hero's superiority to Hercules, who, in the words of the ballad,

had a club,
This Dragon to drub
Or he'd ne'er don't I [done it]
warrant ye:
But Moor of Moore-Hall,
With nothing at all,
He slew the Dragon of Wantley.

The most interesting evidence of literature in connection with the *Courant,* and one of the most interesting evidences of secular literature in all the colonies in 1722 remains to be given. We refer to the list of books in the possession of the *Courant,* and flaunted before the public in the *Courant* of July 2, 1722, number 48, with this cutting introduction: /"We are furnished with a large and valuable collection of Books: which may be of vast Advantage to us, not only in making Indexes, but also in writing on Subjects Natural, Moral, and Divine. . . . We shall at this Time favor you with a small part of our Catalogue, viz." The list, of course, follows. We give the more strictly literary portion of it.

Shakespeare's *Works*
Virgil
Aristotle's *Politicks*
Hudibras
Milton
The Spectator, 8 volumes
The Guardian, 2 volumes
The Turkish Spy
The Athenian Oracle
The British Apollo
The Art of Thinking
The Art of Speaking
The Reader
The Lover

Cowly's *Works*
Burnet's *History of the Reformation*
Burnet's *Theory of the Earth*
Oldham's *Works*
The Tail of the Tub
St. Augustine
A. B. TiUotson Trr 7 Dr. Bates *Works* Dr. South
Mr. Flavel
Mr. Charnock

"We have also ... a vast Quantity of Pamphlets." Much would the inquiring reader like to know if pamphlets of Defoe could have been here included. At least we know that Benjamin Franklin remembered none when he came to write his *Autobiography*. *The Autobiography* records a very early reading of the *Essay upon Projects,37* but when a little later on in the *Autobiography,38* Defoe's conversational method is praised, only those works of Defoe which Franklin imported years afterwards for his book trade in Philadelphia, such as *Robinson*

"*Autobiography,* in *Writings of Benjamin Franklin,* ed. A. H. Smyth, Vol. I, p. 238. " Ibid., p. 251.

Crusoe and *Moll Flanders,* are mentioned, along with the *Family Instructor* which he himself reprinted in 1740, and the *Religious Courtship,* which Keimer had published in his *Universal Instructor.* Evidently these were the prominent things which, in 1771, Dr. Franklin remembered of Defoe.39 Of course these facts indicate nothing definite as to Defoe's pamphlets. There *may* have been any number of them in the *Courant's* library. In any case the method of the *Courant* is never the method of Defoe. Complex irony was not the forte of the Hell-Fire Club. Benjamin Franklin once or twice achieved something of the sort in his maturer years. For instance, his *Prussian Edict,* which was taken seriously in London for some time, and, better still, that Biblical paraphrase which, for once, took the distinguished Matthew Arnold out of his depth. No one will dream of denying that irony too subtle for Matthew Arnold is not simple. It is no wonder that the *Courant* followed easier models. All this, of course, quite apart from the question of pure literary merit. Defoe's *Shortest Way with the Dissenters* may or may not be better literature than the typical *Spectator* essay, but Defoe's typical ironic form was certainly more difficult to imitate than Addison's.

Moreover, there is no external evidence of any other literature which could have furnished the basis of the *Courant* essay, except the volumes of *The Spectator, The Guardian,* and essays of the same general type, themselves imitative, such as *TheReader* and *The Lover,* or the introductory essays in Mist's and Applebee's *Journals.* If the *Courant* had owned any other noteworthy literature whatever, we may be very sure that such would have appeared in the list, since the avowed purpose of this list was to impress "young scribbling collegians." Hence we have another external probability that the *Courant 's* essays were formed on the most conspicuous type of essay periodical.

8"Date of Franklin's commencement of the *Autobiography.*

We have said that the avowed purpose of the pub- lication of the *Courant's* book list was to impress) college folk. One might wonder at the possibility;' of impressing any public whatever, learned or other-1 wise, with such a meager little catalogue, if the Harvard College Catalogue of 1723 were not accessible. By that we know that Addison, Steele, Bolingbroke, Dryden, Pope, Prior, and Swift would have been looked for in vain at Harvard a year *after* the *Courant* had a full set of *The Spectator, A Tale of a Tub,* and Milton. Harvard had just acquired Milton, it is true, and a 1709 Shakespeare; yet these are noted so particularly by literary historians such as Dr. S. A. Green of the Massachusetts Historical Society, that we can infer a new significance for Milton, Shakespeare, Swift and Addison, all in the printing office of an unlearned young Boston printer.

And what about the chief private libraries of the day? In the earliest book catalogue printed in British America, that of Samuel Lee's library, Dr. Green has reckoned about two hundred English titles in a library of a thousand books, almost allLatin and theological.40 This library was too old to contain Addison or Swift (as Samuel Lee left the colonies in the latter half of the seventeenth century), but it has not even a copy of Milton. Nor has a trace of *Paradise Lost* been found in the Mather libraries, though Cotton Mather knew Milton well enough. The Eev. Thomas Prince, learned author of *A Chronological History of New England,* began to collect books as early as 1703. When he died, about 1750, he left a library in two parts; a large theological collection, willed to the Old South Church, and a valuable collection of New England historical pamphlets, willed to the town, and now in the Boston Public Library. Not a trace of secular English literature anywhere in the records, though we may assume safely enough that gentlemen like Mather Byles and Thomas Prince had their copies of Addison. Indeed, there is excellent reason for believing that they had. Nothing, however, can detract from the distinction which belongs to the editors of the *Courant,* of first attempting to introduce and to write literature for its own sake in America.

We have spoken41 of a hitherto unnoted reference to Milton in the *Courant.* It is a news item of January 1, 1721, number 22, to the effect that a "noble Duke is about to erect a Monument in Westminster Abby to the Memory of Milton the Poet." Note the interesting fact that Milton has to be explained as Milton, the Poet. Excepting the reference andquotations in Mather's *Magnalia,* and some verses by Mather Byles, all noted and explained by President Adams in his article42 previously cited in these pages, there is probably no earlier reference to Milton, in Massachusetts, at least. Two quotations from *Paradise Lost* are noted by President Adams, in later issues of the *Courant,* one introduced by the admiring command: "Hear how the lofty Milton sings of this in his own inimitable strain." On the whole, the *Courant* could use Milton about as freely as the Eeverend Cotton Mather himself could or did. Archbishop Tillotson's sermons were in the *Cour- ant's* library, and were quoted in the *Courant* on several occasions. One can but suspect that they proved a handy weapon against the Mathers and the Puritan party in general. Nicholas Clodpate ' certainly represents one of these Puritan divines if not Mather himself, and he gets some vigorous whacks from Timothy Turnstone. "Archbishop Tillotson (whether you know him or no), very justly observes that a small Portion of Wit, and a great deal of Ill-Nature will furnish a Man for Satyr. But, you, Sir, to supply the want of a little Wit, to accompany your Ill-Nature, are obliged to have recourse to a downright Lye in saying that the *Cour- ants* are sent to your Districts by the Author to be read gratis. Good Sir, who but your

Worship . . . desires to read News for Nothing?"43 We know that Benjamin Franklin had a great and life-long admiration for Tillotson, some evidences of which

See *Earliest Book Catalogue Printed in this Country.* In *Ten Fac-simile Reproductions Relating to Old Boston,* pp. 28-31. " Vide supra, p. 13.

Milton's Impress on the Provincial Literature of New England. Published by Mass. Hist. Society in Proceedings, Vol. XLII, p. 154 ff. tt See *The New England Courant,* December 4, 1721.

will appear in a later chapter. The fourth Dogood essay44 represents Plagius (the New England Clergy), in the Temple of Theology, copying Tillot- son's sermons!

The Dogood papers show, of course, more literary influence than any others in the *Cour- ant.* The general *Spectator* form is intensified in the fourteen little essays from Silence Dogood to the Editor. We shall not treat them at length, however, since they have been ably commented on by the late Professor Albert H. Smyth in his edition of Franklin, and are there accessible to every reader. All commentators agree that they are in the manner of the *Spectator;* that they are among the most readable and charming of Franklin's early works; and that they are the first fruits of his days and nights with Addison which he has told us about in his *Autobiography,"5* as all the world knows. The boy was almost twelve years old when an odd volume of the *Spectator,* the third, fell into his hands, and he has recorded the great delight he took in it.46 May we shrewdly suspect that it was somehow his natural desire to see the rest of the *Spectator,* which resulted in the full set in the *C our ant's* library by the time he was sixteen? If so, the literary idea back of the *Courant* would be largely due to him. Without entering into this nice point, we shall pass directly to the discovery of a long paragraph in the fourteenth Dogood paper, quoted verbatim from the one hundred and eighty-fifth *Spectator,* on *Religious*

" See *The New England Courant,* May 14, 1722. 45 See *Autobiography* in *Writings of Benjamin Franklin,* ed. A. H. Smyth, Vol. I, pp. 241-242.

Zeal, which is also the subject of the fourteenth Dogood essay. The authors of the quotation are not named, except as "ingenious gentlemen." The word "ingenious" is used, indeed, nine times in the short Dogood essays; and, while common enough in this sense, in the early eighteenth century, there is no source so likely to have suggested it to Franklin as the *Spectator.*

But the *Courant,* as a whole, is not literature. It took over a literary form, it used purely literary sources as they had never been used in America before, and if the time had been ripe for the " renaissance of New England"47 in secular culture, no doubt the *Courant* would have become a contributory influence. Certainly there was no lack of wit or ability in the enterprise. The *Courant* is entertaining from first to last. But the editors forgot the urbanity of Mr. Spectator, – forgot that one considerable element in the success of their distinguished model was his genial, imperturbable, impersonal kindliness of manner. To be sure, Mr. Spectator himself might have had rather a hard life in Boston in the year of our Lord 1721. But he would have kept at least on bowing terms with Cotton Mather, and assuredly we may believe that he would not have been on the wrong side of a public question like inoculation.

The truth is that the *Courant* represents a violent ani almost coarse reaction against clerical domination of New England. This of itself would not prevent its becoming literature. But the insolent

See *Literary History of America.*, by Professor Barrett Wendell.

personalities do, unfortunately. All its personal enemies are openly vituperated more than once. The "villainous postmaster," who had taken the printing of the *Gazette* from Franklin, is irreverently addressed, in a pretended letter, as Old Muss ;48 we have seen how John Campbell of the *News-Letter* was "reflected on." Cotton Mather is thus insulted: "The first Passage concerning Inoculation (in the writing of the young, scribbling collegian) is no more to be found in the *London Mercury* here on the Table, than Cotton Mather, D. D. is to be found in the List of the Royal Society affixed at the other end of the Room."49 We must admit . thafinis is a far cry from the *Spectator.*. Yeifone hates to give up . altogether the litfrary claim for the *Courant.* The yejy elegance of the model puts the native talent-'in'"a meaner light. Grotesque, no doubt, crude, and sometimes coarse, as this native output is, a genuine humor and shrewd satiric truth of life, a spontaneous freshness, breaks through continually. We have the beginnings of something like a native American literature, which refuses to be literally imitative in all particulars. The next Colonial newspaper which we examine, *The New England Weekly Journal,* will show a much closer fol- , lowing of literary models, in letter as well as in spirit, yet we shall also find a stiff, school-boy quality quite absent from the *Courant.* A slight illustration of the difference may be found in a word for word comparison of the famous introductory sen-

" See *The New England Courant,* No. 25, Jan. 22, 1722. " Ibid.

tence of the first *Spectator* with the introductory sentences of the first Dogood paper, and the first literary essay of *The New England Weekly Journal* respectively.

New England Journal, Spectator, No. 1. *Dogood Paper,* No. 1. No. 3.

I have observed that And since it is ob- An ingenious Author a reader seldom pe- served that the gen- has observed that a ruses a book with pleas- erality of people, now-Reader seldom peruses ure until he knows adays, are unwilling a book with pleasure, whether the writer of either to commend or till he has a tolerable it be a black or a fair dispraise what they Notion of the Physi- man, of a mild or cho- read, until they are ognomy of the Author, lerie disposition, mar- in some measure in- the year of bis Birth ried or a bachelor, with formed who or what and his Manner of liv- other particulars of the the author of it is, ing, with several other like nature, that eon- whether he be poor or Particulars of the like duce very much to the rich, old or young, a Nature, very necessary right understanding of scollar or a Leather- to the right Under- an author. apron Man, etc, and standing his Works,

give their opinion of
the Performance, ac-
cording to the knowl-
edge which they have
of the author's cir-
cumstances, it may not
be amiss to begin with
a short account of my

Past Life and present
condition. . . .

Now Mather Byles, or whoever wrote *The New England Weekly Journal* essay, obviously wrote with his *Spectator* at hand; how stiff his transcription of Addison's "black or fair man," into "Physiognomy" ! But how true a note from genuine firsthand life in Franklin's "Leather-apron Man"! A note not even suggested by the *Spectator*. This isa minute point, of course, and will have to be carefully supported by investigation of all the many literary efforts in *The New England Weekly Journal.* Meanwhile it would be scarcely fair to take our leave of the *Courant* without expressing a suspicion that when the Massachusetts Historical Society publishes its treasured, morocco-bound volume, some people may find it better reading than Sewall's *Diary* or Cotton Mather's *Magnalia.* CHAPTER II

The New England Weekly Joubnal

'Mourn, all ye scribblers who attempted fame,
Screened by the umbrage of his pow'rful name;
No more you'll write beneath his shade conceal'd
But in full dulness be abroad reveal 'd."

*An Elegy on the long expected Death of Old Janus.1 " * He's gone! Thanks for his death! who dy 'd to give The world a poet who deserves to live.

Harvard's honour, and New England's hope,
Bids fair to rise, and sing, and rival Pope."

On the Foregoing.2

Thus the Harvard poets and wits ushered *The New England Courant* out of existence. The *Collection of Poems by Several Hands,* published in 1744, must have been written by 1727 or 1728, for the most part, since a portion of *On the Foregoing* is quoted in *The New England Journal* of August 5, 1728, number 72. Naturally the *Elegy on Old Janus* would appear soon after the *Courant* ceased to exist, in the early ; part of 1727.3 There can be no doubt that educated , young ecclesiastics had been teased and insulted by

1 In *A Collection of Poems by Several Hands,* published by B. Green & Co., Boston, 1744.

'Ibid.

See *Transactions of the American Antiquarian Society,* Vol. VT, p. 38. The last extant number of the *Courant* is No. 252, June 4, 1726. But Isaiah Thomas would be likely to know the year in which it was given up.

the *Courant,* to the point of severe retaliation. The Franklins hated and at the same time bitterly envied "young, scribbling collegians," such as Mather Byles. The college party tried its best to despise such unwelcome adversaries, but never quite succeeded. As a Dunciad, the *Elegy on the long expected Death of Old Janus* is ridiculously wide of the mark. Dulness is about the only fault that could not be laid at his door. Would-that the same might be said of "Harvard's honor, and New England's hope"!

Mather Byles was undoubtedly the hope referred to, who "bade fair to rise, and sing, and rival Pope." If his genuine literary culture and his concentrated literary effort could have been combined with Franklin's originality, we might have had a really great name in pure letters before the Revolution. A full treatment of his work would lie outside the scope of this discussion. Our present interest is in his shaping influence on *The New England Journal,* and his large contributions thereto.

It is an interesting and significant coincidence that the second newspaper in Massachusetts with , literary pretensions should have been organized under circumstances similar to the first. Samuel Kneeland, already mentioned in these pages4 as the printer who succeeded James Franklin in the office of the *Gazette,* was ousted in his turn when a new postmaster, Henry Marshall,5 took over the *Gazette.* Kneeland immediately made plans for a new journal, just as James Franklin had done before him; ! and, like Franklin again, he was cut off from the i most natural and official method of getting the news, pure and simple. In his prospectus, however, sent out March 20, 1727, he informed his public that he- had made arrangements with suburban reporters, as we should call them; in his elegant phrase they are "the most knowing and ingenious Gentlemen in the several noted Towns in this and the Neighbor- Provinces, who may Take particular Care seasonably to Collect and send what may be remarkable in their Town or Towns adjacent, worthy of the Public View." As a matter of fact, the *Journal* became a better newspaper than the *Courant.* But ' the notice in Kneeland's prospectus of special interest in the present investigation is the following suggestive hint of its large aim, independent of the news:

1Vide supra, chap. I, p. 10.

8 See *Transactions of the American Antiquarian Society,* VoL VI,

"This may serve as a Notification, that a Select number of Gentlemen, who have had the happiness of a liberal Education, and some of them considerably improv'd by their Travels into distant Countries; are now concerting some regular schemes for the Entertainment of the ingenious Reader and the Encouragement of Wit and Politeness ; and may in a very short time, open upon the Public in a variety of pleasing and profitable Speculations."

Such an attempt, following directly upon the steps of the *Courant,* suggests that the writers for the *Journal* were using the purely literary idea of their predecessors with no competitor now in the field, and the suggestion of Mr. Delano Goddard6 that one

See *Press and Literature of the Provincial Period,* in *Memorial History of Boston,* Vol. II, chap. XV, p. 396, note.

of the members of the Hell-Fire Club, Matthew Adams, probably wrote for the *Journal* after the *Courant* ceased, seems reasonable. Indeed, it would seem reasonable that the *Journal* should use as many as possible of the writers for the *Courant,* did we not know that they had made themselves obnoxious to the community. Their most brilliant apprentice had long since gone to Philadelphia;7 so that, on

! the whole, we are dealing with a wholly new organization, this time truly made up of respectable char-

acters, with the best traditions of culture in the province behind them.

First, as to Samuel Kneeland himself. He had served his apprenticeship with Bartholomew Green, printer for the College, and publisher of the *News- Letter* after 1722. Bartholomew Green was a son of the Samuel Green of Cambridge, who printed John Eliot's Indian Bible, who even had business relations with the great Robert Boyle, at that time Governor of the corporation in England for propagating the Gospel among the Indians. This Samuel Green, as a mere lad, had come over with Governor

Winthrop in 1630, and "used to tell his children that, upon their first coming ashore, he and several others were for some time glad to lodge in empty casks, to shelter them from the weather."8 Such stories of his father and his father's friends would Bartholomew Green undoubtedly have to tell young Kneeland. Both were members of the Old South Church, where Green was deacon for many years. The principles of Bartholomew Green, also, wouldhave their undoubted influence; for we are told of his "eminency for a strict observing the sabbath; his household piety; his keeping close and diligent to the work of his calling; his meek and peaceable spirit; his caution of publishing anything offensive, light, or hurtful; and his tender sympathy to the poor and afflicted."9 Kneeland certainly acquired, a meek and peaceable spirit, and with it " a caution of publishing anything offensive or hurtful." The *Journal* had a distinguished and successful career. Four months after the establishment of his paper, Samuel Kneeland formed a partnership with Timothy Green, a grand-nephew of Bartholomew Green. This young man's grandfather, a son of the Cambridge Samuel Green, had been one of the earliest Boston printers, and his work had been under the supervision of the famous Samuel Sewall, who, for a time, controlled the press rights in Boston.10 Sewall had a flourishing book store at the time, and must, in many ways, have brought literary matters to his printer's notice. Evidence that the latter had used these opportunities exists in the complimentary reference to him in John Dunton's *Life and Errors.* Dunton, a London bookseller, visited Boston in 1686, and reported his delight in Samuel Green's interesting conversation.11 In brief, the new firm, Knee-

In 1723, as nearly as can be ascertained.

8 See *The Boston News-Letter,* January 4, 1733.

Ibid.

10 See *Transactions of -the American Antiquarian Society,* Vol. V, p. 86.

""I contracted a great friendship for this man; to name his trade will convince the world he was a man of good sense and understanding; he was so facetious and obliging in his conversation that I took a great delight in his company, and made use of his house to while away my melancholy hours." Dunton*'a Life and Errors,* London, 1705, p. 129.

land and Green, had closer and more direct traditions of English culture than was usual in the provincial period. Kneeland soon left the actual printing business to his new partner, young Timothy Green, while he himself opened a book shop in King Street. The advantages of a book store to the literary side of the paper will be obvious at once. Any writer for the *Journal* had access to some sort of secular literature.

We have said that Samuel Kneeland was a member of Old South Church. Probably young Timothy Green would be identified with the same body, also, since his Uncle Bartholomew was a deacon there. What more natural than that they should interest their pastor, the Rev. Thomas Prince, in the new undertaking? One of Thomas Prince's friends was the Rev. Mather Byles. Hence the "Select number of Gentlemen, who have had the happiness of a liberal Education" willing to give their services to a new literary journal that should be without offence to religion. This connection of events, simple though it is, has not seemed to occur to historians of the colonial press, and would remain an unsupported assumption were it not for the definite tradition voiced by Isaiah Thomas in his *History of Printing 'in America.12* He named Thomas Prince,

Judge Danforth, and Mather Byles, as editors and even correctors of the Press. The literary output of the *Journal* confirms this tradition, as well as the entire naturalness of the situation. Moreover, Isaiah

"See *Transactions of the American Antiquarian Society,* Vol. "VT, pp. 41-42.

Thomas is an excellent authority in matters of this kind. Though his *History of Printing* was not published until 1810, he had been a printer's apprentice in Boston himself from 1756 to 1766, and had had many pleasant talks with the old printer Gamaliel Rogers, who gave the lad kindly advice. Now Gamaliel Rogers, after an apprenticeship with Bartholomew Green, had actually begun business for himself by 1729. Later on, he became a publisher of note. It is incredible that he should have been ignorant of the journalistic traditions of his early years, and equally incredible that he should not have enjoyed talking of them to the young lad, Isaiah Thomas, who paid him the compliment of visiting him so frequently. In any case, Isaiah Thomas, in his later career as editor and antiquarian, would be more than likely to voice a trustworthy tradition. Later histories of the colonial press merely follow him in the matter.13

In Mather Byles and Thomas Prince a modified ecclesiasticism is already evident. They were not so purely and entirely devoted to theological content, and theological interpretation, as the generation before them had been. Cotton Mather, for instance, the uncle of Mather Byles, read, as we have seen, Milton's *Paradise Lost,* even paraphrasing sections of it,14 to fit Massachusetts conditions, andto draw a moral; but he never dreamed of discussing the art of *Paradise Lost,* or of imitating it for mere pleasure, either to his hearers or to himself. His nephew, on the other hand, was a Pope enthusiast and a Pope imitator, writing such poems as *Commencement,* in mock heroic couplets, intended, at least, to give pleasure, beginning "I sing the day, bright with peculiar charms" and continuing in such a strain as this:

"See *Specimens of Newspaper Literature,* by Joseph T. Buckingham, pp. 100-111; also, *Journalism in the United States,* by Frederic Hudson, p. 76; also *Press and Literature of the Provincial Period* by Delano Goddard, in *Memorial History of Boston,* Vol. II, chap. XV, pp. 399-400.

14 See his *Magnolia Christi, II,* 568 ff., where *Paradise Lost,* VI, 386- 393, is changed to suit his purpose, entirely a theological and religious one.

And now the sprightly Fair approach the glass,
To heighten every feature of the face.15

The attempt at the style of *The Rape of the Lock* is evident. Two other short poetical nights in the little volume, *A Collection of Poems by Several Hands* are very interesting as establishing Mather Byles's enthusiasm for Pope. They are as follows:

Desiring to borrow Pope's Homer.
From a Lady.
"The muse now waits from 's hands to press
Homer's high page, in Pope's illustrious dress;
How the pleas'd goddess triumphs to pronounce
The names of , Pope, Homer, all at once!"
The Answeb
"Go, my dear Pope, transport th'attentive fair,

And sooth, with winning harmony her ear.

M In *A Collection of Poems by Several Hands,* Boston, 1744. A copy may be seen in the library of the Massachusetts Historical Society.

'Twill add new graces to thy heav'nly song,

To be repeated by her gentle tongue.

Old Homer's shade shall smile if she commend,

And Pope be proud to write, as to lend."

Now in the small, yellow copy of this book of verses in the possession of the Massachusetts Historical Society, the blank spaces shown above are filled out in ink, in a handwriting of long ago, with the name *Byles.* Evidently we have here a trustworthy tradition, especially in conjunction with Byles's long-known letter to Pope, full of extravagant and even fulsome praises.16 Additional evidence of his devotion to Pope as well as to Addison, will be found on examining the *Journal.* Enough has been given to establish our point as to Mather Byles's purely literary interests.

Thomas Prince, on the other hand, was a student of history. His unique collection of New England Pamphlets has already been noted, as well as his *Chronological History of New England,* which, though it began with Adam, had, on the whole, less theological purpose than the *Magnalia Christi.* As to his religious affiliations, Prince was an ardent champion of George Whitefield, and therefore an adherent of emotional religion. This in itself argued some literary quality, according to the famous dictum of the London bookseller in conversation with Parson Adams, that, although sermons as a rule were poor "copy," he would "as soon print one of Whitefield's as any farce."17

"See Buckingham's *Specimens of Newspaper Literature,* p. 110. 11 See *The Adventures of Joseph Andrews,* by Henry Fielding. Sterling Edition, Chap. XVII, p. 95.

The Speculations announced in the prospectus of the *Journal* began with number 3, April 10, 1727. They have not remained unnoticed by'historians of the early press. Isaiah Thomas, in his *History of Printing, 13* says: "During the first year of the *Journal,* several literary gentlemen furnished it with short essays on miscellaneous subjects." He goes on to give a brief account of the essays, but no analysis, and no criticism. HE credits Mather Bytes with "many of the poetical and other essays,"19 and notes the tradition that Judge Danforth and Eev. Thomas Prince also took an important part in writing for the paper, and even in editing it.

Buckingham, in his *Specimens of Newspaper Literature,* devotes one interesting chapter20 to *The New England Journal,* reprinting the first three essays with this warm appreciative comment: "The introductory paper ... is not inferior in easy and quiet humor to those, in which Steele, Addison, and Mackenzie introduced themselves to the readers of the *Tattler, Spectator,* and *Mirror.* ... In his next paper the writer proceeds, agreeably to the example of his great prototypes of the *Tattler* and *Spectator* – then in the height of their popularity – to give an account of the members of 'the Society.' " Several poems from the *Journal* are reprinted in Buckingham's chapter, and attributed, reasonably enough, to Mather Byles, together with an *Essay on Terror.*

"See *Transactions of fhe American Antiquarian Society,* Vol. "VT, p. 39.

"Ibid., p. 42.

20 See *Specimens of Newspaper Literature with personal Memoirs, Anecdotes and Reminiscences,* by Joseph T. Buckingham. Boston, 1852. Vol. I, pp. 89-111.

Several of the essays had previously been repub- lished in *The Emerald,* a Boston paper, in 1807 and 1808. "Some of them," says the editor of *The Emerald,* in introducing them to his readers, "are not inferior to the numbers of the *Spectator;* and their writer seems to follow, and not sub longo in- tervallo, the footsteps of Addison." He conjectures that they were written by some "English gentleman of education, then resident here." Isaiah Thomas's information as to the authors had not appeared at that time.

Hudson's *Journalism in the United States* merely gives a brief note, based on previous authorities.21 One or two interesting new suggestions in the article by Delano Goddard, on *The Press and Literature of the Provincial Period22* will be noted in the course of this discussion.

So then, these *Journal* essays have been mentioned as imitations of Addison. They have never been really examined, however, either for stylistic evidence, or for definite literary references. Such an examination may perhaps make a slight change in the history of American Literature. The dates of its conscious beginnings will be set backward a number of years.

The opening sentence of the first essay in the *Journal* has been given, in a previous chapter.23 The fictitious author of ensuing Speculations introduces himself very fitly as an *imitator.* He can personate animals or men, at will, and intends to

See *Journalism in the United States, by* Frederic Hudson, p. 76.

See *Memorial History of Boston,* Vol. II, chap. XV. "Vide supra, p. 29.

banter a folly by representing it as in a glass. First, he will give an account of himself, "and this," he says,24 "I shall do, (as an ingenious Author whom I am now imitating has admirably expressed it) *in a very clear and concise manner."* Later references in the *Journal* prove that Addison was meant.25 Readers are informed that they may address the new Spectator of men and manners, under the name of Proteus Echo, Esq., who, by a rather clumsy device, has forgotten his own name.

The contrast between Franklin's Dogood papers and the Proteus Echo Speculations is both striking and suggestive. Not only is young widow Dogood a wide variant from the usual type of Spectator, but she gives in her own person the unliterary ideas intended to fit homely New England conditions. Proteus Echo, Esq., proceeds to form a club in very close, and very exact imitation of the Spectator. As to his speculations, they are sometimes ludicrously inapt in the Boston of 1727, as when he is pleased to make merry over the farces of D, ick Grub- street, "whose Plays have very frequently been clapt upon the Stage, and as often, to his great mortification, hissed off."26 What did Boston know of Dick Grubstreet's plays, or of Shakespeare's, either, for that matter, in 1727 ?

The club or "Society" of Proteus Echo is ranged in a semi-circle and sketched for us by the limner in the second ess'ay, which proceeds exactly as the second number of the *Spectator.* First comes the Honourable Charles Gravely, a merchant of considerable eminence, who "has traded for many Thousand of Pounds in Wit and Eloquence." Apart from this ambitious sally in word playing, the Honourable Charles Gravely hardly exists. He does not appear in the following papers.

M See *The New England Weekly Journal,* No. 3, April 10, 1727.

Ibid., Nos. 12, 16, 17.

Ibid., No. 12, June 12, 1727.

Mr. Timothy Blunt represents a distinct, and hitherto unnoted attempt to create a New England version of Sir Eoger de Coverley. He lives at some distance from the town of Boston, but rides in every week, often bringing his "Wallet ballanced with two Bottles of Milk, to defray his necessary Expenses." This last is a Yankee touch indeed. Imagine Sir Eoger economizing on a midday meal! The sketch of Mr. Timothy Blunt continues: "His Eeriwigg has been out of the Curl ever since the Eevolution and his Dagger and Doublet are supposed to be the rarest Pieces of Antiquity in the Country." If it had not been for an unlucky stroke to his Intellectuals in his infancy, "he would have stood the fairest of any of his Contemporarys to have found out the Philosopher's Stone." We remember how Sir Eoger wore " a coat and doublet of the same cut that were in fashion at the time of his repulse."27 Those singularities of behavior which have endeared Sir Eoger to the world, came, of course, from his love for the widow; but they were no less a slight "stroke to his Intellectuals." Both characters are represented as advanced in years. Timothy Blunt appears once again in the essays, when Dick Grub- street complains that he has not been admitted tothe Society, although "you let Timothy Blunt in."28 Christopher Careless and Will Bitterly are just what their names suggest. Mr. Careless has "by a close and vigorous Application to Business, sunk a very plentiful Patrimony, and reduced his Fortune to a level with his Ambition." Mr. Bitterly is a direct descendant of Old Diogenes.

See *Spectator,* No. 2.

"And now comes the wonderful Mr. Honeysuckle, the Blossom of our Society, and the beautiful Ornament of Litterature; a Person of most extravagant Imagination, and one who lives perpetually upon Tropes and Similes. In his common conversation he stalks in Metaphor and Hyperbole."

Mr. Will Honeycomb, himself, translated into a poet! This direct imitation has never been commented upon. Will has become something of a painter, too, in his apotheosis, and has obliged the club room with "the Draught of a Beau, a Clown and a Coquet." Still keeping his old character in a milder way, he is mentioned once again, casually, in a later essay, when Proteus talks and walks with Mr. Honeysuckle.29

Last of all there are the two divines who "sometimes do us the Honour to set with us half an Hour, and improve us with their Excellent Conversation." Undoubtedly we have here a reflection of the good clergyman who sometimes visited the Spectator Club,30 as well as possibly a literal statement of fact. Mr. Delano Goddard's interesting suggestion that

M See *The New England Weekly Journal,* No. 12, June 12, 1727.

" Ibid., No. 38, December 25, 1727.

10 See *The Spectator,* No. 2.

the two clergymen of Proteus Echo's club represent Mather Byles and Thomas Prince, is bofh ingenious and probable.31 Why, if not in deference to some literal, present circumstance, should the one clergyman of Addison, have become two? We can be further guided by the very important fact, mentioned in the closing sentence of the second *Journal* essay which we have been so long considering: ' These Gentlemen will have no inconsiderable Hand in these Weekly Entertainments." Since we have every reason to believe that Mather Byles and Thomas Prince often wrote for the *Journal,* they are quite probably intended here, even if one of them wrote the passage.

From this slight sketch of Proteus Echo's Club, it will be evident that the characters show some good strokes. Timothy Blunt and Mr. Honeysuckle are real creations, and they represent a conscious attempt at a purely imaginative literature *for its own sake,* thirty years before the first conscious attempt recognized in Professor Barrett Wendell's *Literary History of America.* That most of the characters in Proteus Echo's Club did not really live, will be readily admitted. They did not "get over the footlights." The imagination which conceived them could not realize them, partly perhaps because they were studied from literature and not from life. Yet surely it makes some slight difference in the story of New England literature that some of its orthodoxclergy bent their stiff, unused imaginations for art's sake in 1727.

n See *Press and Literature of the Provincial Period,* in *Memorial History of Boston,* Vol. II, chap. XV, p. 399. " Tradition has neVer conjectured to whom these characters belonged, if indeed they were not entirely imaginary." He hazards the suggestion given above.

The third essay is excellent. *The Art of Incorrect Writing* is its title, and Mr. George Brimstone's *Panegyrick on Beacon-Hill* becomes the text for much good satire on bombast. The number of Celestials, Immortals, Everlastings, Infinites, Un- boundeds, in Mr. Brimstone's love poetry are all counted, while his *Poetical Description of a Game at Push Pin,* given in full, offers a fine burlesque on heroic extravagance. The essay, including the verse, was probably written by Mather Byles, since we have Isaiah Thomas's authority for supposing that Byles wrote many of the poetical essays,[32] and the further authority of *The New England Journal* itself for the fact that one of its contributors wrote the poetry,[33] and signed himself with a letter of the word Musae.[34] His verse is, of course, always imitating Pope; we shall see in a later essay that he avowed Pope as the master of his muse. The ideas of simplicity, naturalness, and conciseness of diction, however, he certainly took in part from Addison. The prose style of his essays, on the whole, follows these lines. When he came to write serious poetry, such as an *Elegy on George I,* unfortunately, Mather Byles could more than equal his own Mr. Brimstone on Beacon Hill, or the wonderful Mr. Honeysuckle. ! Essays purely moral soon follow, naturallyenough, and, at intervals, appear throughout the entire series. Even the *Spectator* has its full share of these. The remarkable thing about the didactic efforts of Proteus Echo is that, either from the benign influence of the *Spectator* or from a certain milder theological quality already stealing over New England thought, they are usually ethical rather , than dogmatic or even religious. They are on merit, ' on covetousness or idleness, even on the vapors,[35] concerning which there is one very sensible essay, analyzing the causes of the affliction as loose living, idleness, solitude, rattle of tongue, immoderate laughter, and recommending the wholesome cure of work for the benefit of the world, – and, wonder of wonders, some innocent diversion if we feel the vapors stealing over us! Could the New England clergy have countenanced such an idea?

M See *History of Printing in America.* In *Transactions of the American Antiquarian Society,* Vol. VI, pp. 40-42.

88 See *The New England Weekly Journal,* No. 52, Apr. 1, 1728. "See Essay No. 46, *New England Weekly Journal.*

In the sixth essay36 some admirer of Mather Byles wrote a poem on Eternity – "Dedicated to the Instructor of my Muse," and praising Byles very literally to the skies; Byles responded in the ninth essay37 with a poem in which he disclaimed all credit, giving the praise of his entire poetic performance to Pope, and hailing his master in terms of extravagant, almost fulsome eulogy. Pope's, he said, were the rules of poetry which he followed.

" 0 Pope! thy fame is spread around the sky

Far as the waves can flow, far as the winds can fly!"

This, of course, is direct evidence of the following of Pope in all Byles's verse.

See *The New England Weekly Journal,* No. 8, May 15, 1727.

" Ibid., No. 11, June 5, 1727.

Equally direct is the confession that he and his friends who wrote the prose essays, followed Addi- son. In the tenth essay of the series, appeared a ridiculous letter from Dick Grubstreet,38 a hack writer, accusing the editor of stealing a great many strokes of low humor from Dick's works. Proteus answered grandly: "I was defending myself from his Imputation by the Name and Authority of Mr. Addison, when at once he was struck into Silence."

The fourteenth essay39 is modeled directly on the famous *Spectator* number 34, in which the members of the club have a chance to criticise the paper. All sorts of different trades criticise Proteus Echo, but without the exquisite humor of Addison's characters. Instead, there are dull puns. The Shoemaker hopes that every page may be his *last,* and so on. Finally it is the Scholar's turn. We will hear Proteus himself on this: "I have been Credibly informed of a Young Scholar who has given himself the Trouble, in all Companies to demonstrate by Plain, undeniable Arguments, that some Papers in the *Spectator, Tatler,* or *Guardian* are rather better than many of my *Journals.*"

In the next essay, the fifteenth, Will Pedant writes a saucy letter, saying, "For your Mortification I'll assure you, you don't write so well as the Spectator, tho' I can a great deal better."

Again in the twenty-eighth essay, we have a letter to Proteus Echo, beginning:

88 See *The New England Weekly Journal,* No. 12, June 12, 1727. Ibid., No. 16, July 10, 1727.

Sir:

The *Spectator, Tatter,* and *Guardian,* whose Labours you profess to imitate, have been very particular in the secret History of Clubs.

The letter continues with a brief account of the clubs mentioned by the *Spectator,* such as the Confederation of the Kings, the Association of the Georges, the Company of the Duelists, the Humdrum Club, the Fat Club, the Kit-Cat Club, the Mum Club, the Two-penny Club and the famous Everlasting Club.40 "And no sooner did a Ring of handsome Faces smile round a Table, but the Spectator himself was envious enough to confront them, and without any more ado, thrust his short visage into a Circle of Scare-crows. Indeed so fond was his Taciturnity of these neighborly Assemblies and such a universal Patron of them, that he has by indisputable Right merited the Appelation of King of Clubs."

Could anything show closer reading of Addison and Steele's literary periodicals? Not only is the acquaintance with the general content, ideas and characters evident, but the very phraseology is interesting as compared with that of the Spectator, who says in his first number:" Sometimes I am seen *thrusting my head into a round* of politicians at Will's, and listening with great attention to the narratives that are made in those little *circular audiences."*

But the interesting matter in the letter to Proteus Echo has not been exhausted yet. Its whole point is the description of a Laughing Club, whose prominent members are Mr. Gorgon Grin and Mr. Titus Titter. The chief business of members seems to be that of laughing at their own jokes. And the whole is signed " Your humble Servant, Jack Sneer." Evidently this entire letter was thought to be a piece of delightful pleasantry in Addison's manner. How far it actually succeeded in attaining the Addisonian charm, the reader may be left to determine, since literary accomplishment is not for the moment, of main importance; we must not forget to notice, however, that Gorgon Grin is a reflection of the grinning cobbler who won the prize for grinning in the match described in the *Spectator.41*

See *The Spectator,* No. 9.

If it seemed worth while to make a word for word study of the *Journal* essays with the *Tatler,* the *Guardian,* and the *Spectator* in hand, many actual verbal correspondences could probably be established beyond question. Some of these have already been indicated. But since the direct and avowed purpose of the papers is so clear that Proteus Echo is actually often addressed as Mr. Imitator,42 the further task of establishing verbal proof is unnecessary. What we want to know is the method of using a literary model. Sometimes the *Journal* writer simply takes the same kind of subject, such as the description of a club, or some form of satire on absurd contemporary customs; in that case the thought, as well as the manner of the original, is likely to appear. Sometimes, however, we have an odd, unexpected use of a phrase or an incident from

"No. 173.

See *The New England Weekly Journal,* Nos. 17, 22.

the *Spectator,* in the midst of a highly moral discourse, of a totally different order. It is as if the Reverend Mather Byles were seeking illustrations for his Sunday morning sermon, and naturally turned his week's reading to account. An instance of this may be found in the essay on the merciful uncertainty of death in the *Journal:3* "I know not by what happy Providence it is," the essay begins, and goes on to make the general point that we should adore the Creator for concealing the manner of our death. This leads to the general subject of dying, and we are told the "well known Story of the Lady who bled to death by the Prick of a Needle at her Work." The moral essayist has "often beheld her Statue in Westminster Abbey, in which is emblematically intimated the Manner of her dying." We should be fairly certain by this time that our author had read of Sir Roger's visit to Westminster Abbey, with the Spectator,44 on the happy occasion when this very statue was pointed out to Sir Roger, and he wondered that "Sir Richard Baker has said nothing of her in his Chronicle." But as if to make assurance doubly sure, Mather Byles, or whoever wrote the *Journal* essay, called the unhappy lady a "Martyr to Diligence and good Housewifery." Addison's phrase is "Martyr to good Housewifery." Another edifying essay on Envy of the Great45 resolves itself into Patrick Henry's theme in a novel form. Caesar had his Brutus and Cassius, we are told, Virgil his "vile Obloquies," and even the *Tatler*

"Ibid., No. 20.

" See *The Spectator,* No. 329.

"See *The New England Weekly Journal,* No. 20.

and *Spectator* could not escape! "The *Tatler* was writ in too fine a spirit," the essay continues, "and too much thrown out of the common road of thinking, not to alarm the Men of little Genius, while the *Spectator* which will be admired by Posterity could not escape the impotent Lashes of the *Examiner."* So the paean of tribute and admiration goes. In one way or another, we meet traces of it everywhere.

Many of Mather Byles's poems were published in the *Journal* before they were gathered together for the little volume of 1744; such are the *Verses written in Milton's Paradise Lost,6* the *Elegy of George I,"* *Belinda,* a *Pastoral;48* other poems published in the *Journal* and almost certainly his, are the *Sequel of Commencement,9* the *God of Tempest,50* a paraphrase of the *One Hundred and Fourth Psalm,51* a *Congratulatory Poem,52* addressed to Governor Burnet, who had just been appointed. Some of these effusions have the pompous nourish of his serious heroic style, while some, like *Belinda,* and *Commencement,* effect the gay mock-heroic; but all alike imitate Pope. Even when he is writingverses in his *Paradise Lost,* showing his admiration of Milton, it would be hard to find many traces of its effect on his own poetry: and we have seen his acknowledgment of Pope as his master. The last of the Proteus Echo essays, the fifty-second, in the *Journal* of April 1, 1728, announces with a flourish, the new book, "now preparing for the Press," namely *A Miscellany of Poems,* "by several Hands, and upon Several Occasions: some of which have already been published, and received the Approbation of the best judges, with many more, very late Performances, of equal if not superior Beauty, which have never yet seen the Light. Any ingenious gentlemen may contribute toward its publication by sending to Mr. Daniel Henchman, *or* the Publisher of this Paper." The book is that same little collection from which we have so often quoted, and the advertisement furnishes one more clear proof of the close connection between Mather Byles and the publishers, Kneeland and Green.

See *The New England Weekly Journal,* No. 22, August 14, 1727.

" Ibid., No. 24, August 28, 1727.

" Ibid., No. 54, April 1, 1728. -." Ibid., No. 15, July 3, 1727.

Ibid., No. 33. Six stanzas of this poem appeared in Dr. Belk- nap's collection of *Sacred Poetry,* and are there attributed to Mather Byles.

51 Ibid., No. 35.

" Ibid., No. 71. See Drake, *History of Boston,* pp. 581-582; Kettell, *Specimens of American Poetry; Memorial History of Boston,* Vol. II, chap. XV, p. 399, note.

The fifty-second essay was announced in the *Journal* as "the last piece which will be published by the gentlemen who begun and have till now supplied this paper." Yet they evidently continued their editorial services,53 and the essay certainly remained for many years a main feature of the *Journal's* front page. Such essays in the later years are not always linked together, of course, by a fiction like that of Proteus Echo and his club; but some of the later attempts are just as well written in themselves.

See *Transactions of the American Antiquarian Society*, Vol. VI, p. 41.

One series of eighteen, beginning January 6, 1729, has been traditionally ascribed to Governor Burnet. Isaiah Thomas's reasons for accepting the ascription seem to be sound enough.54 He had seen a file of the *Journal*, belonging to one of its distinguished first editors, with an index written in the latter's own hand; and in this index the eighteen numbers in question are listed thus: *"Speculation* – Govr No. I," "No. II," and so forth. If Governor Burnet did write the new series, he proved himself a wielder of sensible pedestrian prose, not so close to Addison, either in form or content, as the fifty- two essays of Proteus Echo, but showing a large reading in the philosophy of the day, and a considerable knowledge of literature. His seventh paper55 begins characteristically enough: "Mr. Addison has given us a Chain of entertaining Thoughts upon the Instinct of Animals, in the *Spectators* No. 120, and No. 121. As I was reading these Papers over, I was led to think, that Instinct was not confined to the lowest Orders of Beings, but might perhaps take place in Human Creatures in many cases." This far-away philosophy is just the sort of thing he would draw from Addison, instead of the more human elements; that is, Governor Burnet was really writing *Speculations,* in the exact sense of the word.

After the publication of the Governor's essays, we find, in the *Journal* of June 22,1730, a high-flown discourse on the "spangled concave" above us, treating the beauties of knowledge in general, and the injustice of its being denied to women. All periodicals that followed the *Spectator* took an interest in women's training and education, confidently preaching the betterment of the sex. There are essays also on education in general, on the poetry of Horace, on emulation, on happiness, on business, and kindred subjects. Who wrote them, can only be dimly guessed. The pastors may have continued to furnish an occasional speculation. Samuel Knee- land himself, or his partner, Timothy Green, after all their association in business with the best educated men in Boston, can hardly be supposed incapable of turning off a neat essay upon occasion. In any case, they had the wit to present one startling novelty to their readers. On February 14, 1732, they began publishing *The London Merchant, or the History of George Barnwell,* without naming the author, Lillo. One of the most noteworthy realistic tragedies of the eighteenth century was thus reprinted in the Puritan stronghold of America, within a surprisingly short time of its first appearance. This fact seems to have escaped observation until now. Probably a stray copy of the play had found its way into Kneeland 's book-shop. We cannot suppose that it had a place in the Prince or Byles libraries! Evidently Boston readers were rather more liberal in their tastes than we have been accustomed to think.

51 See *History of Printing in America*. In *Transactions of the American Antiquarian Society,* Vol. VI, p. 40. K See *The New England Weekly Journal,* March 10, 1729.

But the need of inventing amusement from literary models was passing. The *Journal's* first page gradually became a reprint of selections from *The Universal Spectator, The Political State, The Weekly Register, The London Magazine, Applebee's Journal, The Free Briton,* and finally, *The Gentleman's Magazine.* Although these now and then included a selection from Steele,56 or Sir William Temple,57 or once, even, from Milton,58 they tended I rather to discuss contemporary questions of polit- i ical, economic, or scientific importance. That is, *The New England Journal* was selecting more and more the material appropriate for a newspaper. When its publishers bought out the old *Boston Ga-*

' *zette,* in 1741, and combined the two papers into one, the resulting *Boston Gazette and Weekly Journal* began already to have the look of a modern newspaper. It needed only the establishment of the monthly magazine to make the separation from literary sources complete.

f-' Henceforth the literary periodical would be one thing; the newspaper would be quite another.

Steele '*a Englishman,* No. 11, is quoted in the *Journal,* June 17, 1734.

"Sir William Temple's *Essay on Popular Discontents* was printed in the *Free Briton* of June 8 and 15, 1732, and included in the *Journal* of Nov. 20, 1732.

"Milton's passage, "Hail, Wedded Love," quoted in *The Weekly Register* of Sept. 30, 1732, and included in the *Journal* of Feb. 5, 1733.

4

SECTION 4

CHAPTER III

   "the Hue And Cby Afteb The Busy-body"

   Bbadfobd's Amebican Mebcuby

   It is now time for us to return to the fortunes of that brilliant run-away apprentice of James Franklin, who advertised in 1723 for "a likely lad," doubtless to fill the vacancy in his printing office. As Paul Leicester Ford has put it, "A likely lad may have been forthcoming, but *the* likely lad was lost to Boston for all time."1 The thrilling story of his next six years is known to every school-child. Only a comment or two will be needed here.

   The literary output of these years in no way justified the promise of the Dogood papers. There stand to his credit between 1723 and 1729, only the so-called "wicked tract" on Liberty and Necessity, a dissertation more dull even than wicked; the Journal of his Voyage from London home to Philadelphia; and the Rules for his little Junto. Nothing could be clearer, however, than the continued intensity of his literary interests during those varied and exciting years. Apparently he selected his friends for their libraries or their love of reading. And when writing his autobiography years afterwards, he remembered and was at pains to note the little facts that establish his continued passion for reading. His friend Collins's library, *"a* pretty collection of

Mathematicks and natural philosophy,"2 was to go by boat with Franklin to New York. His chief acquaintances at this time were ". . . all lovers of reading."3 One of them, James Ealph, besides being a tolerable versifier, must have imbibed along with Franklin's Deism, some of the latter's ambition to write prose, for when the two friends were looking about for employment in London, Ealph "propos'd to Eoberts, a publisher in Paternoster Eow, to write for him a weekly paper like the *Spectator."4* The Philadelphia library grew out of the mere collecting of the books of Franklin's club into one room.5 His very original, private manual of perfection was headed by a quotation from Addison's *Cato.6*

1 In his *Franklin Bibliography,* p. xv.

Indeed, long after Benjamin Franklin had become the great man of affairs, he retained his warm interest in the literary models of his youthful days. The little pamphlet which he wrote and distributed in 1749, on *The Education of Youth in Pennsylvania7*proposed that English grammar be taught by reading Tillotson, Addison, Pope, Algernon Sidney, Cato's Letters; his plan for an English education to be adopted in the Philadelphia Academy, sketched in full for the trustees in 1750,8 gave reading lessons in the easier *Spectators* to the young students of the second class, would have the fifth class rework the "Sentiments of a *Spectator,"* in Franklin's own early manner, and the sixth class read and study Tillotson, Milton, Locke, Addison, Pope, Swift, the higher papers in the *Spectator* and *Guardian,* with translations of the classics, in which Franklin took a special interest. It was his original plan of an English education for students of the Academy, that he remembered and advocated again at the age of eighty-three, when the plans of the trustees were sadly confused.9

2 See *Autobiography,* in *Writings of Benjamin Franklin,* ed A. H. Smyth, Vol. I, p. 262.

8Ibid. The entire *Autobiography* testifies to the same fact.

Ibid., p. 277.

" Ibid., p. 312.

' Ibid., p. 331. " This my little book had for its motto these lines from Addison's *Cato:*

'Here will I hold. If there's a power above us
(And that there is, all nature cries aloud
Thro' all her works), he must delight in virtue;
And that which he delights in must be happy.' "

Act V, Sc. I, 11. 15-19.

1 *Proposals relating to the Education of Youth in Pennsylvania,* 1749.

Early in 1729, however, Franklin saw a profitable opportunity to compose again the little pieces modeled on the *Spectator,* such as he had formerly written for *The New England Courant.* This time he wished to put an inconvenient rival out of business. The story need be given here only in barest outline. Samuel Keimer, Franklin's old master in his first years in Philadelphia, having heard that his former journeyman intended to establish a newspaper, hastened to forestall him by issuing the first number of his cumbrous *Universal Instructor*

8See *Writings of Benjamin Franklin,* ed. A. H. Smyth, VoL III, p. 21.

"See *Observations relative to the Intentions of the original Founders of the Academy in Philadelphia,* 1789. In *Writings of Benjamin Franklin,* ed. A. H. Smyth, Vol. X, p. 9.

/ in all Arts and Sciences, and Pennsylvania Gazette, December 28, 1728. The instruction in all arts and sciences consisted in regular extracts from Chambers's *Universal Dictionary,10* beginning with A and going steadily on toward Z, followed in each issue by a weekly instalment of Defoe's *Religious Courtship,* which is introduced with a flourish in the *Universal Instructor,11* as "a scarce and delightful piece of History called *Religious Courtship,* which more especially regards Young People." Although the author is not mentioned by name, the authorship of *Religious Courtship* was probably no secret to Keimer, who was a personal friend as well as an admirer of the great dissenter. And Keimer's admiration was natural, since he himself had been a French "prophet," probably a Camisard of the Cevennes.12 His ignorance and fanaticism have been ridiculed once for all in the *Autobiography,13* yet in one or two particulars Franklin seems to have done him scant justice, admitting grudgingly, however, that he was "something of a scholar."14 A diligent search through the publications of the colony of Pennsylvania reveals the fact that Keimer, who had conducted a newspaper, and printed pamphlets on the Protestant Succession,15 in London, issued a number of by no means uninteresting reprints from his Philadelphia press, among them *Epictetus, His Morals,* in 1729, and Steele's *Crisis.* Even stray connections with the literary world are worth noting in the wilderness of colonial treatises on *The Fatal Consequences of Unscriptural Doctrine* or *Twenty Considerations against Sin.*

10 Chambers's *Universal Dictionary of all the Arts and Sciences.*

11 No. 18, Feb. 24, 1729; it ran through No. 35, filling a page or more each week.

12 See *Writings of Benjamin Franklin,* ed. A. H. Smyth, VoL I, p. 257, note.

a Ibid., p. 258, and passim. " Ibid., p. 257.

"Such as *The Protestant Jubilee: A Thanksgiving Sermon on that Doubly Remarkable Day, The Twentieth of January.* "Appointedfor Celebrating the Praises of God, for our Wonderful Deliverance, by the Happy Accession of His most Gracious Majesty King George to the Throne of Great Britain, when we were just at the brink of Euin." Printed and sold by S. Keimer, at the Printing Press in Paternoster Eow, 1715.

But Franklin seems to have been accurate in judging Keimer as very ignorant in his business, and in ordinary practical affairs; certainly it was not difficult for Franklin to compose something more sprightly than the *Religious Courtship.* He began the series of *Busy-Body* essays, and sent them to the *Mercury,* Bradford's long established paper, t give it a temporary popularity exceeding that o Keimer's *Instructor.* The vogue of the new Spectator of men and manners seems to have been immediate, and Franklin was able to buy *The Universal Instructor* for a song, after it had dragged through / forty numbers. He made it *The Pennsylvania Gazette,* of deserved fame.

But to return to the *Busy-Body.* Franklin was twenty-three when he wrote the six numbers known to be his; the first five, and the eighth. He neverx excelled them in his consciously imitative work. ? Later papers, such as the famous prefaces to *Poor Richard,* represent a distinctly more self-realizing, native humor, closer to the soil, daringly, deliberf ately bourgeois. Here in the *Busy-Body* he is still, on the whole, elegant, lofty, a Censor Morum as Isaac Bickerstaff in the *Tatler* had been before him. Eidentius and Eugenius, Cato and Cretico, Patience and Titan Pleiades make up the rather impressive list of imaginary characters, pointing various morals. No homely Bridget Saunders, drawn to the life that Franklin knew, meets us with "What a-peasecods! ... all the World must know that Poor Dick's Wife has lately taken a fancy to drink a little Tea now and then."16 In style, also, the *Busy-Body* is admittedly very close to Franklin's favorite literary models, the *Spectator* and the *Tatler.* Passages like the two following carry their own evidence in them.

"One of the greatest Pleasures an Author can have, is certainly the Hearing his Works applauded. The hiding from the World our Names, while we publish our Thoughts, is so absolutely necessary to this Self-Gratification, that I hope my Well-wishers will congratulate me on my Escape from the many diligent but fruitless Enquiries, that have of late been made after me. Every Man will own, That an Author, as such, ought to be try'd by the Merit of his Production only; but Pride, Party, and Prejudice at this Time run so very high, that Experience shews we form our Notions of a Piece by the Character of the Author. Nay, there are some very humble Politicians in and about this City, who will ask on which Side the Writer is, before they presume to give their Opinions of the Thing wrote. This ungenerous Way of Proceeding I was well aware of before I publish'd my first Speculation, and therefore concealed my Name."17

TM See *Preface by Mistress Saunders to Poor Richard,* 1738. " *Busy-Body,* No. 8, March 27, 1729.

"There are little Follies in the Behaviour of most Men, which their best Friends are too tender to acquaint them with; There are little Vices and small Crimes, which the Law has no Regard to or Remedy for: There are likewise great Pieces of Villany sometimes so craftily accomplish'd, and so circumspectly guarded, that the Law can take no Hold of the Actors. All these Things, and all Things of this Nature, come within my Province as Censor:"18

Of course Franklin would not have been Franklin if he had sustained this high tone throughout any series of essays. The flippant, jaunty insults he had learned to give rivals and enemies in *The New England Courant* were bound to mar the effect of his assumed literary decorum. In fact, however he might assume the *Spectator's* office of censuring small follies, the aim of publishing the *Busy-Body* papers was very different. The personal sting often lurks in the careless little postscripts, apparently so pointless.

As to the actual subject-matter of the *Busy-Body,* Franklin never found himself in the predicament of the *Spectator's* more slavish imitators, – a predicament described forcibly enough in the English paper, *Common-Sense,* June 11, 1737: '-The *Spectator,* of moral and facetious memory, reformed the periwigs, the canes, and the sword-knots of the fops; nay, he tripped up their red heels, if I may be allowed that expression. ... In a word, whenever I take up the *Spectator,* I am ready every minute to break out into the same exclamation that a poet of Gascogny uttered upon reading over a beautiful ode of Horace.

"Busy-Body, No. 5, March 4, 1728-29.

'D – n these ancients (says he), they have stolen all my fine thoughts.' "

The *Spectator* never stole any of Franklin's best thoughts. When he read Addison's charming papers on women's follies, he could use the general idea, which he undoubtedly drew from the *Spectator* and the *Tatler,* to create vividly realized characters of his own, such as Patience, in *Busy-Body* Number 4, with her thrifty little shop to mind, and her complaint of impertinent visitors who wasted her valuable time. The very notion of impertinent visits he may have taken from the twenty-fourth *Spectator,* where Thomas Kimbow's letter mentions the grievance in a very different connection.19 He could adapt the endless essays on scandal and defamation in the *Tatler* and *Spectator* to his own private enemies! From Addison's sober remarks on laughter and ridicule,20 he probably created the two characters Eidentius and Eugenius in the second *BusyBody;* wooden enough stalking horses they are, to be sure, but they furnished an opportunity for some good original sentences,21 and the whole conclusion of Franklin's paper turns abruptly away from that of the *Spectator,* which becomes a discussion of comedy and burlesque, somewhat on the order of Fielding's later discussions. The "renowned Tiff- Club," of which Franklin advertised an account in his fourth *Busy-Body* follows more closely the "King of Clubs," but, on the other hand, the tale of Vulcan's dogs in the five hundred and seventy- ninth *Spectator* furnished evidently a bare hint for the coarser episode of Pug, the monkey, in the fifth *Busy-Body.* When Franklin read the *Tailer's* account22 of distinguishing various callers by their raps, he drew from it a suggestion for the development of Cato's character,23 that model of homespun virtue in his third *Busy-Body.*

18"Mr. Spectator, if you have kept various company, you know there is in every tavern in town some old humorist or other, who is master of the house as much as he that keeps it. The drawers are all in awe of him, and all the customers who frequent his company yield him a sort of comical obedience. I do not know but I may be such a fellow as this myself. But I appeal to you whether this is to be called a club, because so many impertinents will break in upon me, and come without appointment."

20" The talent of turning men into ridicule, and exposing to laughter those one converses with, is the qualification of little ungenerous tempers. A young man with this east of mind cuts himself off from all manner of improvement. ... If the talent of ridicule were employed to laugh men out of vice and folly, it might be of some use to the world; but instead of this, we find that it is generally made use of to laugh men out of virtue and good sense, by attacking everything that is solemn and serious, decent and praiseworthy in human life." *Spectator,* No. 249.

21" Among these witty gentlemen let us take a view of Ridentius. What a contemptible figure does he make with his train of paltry admirers! This wight shall give himself an hour's diversion with the cock of a man's hat, the heels of his shoes, an unguarded expression in his discourse or even some personal defect; and the height of his low ambition is to put some one of the company to the blush, who perhaps must pay an equal share of the reckoning with himself."

B"A very odd Fellow visited me to Day at my Lodgings, and desired Encouragement and Recommendation from me for a new Invention of Knockers to Doors. . . . He then gave me a compleat Set of Knocks, from the Solitary Rap of the Dun and Beggar, to the Thun- derings of the Sawcy Footman of Quality, with several Flourishes and Ratlings never yet performed. He likewise played over some private Notes, distinguishing the familiar Friend or Relation from the most modish Visitor; and directing when the Reserve Candles are to be lighted." *Tatter,* No. 105.

"" Cato had Business with some of them, and knock 'd at the Door. The most trifling Actions of a Man in my Opinion, as well as thesmallest Feature and Lineaments of the Face, give a nice Observer some Notion of his Mind. Methought he rapp'd in such a peculiar Manner as seem'd of itself to express there was One, who deserv'd as well as desir'd Admission." *Susy-Body,* No. 3.

If he saw the *Censor,?* one of the numerous early imitations of the *Spectator,* he probably took the account in one of its numbers of Sarah Skelborn,215 the Speculatrix, asahint, butonlyahint, for his nameless correspondent with the gift of second sight in the fifth *Busy-Body.* Second sight was one of the serious superstitions of the day, and the *Censor* tells us that "many ladies have as high an opinion of the Dumb Doctor26 as of the great Meade," and that "Partridge is daily preferred to the immortal Sir Isaac Newton." Whether Franklin ever saw this number of the *Censor* or not is entirely problematical, since there is no evidence to guide us. Stray copies of English papers did cross the Atlantic. The account of Sarah Skelborn, however, he could have read in Lilly's History of his Life and Times, or he could have read similar accounts of similarly gifted persons almost anywhere. The important thing to note is that some such hint served him for the fifth as well as the delightful eighth number of the *Busy-Body,* in which he warns his country-folk against the "odd Humour of Digging for Money, thro' aBelief that much has been hid by Pirates formerly frequenting the River." Astrology and "second sight" were frequently resorted to for information as to mysterious treasure.

24 *The Censor* is probably Theobald's paper.

""And, therefore, when he (Lilly in his History) says, that Sarah Skelborn, the Speculatrix, had the best eyes for second sight that ever he saw, he will certainly be believed; because it is a received maxim with the ignorant that every one has not the faculty of discerning spirits and future contingencies." *Censor,* No. 11, May 4, 1715.

28 The " Dumb Doctor" referred to is Duncan Campbell, the hero of Defoe's book.

The passages giving the avowed aim of the *Busy- Body* show the greatest direct imitation of the *Spectator* to be found in the essays. Even here, however, the resemblance is seldom verbal. There is a vital use of the thought borrowed for new ends. It may be clearer at this point to quote parallel statements of purpose in the *Spectator* and *Busy-Body* respectively:

The Spectator.

"If Punch grows extrara- gant I shall reprimand him very freely; if the stage becomes a nursery of folly and impertinence, I shall not be afraid to animadvert upon it. In short, if I meet with anything in city, court, or country, that shocks modesty or good manners, I shall use my utmost endeavors to make an example of it. I must, however, entreat every particular person, who does me the honor to be a reader of this paper, never to think himself or any one of his friends or enemies, aimed at in what is said; for I promise him, never to draw a faulty character which

The Busy-Body.

"With more concern have I continually observ'd the growing Vices and Follies of my Country-folk; and, tho' Reformation is properly the concern of every Man; that is,

Every one ought to mend One; yet Tis too true in this Case, that what is every Body's Business is nobody's Business; and the Business is done accordingly. I, therefore, upon mature Deliberation, think fit to take Nobody's Business wholly into my own Hands; and, out of Zeal for the Publick Good, design to erect myself into a Kind of *Censor Morum;*

does not fit at least a thousand people; or to publish a single paper, that is not written in the spirit of benevolence, and with a love to mankind." No. 34.

"I am sensible I have in this Particular undertaken a very unthankful Office, and expect little besides my Labour, for my Pains. Nay, 'tis probable I may displease a great Number of your Readers, who will not very well like to pay 10 S. a Year for being told of their Faults. But, as most People delight in Censure when they themselves are not the Objects of it, if any are offended at my publickly exposing their private Vices, I promise they shall have the Satisfaction, in a very little Time, of seeing their good Friends and Neighbours in the same Circumstances." No. 1.

" Tis to be observ'd that if any bad Characters happen to be drawn in the Course of these Papers, they mean no particular Person, if they are not particularly apply'd. Likewise, that the Author is no Party-Man, but a general Meddler." No. 3.

"But there are none to whom this paper will be more useful than to the

"However, let the Fair Sex be assur'd that I shall always treat them and theirfemale World. I have often thought there has not been sufficient pains taken in finding out proper employments and diversions for the Fair ones. Their amusements seem contrived for them, rather as they are women, than as they are reasonable creatures; and are more adapted to the Sex than to the species. The toilet is their great scene of business, and the right adjusting of their hair the principal employment of their lives." No. 10.

"I look upon myself as (t kind of guardian of the fair, and am always watchful to observe anything which concerns their interest." No. 423.

Affairs with the utmost Decency and Kespect. I intend now and then to dedicate a Chapter wholly to their Service; and if my Lectures any Way contribute to the Embellishment of their Minds and brightening of their Understandings, without offending their Modesty, I doubt not of having their Favour and Encouragement." No. 1.

– Tenet insanabile multos Scribendi cacoethes. Juv.

"There is a certain distemper, which is mentioned neither by Galen nor Hippocrates, nor to be met with in the London Dispensary. Juvenal, in the motto of my paper, terms it a *cacoethes,* which is a hard word for a disease, called, in plain Eng-

" The Censor observing, that the Itch of Scribbling begins to spread exceedingly, and being carefully tender of the Reputation of his Country in Point of Wit and Good Sense, has determined to take all manner of writings in Verse or Prose, that pretend to either, under his immediate Coglish, the itch of writing. This caeoethes is as epidemical as the small-pox, there being very few who are not seized with it some time or other in their lives. There is, however, this difference in these two distempers; that the first, after having indisposed you for a time, never returns again; whereas this I am speaking of, when it is once got into the blood, seldom comes out of it. The British nation is very much afflicted with this malady, and though very many remedies have been applied to persons infected with it, few of them have ever proved successful.

Some have been cauterized with satires and lampoons, but have received little or no benefit from them; . . . I suffered them (the scribblers) to ray out their darkness as long as I was able to endure it, till at length I came to a resolution of rising upon them, and hope in a little time to drive them quite out of the British hemisphere." No. 582.

nizance; and accordingly hereby prohibits the Publishing any such for the future, till they have first pass'd his Examination, and receiv'd his *Imprimatur;* for which he demands as a Fee only 6 d. per Sheet." No. 5.

A glance will make it plain that the imitation here hardly extends further than the general purpose and form, with now and them a haunting likeness in a phrase, a word, a paragraph. Since Franklin's early work is popularly regarded as the most noteworthy colonial imitation of Addison, the results of investigation into other papers such as *The New England Weekly Journal* may appear the more striking as we proceed.. In Franklin's case, we simply have the advantage of knowing his models, beforehand. And it happens that Keimer's *Universal Instructor,* dull as its pages are for the most part, affords us here a piquant piece of external evidence, hitherto buried along with the articles copied from Chambers's Encyclopedia. Keimer was by no means poor-spirited enough to abandon his own cause, when he saw the *Busy-Body* taking the town by storm. He attacked his unwelcome rival boldly; and his attack consists in accusing him of copying the *Tatler* and, the *Spectator!* So we have excellent first hand evidence that Franklin's love for Addison and Steele was well known to his contemporaries.

Keimer took the character of Cretico in the third *Busy-Body* as a portrait of himself, which indeed it probably was. "0, Cretico! thou sowre Philosopher!" wrote Franklin, "When wilt thou be esteem'd, regarded, and belov'd like Cato? ... Be advised by thy Friend. Neglect those musty Authors; let them be cover'd with Dust, andx moulder on their proper Shelves; and do thou apply thyself to a Study much more profitable, The knowledge of Mankind and of thy Self." Doubtless the "mustyauthors" referred to Chambers's Encyclopedia and various Seventh Day or other religious tracts. Keimer retorted in a prominent column of his paper,27 with the conspicuous headline, "Hue and Cry after the Busy-Body." A bit of yellow journalism it was, and, as might have been expected, it only made the *Busy-Body* loom larger in the public eye. Keimer dabbled in verse, so it was natural enough that he should try his hand on his rival. This is the withering little satire which introduces his remarks.

"But prithee tell me, art thou mad,
To mix good Writing with the bad?
Fie, Sir, let all be of a Piece,
Spectators, Swans, or Joseph's geese:"

"Joseph," of course, refers to Franklin's co- worker on the *Busy-Body,* Joseph Breintnal, whose papers by no means always deserved the slur. Keimer followed these spirited lines with prose criticism of the third *Busy-Body,* in which, we remember, the characters of Cato and Cretico are contrasted, Cato being distinguished by his knock.28 Keimer calls this "ridiculous rant about knowing a man for his rap," yet not without example, "for," he writes, "I remember the *Taller29* says 'A very odd fellow visited me to-day at my Lodging, and desired Encouragement and Eecommendation from

" See *The Universal Instructor in all Arts and Sciences and Pennsylvania Gazette,* No. XII, January 13, 1729. Keimer must have made a mistake in dating his paper, for the *Busy-Body* did not begin until Feb. 4, 1729.

"Vide supra, pp. 65-66.

" Tatler, No. 105. Vide supra, p. 65, note 22.

me.'" Then follows the "odd fellow's" lesson in raps, which Keimer quotes in full from the *Tatler,* ending with, "He likewise played over some private notes, distinguishing the familiar Friend, Eelation, etc." The comment which Keimer makes on the *Busy-Body's* indebtedness to the *Tatler* is intended to be full of wit and sarcasm. "Egad," he says, "I fancy Cato's an odd Descendant of that very odd Fellow; and his Knack of Knocking comes by Inheritance." Franklin did indeed, in all probability, get his idea of Cato's Knock from the *Tatler,* as we have seen.30 Not to be outdone in the knowledge of polite literature, Keimer proceeds himself to quote from the "sentiments of that generous Man, to whom the World is So highly obliged for the elegantest System of Wit, Politeness, Oeconomy, and all the social and Christian Vertues that form that shining Character, A Gentleman! who was as justly rewarded by an unenvy'd Applause and an uninterrupted Bun of Eeputation." These are Keimer's glowing words in praise of Addison.

The next week another article appeared in *The Universal Instructor,31* proving again that Keimer was something of a man of letters, for he quotes the *Essay on Criticism,* and condemns in round terms the "servile Imitation" of the *Spectator* in the spurious ninth volume. "The Fate of this Book," he says grandly, "in some sort falls on all that have endeavour'd to succeed in that way." Thus he tried to stem the popularity of the *Busy-Body.* But the

"Vide supra, p. 65.

"See *The Universal Instructor,* No. XIII, Jan. 20, 1729. Again, Keimer must have been wrong in his date.

reading public delighted in the novelty of essays in any form, imitative or not, after years of stale news from Hungary or Italy. In a few months Keimer had sold his paper to Franklin and left for the Bar- badoes, where he established a newspaper, called *The Barbadoes Gazette.* It contained a number of essays and letters imitative of the *Tatler.32* Thus Keimer would seem to have profited by Franklin's example.

Not all the credit of the clever work that ruined a rival's business belongs to Franklin, however. Only six of the *Busy-Body* essays are his, and not even all of these. His share has been indicated in the second volume of the late Professor A. H. Smyth's edition of Franklin's Writings. Joseph Breintnal wrote the rest. The papers in which Franklin had no share have been passed over as dull, forgotten rubbish.

A word about Breintnal. In the *Autobiography* he is described first among the members of the Junto. A copyer of deeds, he probably held a slightly higher position at that time than many of Franklin's friends. "A good-natur'd, friendly, middle-ag'd man," we are told in the *Autobiography,33* "a great lover of poetry, reading all he could meet with, and writing some that was tolerable; very ingenious in many little Nicknackeries, and of sensible conversation." Franklin evidently valued him also for his

M*Caribbeana,* "containing Letters and Dissertations, together with Poetical Essays on various subjects and occasions, chiefly wrote by several hands in the West Indies." Published in London, 1741.

"See *Writings of Benjamin Franlclin,* ed. A. H. Smyth, Vol. I, p. 299.

influence in recommending solid business to the printing-house, for which Breintnal procured from the Quakers the printing of forty sheets of their history.34 This fact, and the papers against Infidelity in the later numbers of the *Busy-Body* indicate that Breintnal was untouched by Franklin's Deism, and, indeed, as a middle-aged man, he would be little likely to attend to the religious opinions of a young fellow of twenty-three. None the less did he. devote himself to the young fellow's interests; and none the less was he profoundly influenced by the literary and economical enthusiasms of Franklin, as an examination of his papers shows. When the members of the Junto merged their private books in the common library, doubtless Breintnal's formed no small share. There is indeed some evidence for this supposition in the fact that he presented to the later Library Company Plutarch's *Morals* (in English) and *Animadversions upon Hobbes's Leviathan,* by Alexander Eosse, a London publication of 1653. Political and philosophical thought interested him keenly.

Thirty-two *Busy-Body* papers were sent to the *Mercury.* Breintnal wrote twenty-six, and collaborated on two of the others, so that, as a matter of fact, Franklin only started the series, evidently with the understanding that Breintnal should continue in the same general manner. This Breintnal succeeded in doing. He had none of Franklin's teasing, witty effrontery, yet several of his social satires compare favorably enough with the best of Franklin's. Indeed, there is a double imitation here, interesting to observe. On the one hand, Breintnal followed the *Spectator.* No doubt he had his own copy at hand, but in any case a member of the Junto would have access to all the books of the club. The general plan of Breintnal's essays resembles the *Spectator* more closely than Franklin's. There are letters from Florio and Matilda, from Amy Prudent, Lucy Wid- owless and Marcia, all with grievances such as the Amorets and Deborahs bring to Mr. Spectator. Then, too, Breintnal was naturally trying to be like Franklin. In one instance,36 he succeeded so admirably that one almost suspects Franklin of a share in the paper, – a rather unworthy and unnecessary suspicion, however, since there is no other evidence for it. As this clever little piece may be seen only in the dusty files of the *Mercury,* we may profitably examine it in more detail than the well-known and often-reprinted essays of Franklin.

" Ibid., p. 300.

Breintnal begins with a petition, having all the conviction of reality, from the young tradesmen and artificers of the city of Philadelphia to the Busy- Body, showing first of all why they cannot marry. " The gay and splendid appearance which the young Ladies about our own Station universally affect, makes it very difficult to distinguish them from People of the best Estates in Town, which very much perplexes your Petitioners, lest by addressing Themselves to their Superiors they should fall under the Imputation of Impudence and Presumption, which your Petitioners hope they shall always have more

" See *Susy-Body,* No. 15, in *The American Mercury* of May 22,1729.

'Grace than to incur. . . . Your Petitioners are likewise so unbred as to have no true Relish for Tea, neither can they clearly distinguish the Taste of Bohea from Green: Besides which there are great Variety of Utensils belonging to the Tea-Equipage which your Petitioners despair of ever learning the Name, and Use off; And this ignorance of theirs, they are sensible, must make them appear excessively awkward and ridiculous, when they come under the Tuition of Polite Spouses, who count the knowledge of these particulars of the greatest Importance. Your Petitioners have heard also, that all these Things are very chargeable; viz., That one Ounce of Tea often costs as much as Fifty Pounds of Flour, That a Sugar Loaf is worth a Quarter of Beef, and That the Tea-Table and Appertenances, are of as much value as the Furniture of a Room; Which Account to your Petitioners appears altogether extravagant and surprising." Accordingly they beg that the Busy-Body will lay his injunctions upon the fair ones of their rank, that they may no longer be "thus guarded with an Air of Quality, and entrench'd behind double Rows of China-Ware."

Here indeed are all the favorite economic ideals of the man who took his morning porridge with a pewter spoon, and wrote Poor Richard's Almanac. The petitioners' letter immediately suggests the later effusion of Anthony Afterwit in the *Gazette;36* Franklin makes Afterwit complain of the " Tea- Table with all its Appertenences of China and Silver," as well as other feminine extravagances. Yet there is a certain sly urbanity in BreintnaPs respectful and even complimentary hints, which, one fancies, would have made Philadelphia young ladies more kindly disposed toward the good advice than they were toward Franklin's derisive fun.

See *Pennsylvania Gazette,* July 10, 1732. This letter of Anthony Afterwit has also been reprinted in *Writings of Benjamin Franklin,* ed. A. H. Smyth, Vol. II, p. 182.

As a matter of fact both papers probably had the same ultimate source in the three hundred and twenty-eighth *Spectator* of the collected edition,37 where a grieved husband sets forth his wife's extravagance in embroidery and tea. "Coffee, chocolate, green, imperial, Pekoe, and Bohea Tea, seem to be trifles; but when the proper appurtenances of the tea-table are added, they swell the account higher than one would imagine." Steele's word "appurtenances" would not come very naturally to either Breintnal or Franklin unless they had seen it in some rather formal, literary connection. It has no concrete, mechanical significance, such as tradespeople would need. Elegant conversation, much more formal in the eighteenth century than now, might have supplied it; and we know that the Junto tried to present their arguments in what was regarded as excellent form. Then, too, there are a thousand literary sources, books and pamphlets, in which they could have found it, as well as the *Spectator.* Nothing more than a probability that they took their *literary* expression of the growing custom of tea-drinking from this source, can be even contended for. The great similarity in the context, the fact that the connection of words and thought is precisely the same

"March 17, 1712.

in all three, strengthens the probability. Moreover, it must not be forgotten that before 1730, – before the days of the *London* and *Gentleman's Magazines,* stray English essays on the *Spectator* model did not reach the provinces frequently. Eeaders were far more dependent on bound volumes of standard books; and of these none that we know were so often imitated as the various periodicals of Addison and Steele.

Another good paper from the hand of Breintnal treats of idleness. The sermon is well disguised by a coating of sugar.28 Octavus, complaining that he has so little to do, begs to be admitted into the Censor's service as a sort of Under Busy-Body. " It is my Misfortune, Sir," he explains, "since the renowned Don Morisini, and the ingenious Mr. P. left this Place, to have no Company, nor any Thing in the World to employ my Time in, except sauntring idly up and down, swinging my Cane in my Hand, and counting the Pillars in the Market-House." The cane was one of the conspicuous contemporary accessories of a fop39 in England, and it is interesting to see the *Busy-Body* taking note of the same characteristics in provincial Philadelphia.

The fourteenth *Busy-Body* has also a very lively letter from Matilda to the Censor, headed tragically enough with the motto, "0 Temporal 0 Mores!" and saying that Florio, "the gayest, prettiest Gentleman about Town," has made love to both Flavia and herself. The Busy-Body promises to avenge her, in Breintnal's more melodramatic strain. "I must confess so great an Enormity acted even under the Eye of our Censorship transports me with Indignation. And thou discourteous Knight, thou shame to the Honour of thy Profession, thou that hast basely falsified thy Word, make immediate Eeparation, or my Sword shall seek thee; among the Steely Squadrons will I pursue thee; In vain tho' thou hidest thyself in the Center of the Macedonian Phalanx; in vain tho' Hector and Achilles fought on thy side, and the Seven Champions of Christendom battled on thy Eight Hand."

88 See *Busy-Body,* No. 14, May 15, 1729.

" See *The Tatter,* Nos. 26, 28, 71, 77, and 103 for descriptions of the English fop, with his red-heeled shoes, and his amber-headed cane tied at his button.

Presently we hear from the distracted Florio,40 whose defence becomes in itself an amusing hit at the hard-hearted coquette. " I Ve sigh 'd, I 've sworn, and pin'd almost to Death, and like an Amorous Fool composed Ten thousand Stanzas fill'd with the Praises of Matilda's Form." In this distressing crisis, Flavia took pity on him. What should he do? Eefuse the proffered balm? The Busy-Body leaves his question quietly unanswered. But we learn from Marcus, in a later number,41 that the ladies began to resent the Censor's attempt to reform modish follies, and whether this be fiction or not, the next essay42 changes the emphasis to the faults of the other sex. In fact, there are no more satires on the ladies. Instead, Amy Prudent is allowed to show the enormity of the Meridional Club. What, indeed, could "Twelve a Clock Punch Drinkers," as she calls the members, have to say to afternoon tea? Lucy Widowless, too,43 writes of the sad neglect and abuse received from her husband, contrasting such treatment with the days of courtship.

See *Busy-Body,* No. 16, May 29, 1729. " Ibid., No. 19, June 19, 1729. "Ibid., No. 20, June 26, 1729.

The last number of the *Busy-Body* has an amusing as well as sensible letter of advice to voters before the fall elections. Apparently men were even more in danger of over-excitement then than now, if we may judge by the Busy-Body's warning in regard to the diet best adapted for keeping a cool head. "I advise you, therefore, now Dog days are past, to drink water moderately, and no wine."

Breintnal wrote several more or less political papers, showing not only that he had his Plutarch at his fingers' ends, but was supplied with *Cato's Letters46* and the *Guardian,* as well as miscellaneous classical tales and instances of one sort and another. No doubt he owned Plutarch's *Lives* together with the *Morals,* which we know he presented to the Library Company. *Cato's Letters* were popular enough in the colonies to be quoted in every colonial newspaper from Boston to Savannah, and must have had no small share in bringing about that amazing unity of political feeling which we find by 1760 in civilizations so fundamentally opposed as those of Charleston and Boston. Indeed, these political papers of Thomas Gordon and John Trenchard, published in *The London Journal* before 1723, develop a theory of representative government similar in most respects to that which underlies the Declaration of Independence. Often the very phrases of *Cato's Letters* sound like American commonplaces. For example, we read in the fifteenth paper: "The Administration of Government is nothing else but the Attendance of the Trustees of the People upon the Interest and Affairs of the People." Or again, in the twenty-fourth: "The first Principles of Power are in the People; and all the Projects of Men in Power ought to refer to the People, to aim solely at their Good, and end in it." As to the Divine Right of Kings, the British Cato is unequivocal: "Some have said that Magistrates, being accountable to none but God, ought to know no other restraint. But this Reasoning is as frivolous as it is wicked." *Cato's Letters* were collected in four volumes by 1724, and could therefore be more easily circulated in America than current periodicals. The colonial editor could publish his own sentiments in safety, if he could advertise them as the opinions of the "Divine English Cato."

Ibid., No. 28, August 21, 1729.

" Ibid., No. 32, September 18, 1729.

"Cato's Letters or *The British Cato.* The political papers of Thomas Gordon and John Trenchard, published every Saturday from Nov. 5, 1720, to July 27, 1723. The earliest numbers were printed in *The London Journal,* later ones in *The British Journal.* The New York Public Library has four editions of *Cato's Letters.*

So Breintnal "finds the subject better treated by Cato,"46 and proceeds to give along extract verbatim on the reasonable desires of men.47 He takes a

"See *Busy-Body,* No. 10, April 10, 1729.

"" The first reasonable Desire which men have, is to be in easy- Circumstances, and as free from Pain and Danger as humane Condition will permit; and then all their Views and Actions are directed to acquire Homage and Respect from others; and, indeed, in a larger Sense, the latter are included in the former. Different Ways are

letter entire48 from a "late famous political Writer in England," on peace and conciliation with the Colonies.49 He also uses Plutarch's *Life of Timoleon* for a similar purpose, and relates at length the incident leading up to Timoleon's famous saying, "Rejoice to see the time when every man in Syracuse may freely speak what he thinks."50 He publishes in the same number of the *Busy-Body,*61 an essay entire from the *Guardian,* with this little notice: "The following Essay on the Political Lion, taken from the *Guardian,* is sent me by a Correspondent, as proper to be published at this Time." The correspondent was probably fictitious.

But it must not be supposed that there are no dull stretches in Breintnal's *Busy-Body* papers. His essays on general topics such as the manners of the poor and the rich,52 the dependence of different members of society upon one another,53 youth and age,54 a catalogue of virtues and vices,55 are insufferably tedious; while if he was indeed, as Franklin said,56 a tolerable writer of verse, we get no hint of it in the dull couplets which he ground out for the*Busy-Body*. *TM* We should not even guess that he was "a great lover of poetry,"58 unless his occasional slips in grammar indicate a poetic license. Not infrequently he mistook a temporal or conditional clause for a complete sentence ;59 and he was capable of turning out a stupid medley of phrases like the incoherent letter of Amicus Curiae in the twenty- second *Busy-Body.60* Such hack work he probably did in haste to meet the emergency of the moment. The remarkable thing is, not that an obscure, middle- aged clerk sometimes wrote a dull rehash of moral commonplaces, but that such a man composed a dozen little pieces sparkling with wit, or full of genuine thought, – pieces that can bear comparison with Franklin's best. Keimer spoke truly enough, perhaps, in his jibe. The *Busy-Body* may have been made up of

taken to attain this End." And so on. See *Cato's Letters,* Nos. 108-115, inc., for a series of philosophical speculations on instincts, on the origin of good and evil, on liberty and necessity, and other subjects of a similar nature.

" See *Busy-Body,* No. 11, April 24, 1729.

See *Cato's Letters,* No. 106. *Of Plantations and Colonies.*

M See *Busy-Body,* No. 9, April 3, 1729.

"Ibid.

"Ibid., No. 12, May 1, 1729.

58 Ibid., No. 25, July 31, 1729.

84 Ibid., No. 30, Septmeber 4, 1729.

" Ibid., No. 24, July 24, 1729.

"Vide supra, p. 74.

Spectators, swans or Joseph's geese,

– but some of Joseph's geese were swans too.

The last number of the *Busy-Body* – the thirty- second61 – closed the series abruptly. Probably Franklin was already negotiating with Keimer for his *Universal Instructor,* and precisely two weeks afterward the first number of the new *Pennsylvania Gazette* appeared, being the fortieth number of the *Instructor,62* shorn of its ponderous superfluities.

" On the subject of a Philadelphia street, *Susy-Body,* Nor 18, June 12, 1729.

"Vide supra, p. 74.

" See *Busy-Body,* No. 12, May 1, 1729. Ibid., No. 13, May 8, 1729.

""July 10, 1729.

"September 18, 1729.

M October 2, 1729.

Henceforward neither Franklin nor his friends would write entertaining articles for *The American Mercury.* Quite the reverse. All that wit and ridicule and superior enterprise could do to drive the *Mercury* out of business was to be done with a kind of merciless good-humor. Andrew Bradford had a more solid position in the community than Keimer, as well as more sober common sense, but little by little the *Mercury* fell behind, until at length its backbone was broken by Franklin's appointment as postmaster in place of Bradford. We have seen before63 how much this office could mean to a newspaper. Bradford dragged on in business, it is true, but the *Mercury* remained a pitiful affair, and its chief permanent importance doubtless lies in its connection with Franklin and the *Busy-Body* papers. Bradford's various book advertisements and reprints will be considered in comparison with those of Franklin's press. The *Mercury* itself, however, is not quite destitute of interest, and it will be necessary to consider some traces of literary influence brought to light by the present investigation.

The American Mercury came within a day of being the second newspaper established in the colonies, since its first issue of December 22, 1719, was only a day later than that of *The Boston Gazette.* The earliest files of the *Mercury* in the Pennsylvania Historical Society have been examined. These quaint little sheets, published when Benjamin Franklin was a boy of thirteen in his brother's printing office, do not differ materially from the old *Boston*

"Vide supra, chap. I.

News-Letter. We find only a few stale foreign items revamped, together with the Philadelphia shipping entries. Certainly there is no original essay until the first *Busy-Body* of 1729; but Bradford could hardly have failed to note the popularity of this literary fashion, new in Philadelphia. He must have taken a hint from Franklin's careless words: "But as few here have the Advantage of good Books, for want of which, good Conversation is still more scarce, it would doubtless have been very acceptable to your Eeaders, if, instead of an old out- of-date Article from Muscovy or Hungary, you had entertained them with some well-chosen Extract from a good Author."64

Remarkers, Cato Juniors, essays both original and copied whole "from a good author," appear in the *Mercury* after 1729. Bradford knew his Addi- son well, and sometimes published a *Spectator* paper, especially when he found it convenient to draw a moral from illustrious authority. Twice he prefaced his selection from Addison with an appreciative comment slyly aimed at his own foes, including Franklin probably in both instances; certainly in one. This is an obvious thrust at Franklin's Deism, which could not have been a secret in Philadelphia, and would very likely be known there as "infidelity" rather than as Deism. A letter to "Mr. Bradford" introduces the well-aimed remarks by which Franklin was to be confronted with his own pet enthusiasms arrayed against him.

"'Tis an Observation of my Lord Bacon," the

*" See *Busy-Body,* No 1, February 4, 1728-29.

letter begins,66 striking a dignified Addisonian note, "' That a little Natural Philosophy inclines Men to Atheism; but depth in Philosophy always brings them about to Religion.' " After deploring the loss of reverence among Americans, particularly young Americans (Franklin was twenty-nine at the time), the letter continues in a still more significant vein: "I am led into these Reflections from reading a Paper of the late Mr. Addison, the justness of whose Sentiments, embellish'd with the naked Beauties and Chastity of his Stile and Language, have deservedly placed him in the foremost rank of Authors. This great Man, as may be seen in many of his Speculations, was not ashamed to own himself a Religious Man, tho' in natural and acquired Knowledge was as much Superior to our Modern Skeptical Refiners, as were Socrates or Plato to a Toland or a Woolston. You may if you please give it Room in your Paper." These unmistakable hints lead up to the four hundred and forty-first *Spectator,* that tender, yet restrained expression of trust in the divine goodness, ending with Addison's own version of the twenty- third Psalm. Franklin would have endorsed every word of it heartily.

Again, and hardly less surely, Bradford was aiming at his rival, when introducing a passage from the *Spectator,* against unfounded suspicions. Bradford, himself, had been accused of slander, as he thought, and a sympathizing letter in the *Mercury*90 promptly administers a rebuke in these apparently simple terms:

See *The American Mercury,* No. 824, October 9, 1735. "No. 738, February 12, 1733-34.

"Whilst three or four of us were talking over this affair, one who admires and often reads over the *Spectators,* sent for his eighth volume, and read over number five hundred and sixty-eight. I shall only write out the Conclusion of it, which runs thus; 'I could not forbear reflecting with myself, upon that gross tribe of fools, who may be termed the Over-wise. ... A man who has a good nose at an innuendo, smells treason and sedition in the most innocent words that can be put together, and never sees a vice or folly stigmatized, but finds out one or other of his acquaintance pointed at by the writer. I remember an empty, pragmatical fellow, in the country, who upon reading over *The whole Duty of Man,* had written the names of several persons in the village at the side of every sin which is mentioned by that excellent author; so that he had converted one of the best books in the world into a libel against the 'Squire, churchwardens, overseers of the poor, and all other the most considerable persons in the parish.' "

We know that Franklin laid great stress on the freedom of his own paper from libel,67 and did not hesitate to expose a slander where he thought he saw one. Probably Bradford fondly hoped to spike the enemy's guns once for all. If so, he was grievously mistaken. The next chapter will show Franklin gaily complimenting himself on his newspaper, and bidding all slanderers to look themselves in the face in the incomparable mirror of truth furnished by the *Spectator!* But, in any case, Bradford's remarks are interesting in themselves. They show ; that he expected his readers to feel the import of a 1 quotation from the *Spectator;* that the idea of set-

" See *Autobiography,* in *Writings of Benjamin FranJclin,* ed. A. H. Smyth, Vol. I, p. 344.

tling all questions by a simple reference to its almost , scriptural authority was at least not unfamiliar, if i less common than in England.

Bacon's various works must have been in the office of the *Mercury* or in Bradford's library, as frequent quotations and one essay68 entirely devoted to an appreciation of Bacon amply prove. Stray quotations from Pope and Addison also add to the literary flavor of scattered pieces69 like the discussion of liberty in the seven hundred and forty-seventh *Mercury, TM* which is solemnly introduced by Addison's lines beginning, " 0 Liberty, Thou Goddess Heavenly Bright."71

The popularity of this subject, liberty, in the eighteenth century was equalled only by that of infidelity, of marriage, and of temperance. When the journalist needed a topic on sudden notice, he could work over the well-worn ideas and apparently never meet the charge of dulness. Sometimes he revamped a famous treatise, and in case he were writing on liberty, he would be likely to use *Cato's Letters.* Certainly Andrew Bradford drew on them liberally in every sense, for he not only published seven of the letters in his *Mercury,72* but also a series of very pompous articles on liberty73 in avowed imitation of Cato. Whether Breintnal's well-known interest in the *British Cato* influenced Bradford, it is impossible to say. The contempt expressed in the *Mercury* articles for low personal satire, for "little stories and calumnies invented" points to some personal bias, probably against Franklin, who had by that time been appointed to the post office by Colonel Spotswood. The duty of a good magistrate, public justice, property, personal liberty in general, are prominent topics in the *Mercury* essays. As literature their merit may be scant, yet they represent a certain attempt at formal essay-writing well worthy of mention.

"See *Mercury,* No. 818, August 28, 1735.

"Pope's *Eloisa* is quoted in the *Mercury,* No. 667, October 12, 1732, and a couplet from the *Essay on Criticism* closes an epitaph on *A Young Lady Lately Dead,* No. 547, June 18, 1730.

1"April 18, 1734.

n See *A Letter from Italy, to the Right Honourable Charles Lord Halifax,* 1. 119 ff.

" Nos. 537-540, April 9 through April 23, 1730, and Nos. 541-545, May 7 through May 28, 1730.

1 Beginning in the *Mercury,* No. 955, April 13, 1738.

/ After 1730 English periodicals of every kind [reached the colonies more regularly and much more 1 frequently. Bradford evidently subscribed to *The London Magazine,* and probably to *The Gentleman's Magazine,* while receiving stray copies of weekly papers like the *Register* and the *Miscellany.* These furnished him a mine of wealth. He regularly exploited *The London Magazine,* boldly copying arti- (cles and essays on the fashions, the power of custom, Jor the English political situation. *The Gentleman's Magazine* appears hardly less often, sometimes continued through number after number of the *Mercury'1* until its miscellaneous offerings are exhausted. The monthly magazines were repositories of news, of publishers' notices, of political editorials open or disguised, of moral and critical essays, and of recent verse. The political sections perhaps had

"*The Gentleman's Magazine* for March, 1734, is quoted August 8 in the *Mercury,* continued in the next week's *Mercury,* No. 763, also in No. 766.

the most eager readers in America, yet neither the essays nor the verse were slighted, if we may judge by the uninterrupted stream of both which filtered into colonial newspapers and the later colonial periodicals. Often an essay from *The Weekly Register,* or *The Universal Spectator,* or the *Miscellany* reached the American paper by way of *The London Magazine* or *The Gentleman's Magazine* in which it had been reprinted as a whole, or in part. Bradford could not have regularly subscribed to all the various weeklies which the *Mercury* used so liberally. Whether it be a little treatise on *Love and Marriage* with Milton's "Hail, wedded Love!" as a motto,76 or a warning *Of Punctilios among the Fair Sex, TM* or *Of Infidelity,77* Bradford probably drew from the monthly reviews, although particular cases would be difficult to establish, since he was quoting from Fog's *Weekly-Journal* in 1729, before the establishment of the magazines.

To continue the list of English periodicals influencing the *Mercury,* or copied directly into its pages, would be tedious and unnecessary. Bradford probably cared little for literature at first hand. He owed his literary interests in the first instance to the quickening of his paper by the *Busy-Body,* and the resulting demand for the essay form among provincial readers; in the second instance, to the fact

"From *The Weekly Begister,* September 30, 1732, quoted in the *Mercury,* No. 688, February *28,* 1732-33.

"From *The Universal Spectator,* No. 405, quoted in the *Mercury,* No. 888, December 28, 1736.

"From *The Weekly Miscellany,* July 21, 1733, quoted in the *Mercury,* No. 723, November 1, 1733.

that English papers of more or less permanent value, reached America in greater numbers after 1730. Bacon he no doubt genuinely admired, as well as Pope78 and perhaps Addison. But on the whole, he was not a book-inspired man, as his various book advertisements will show when compared with Franklin's. His paper, though of immense importance to the student of American life, has a small place in the history of literature; nor indeed was Bradford seriously attempting to make that place larger.

" The *Mercury* of January 13, 1735-36, No. 838, contains the well- known lines from "Mr. Littleton to Mr. Pope,"

Immortal Bard! for whom each muse has wove,

The fairest garland of the Phocian Grove:

Oh! Born our drooping genius to restore,

When Addison and Congreve are no more. CHAPTER IV

The Pennsylvania Gazette

When the subscribers of *The Universal Instructor* read their paper on October 2, 1729, they must have been conscious that the new editorial policy meant a change in the character of the weekly. It was clear that they could no longer doze over encyclopedic information, although if any readers had found this especially delightful, they could look forward to being regaled occasionally in the old manner. Franklin, ever wise and canny, gave up nothing in the *Instructor* that might conceivably have met a demand. He merely provided for clumsy material in a new and convenient way. And how refreshing to most of his readers must have been the new editor's bland announcement1 that "upon a view of Chambers's great Dictionaries ... we find that besides their containing many Things abstruse or insignificant to us, it will probably be fifty Years before the Whole can be gone thro' in this Manner of Publication; . . . and since it is likely that they who desire to acquaint themselves with any particular Art or Science, would gladly have the whole before them in much less time, we believe our Eeaders will not think such a Method of communicating Knowledge to be a proper One."

1 See *Editorial Preface to TJie Pennsylvania Gazette,* October 2, 1729, reprinted in *Writings of Benjamin Franklin,* ed. A. H. Smyth, Vol. H, p. 155.

As to the *Religious Courtship,* which had been "retal'd to the Publick in these Papers,"2 Franklin boldly announced its forthcoming publication, entire. But, unfortunately, neither in the bibliographies of Philadelphia reprints, nor in his own book notices in the *Gazette* can be found any clear evidence that it ever issued from his press. Twice before 1740 it is advertised in the *Gazette3* as "just imported," once along with scales, compasses and sealing wax. Probably the matter had simply drifted along as an intention in Franklin's mind, until he found the book easy to procure from London, when he naturally abandoned the idea of putting a reprint through his own press. Moreover, his publications were almost all of the obviously practical order.

/ The greatest difficulty which confronts us in speak- /ing of the *Gazette* is its very wealth of interest. I Whether its wit, its vivid and remarkable news / items, or its quaint advertisements be in question, we find a mine of unworked material everywhere. Nearly all the best original essays and tales in the *Gazette,* however, have been reprinted in the various editions of Franklin's writings and of ten commented upon. Nearly all, be it noted. One or two unpublished pieces in Franklin's best manner remain to be treated. For the rest, the unworked literary material is largely of a mediocre order, though often interesting and significant from many points of view. But at least it will not be necessary to pause over*The Witch Trial at Mount Holly,* the *Meditation on a Quart Mugg,6* the *Letter from, Celia Single?* the *Apology for Printers,7* or other well-known pieces showing only the barest resemblance in form to a literary model. A bare resemblance to the *Spectator,* certainly will not be denied in the case of the fictitious letters, which had at their best already ceased to be consciously imitative. Franklin was drawing the follies of his own provincial town with bold, free strokes.

' See *Editorial Preface.*

The Pennsylvania Gazette, No. 415, November 18, 1736, and No. 463, October 20, 1737.

At the same time his literary enthusiasms were not less conscious. So late as April 4, 1734, the *Gazette* has a delightful letter, introducing a *Spectator* paper on slander. The introductory remarks gravely addressed to "Mr. Franklin" can be from no other hand than his. The ascription will not be questioned in view of the fact that all his tantalizing wit, all the flavor of his individual method, are in them. No doubt Franklin was gaily answering his rival's taunts as to "a good nose at an innuendo"8 with a counter accusation of direct slander, also supported by a *Spectator* paper, and plainly aimed at the *Mercury,* as the word "weekly" shows. There was no other weekly in Philadelphia at the time. Since this letter in the columns of the *Gazette* furnishes one more direct and hitherto unpublished evidence of Franklin's veneration for Ad- dison, it will be worth while to quote a portion of it."Tho' your News-paper is sometimes as empty as those of others," he begins, merrily addressing / himself, "yet I think you have for the most part / (tho' you were once in one particular a sad Offender) had the Modesty to keep it pretty clear of Scandal, a Subject that others delight to wallow in. These People, probably from some Corruption in themselves . . . seem to think everything around them tainted; But that they may see their own Picture, and learn to know what they are doing *weekly,* pray let your Paper hold the following Glass to them, and as they like the Figure they may proceed for the future; others, however, will find by it what Judgment to make of them. It is a Performance of the immortal Mr. Addison, who to his own and the lasting Honour of the English Nation, labour'd hard, and sometimes with Success, to reform the Follies and Vices of his Country." The four hundred and fifty-first *Spectator* follows.

4 See *The Pennsylvania Gazette,* October 22, 1730.

Ibid., July 19, 1733.

Ibid., July 24, 1732. 'Ibid., June 10,1731. Vide supra, p. 88.

But Franklin did not always use literature to read a lecture to his rivals. Often he inserted a paper, like the four hundred and twenty-second *Spectator,* on raillery,9 or a sermon of his revered Tillotson, Nfor the mere edification of his readers. "I considered my newspaper, also, as another means of communicating instruction," he says in the *Autobiography,10* "and in that view frequently reprinted in it extracts from the *Spectator,* and other moral writers; and sometimes publish'd little pieces of my own, which had been first compos'd for reading in our Junto."

'Reprinted in *The Pennsylvania Gazette,* April 18, 1734. "In *Writings of Benjamin Franklin,* ed. A. H. Smyth, Vol. I, p. 343.

Among these "little pieces" of his own, yet certainly not written for the Junto, nor mentioned in the *Autobiography,* is the letter from Marcus11 on the increase of infidelity. Surely no one else in provincial Philadelphia of 1732 was capable of the Defoe-like irony in this letter. The first half of it might be taken seriously enough as one of the innumerable essays against infidelity found in every eighteenth-century periodical. Slowly it must have dawned upon shocked readers of the *Gazette* as they came to the second half, that "Marcus" was satirizing just such dull, incontestable statements as composed the ordinary treatise on infidelity in general, and, in particular, an unfortunate specimen of the sort in the *Mercury* of the previous week. The irony is not equally well sustained throughout, and could scarcely have deceived his enemies, yet one is tempted to believe that Franklin knew more of Defoe at this time than the *Religious Courtship* and the *Essay upon Projects.*

Marcus attacks the "prodigious Growth of Infidelity among us" with perfect gravity, saying that all persuasions have joined against it. "How unaccountable is this strange Eace of Unbelievers! Often have they been attack'd with great Strength and Judgment, by the worthy Advocates of our common Cause; but never so effectually as in the last Week's *Mercury:* Portius has afforded a Blow that staggers even the stoutest of 'em; and needs only tobe well follow'd to cause their entire Overthrow. I therefore add my Force to his, and, to their utter Confusion, I design in the following Discourse, to advance Five Hundred several Propositions, Doctrines, or Matters of Belief, each of which shall be clear to the Understanding, convincing to the Judgment, undeniable by the most perverse Sceptic. . . . I shall begin, by observing, That whoever abandons a Truth he was once in possession of, may be said to relinquish that Truth; and if, in its room, he cleaves to Falshood, he certainly adheres to Error. This being granted me, I infer, that in order to his Amendment there ought to be a Reformation; because, . . . every Offender is undeniably a Delinquent. "

31 See *The Pennsylvania Gasette,* March 23, 1732. *a* April 13, 1732.

Although Marcus did not deceive, he did confuse his enemies; and several weeks afterwards12 he expressed surprise that "a Gentleman of such profound Thought as the Remarker in the last *Mercury* should declare he cannot understand them (his principles). One would imagine that any Thing might more justly be accus 'd of Obscurity, than Principles so clear and perspicuous, even ready to burst with Self-evidence. But there are certain Birds, of notable G-ravity, whom too much Light rendereth blind." Of course there is no proof that Franklin himself wrote these jesting satires. He had fairly 1 able assistants in his printing business, and the Junto , always at hand to call upon. The one thing certain (is that they are done in Franklin's characteristic manner.

The *Gazette* had more boisterous fun at the expense of the English writer for the *Mercury,* "a coxcomb from Europe," as he is described in the *Gazette.* We are first told of a sagacious farmer who owned pigs of celebrated English breed, and who insisted that " they think they have more Sense and Merit than the rest of my Pigs." The *Gazette* then hastens to make the application: "Had they been brought from some Place near Westminster Hall, who knows but it might have been obvious to everybody?" This was not enough, but the poor Englishman must be lampooned again by a pretended letter to the *Gazette,* purporting to be his own vindication of himself, but really, of course, a more ridiculous exhibition of coxcombry than ever. It is ironically apologetic, hopes there will be no affront to "the Majority of my Eeaders; for considering the little Time I have been in the Country, it cannot be suppos'd they have gain'd much Knowledge of the polite Arts." No doubt Franklin had a very genuine dislike for snobbish pretension of every kind, as well as the desire to lampoon a rival.

Mirth and jesting in the pages of the *Gazette* ex- / tend all the way from dignified irony to puns and / ancient jokes. On one occasion, "Memory" sends a complaint (whether real or pretended we cannot know) to the *Gazette,13* protesting against all the old stories revamped as news. Franklin gravely answers that the letter should have been directed to the *Mercury!* An impartial reader feels that it might have been appropriately enough sent to either

"November 2, 1732.

office. Puns of all sorts abound in the *Gazette,* sometimes elaborately worked out in various conceits, like Chatterbox's history of the box family,14 an imitation of Bickerstaff's genealogy of the staffs.15 Humor of this sort was abundantly relished, and could have been found in many English papers of the period. The genealogy, in particular, came to be !a recognized form of satire, a convenient way of giving your enemy unpleasant forbears. Such Eng- ylish satires as *The Genealogy of a Jacobite* were I eventually reprinted in many American papers.

But neither high nor low comedy always sparkled /-in the *Gazette.* Innumerable mediocre essays filled / the long stretches of dull winters. Some have been attributed to Franklin, on more or less insufficient evidence.16 As a matter of fact, it makes very little difference who wrote *The Waste of Life,17* or *True Happiness,16* since almost any one could turn out such pieces of uninspired moral wisdom on the old model of the *Spectator* essay. The important thing to note is that this model persisted, along with Franklin's own characteristic development of it. The ordinary treatment of benevolence, temperance, simplicity of heart, need not detain us. There are, however, two or three unpublished essays of this sort, with so delightful a flavor of *Poor Richard* about them, that they can scarcely be left withoutmention. It is as if Poor Bichard were to write his philosophy on the deeper values of life, in Addi- sonian phrase, with due regard to all the proprieties of religion and ethics.

" See *The Pennsylvania Gazette,* January 4, 1733. " See *The Tatler,* No. 11.

" See *Writings of Benjamin Franklin,* ed. A. H. Smyth, Vol. II, *Preface.*

11 See *The Pennsylvania Gazette,* No. 414, November 11, 1736. " Ibid., No. 363, November 13, 1735.

One of these charming pieces treats of visiting the sick.19 After the dignified statement that man of all creatures has the greatest number of diseases to his share, and after a solemn exhortation, based on the parable of the good Samaritan as a text, the whole ends with this clinching argument, addressed to those worldly readers whose hard hearts may have been untouched by the above sermon: "If the Considerations of Eeligion and Humanity have not the Effect they ought to have on the Minds of some, perhaps this Observation, which generally holds true, may have its weight with the Self-interested, That there are no Kindnesses done by one Man to another, which are remembered so long, and so frequently return'd with Gratitude, as those received in Sickness, whether they are only present Comforts, or assist in restoring Health."

Another on wisdom,20 or " a prudent Management of ourselves in Affairs and Conversation" has the same philosophy, – the very essence of "Honesty is the best policy," put in literary form. Here there is less preliminary appeal to the lovers of morality for its own sake. "The Cardinal Virtue of Life, with respect to others, is to acquire and maintain a good Eeputation, suited to the station we are placed in. Among an Hundred other weighty Eeasons, thisis one, that a good Eeputation is the most infallible Means of Success in our Aims and Endeavours, that the uncertainty of Worldly Things admits of. A Man who takes Care to preserve a general good Character, will hardly fail of compassing his Ends some Time or other." A more direct application of the same cheerful, worldly morality may be seen in the excellent letter of Philanthropos,21 very much in the general style of the *Spectator,* on the advisability of introducing poor young men of promise to business. "It is no uncommon Thing," says Philanthropos, "to see Men of ingenuous Education, shining Abilities and Largeness of Heart, as the Sand upon the Sea-Shore; who would be capable of adorning almost any Post of Honour and Service, . . . restrained by the Narrowness of their Fortunes, . . . from doing the Good they desire, and are eminently accomplish'd for: Whereas it might have been the easiest Thing imaginable, for Men in superior Circumstances to have introduced them into Business." Now and then the return to the *Spectator* model is even closer, as in the humorous letter of N. N.,22 complaining of the icy streets of Philadelphia, and commending the good old woman who had sprinkled ashes before her door. The unkind ridicule of those passers-by who had laughed at his recent tumble is set forth with amusing seriousness and in a lofty, Addisonian temper. Also, when Z gives an account of himself,23 it is quite in the general manner of Mr. Spectator's first autobiographical hints.24

See *The Pennsylvania Gazette,* March 18, 1731. " Ibid., March 25, 1731.

See *The Pennsylvania Gazette,* June 19, 1732.

" Ibid., January *4,* 1733.

" Ibid., No. 397, July 8, 1736.

'4 See *Spectator,* No. 1.

Verse in the *Gazette,* unless directly quoted from- Milton or Pope, is weak doggerel, especially when compared with the really excellent lines abounding in the Virginia and South Carolina weeklies. Franklin's enthusiasms in poetry were capable of leading him to Stephen Duck, whose effusions appear again and again in the *Gazette.* Duck's personal history, too, is given at length in the *Gazette,* evidently as an example of industry and thrift, – another reinforcement of Poor Eichard's ideas. Indeed, one cannot escape the suspicion that Franklin admired the poetry for the sake of the man. Young Stephen Duck, a poor thresher in a Wiltshire barn, at four shillings six a week, who read his poem on *The Thresher's Labour* before her Majesty at Windsor, was rewarded not only with thirty pounds a year but also with a small house at Eichmond. Franklin readily assumed that the talent which brought such tangible rewards was a real poetic gift; and there is no indication that he thought Duck's poems in need of apology or justification. *The Thresher's Labour,25 The Shunamite,2 On Poverty,27 Royal Benevolence28* are reprinted in all their tedious length in the *Gazette.* Such lines as these make Pope's ridicule seem even mild:

Thus when a tim'rous Man, in Pears grown old,

Reminds the Fairy Tales his Nurse has told;

In the dark Night he oft will sideways squint,

And see a goblin when there's nothing in't.29

See *The Pennsylvania Gazette,* January 19, 1731.

"Ibid., March 11, 1731.

" Ibid., January 26, 1731.

Ibid., December 28, 1731.

"From Stephen Duck's poem, *On Poverty.*

For Milton and Pope Franklin had a very sincere admiration, while he certainly was well acquainted with Thomson, as his private manual30 shows. The stock quotation from Milton, the famous, "Hail, wedded Love!" is given as usual in an essay on marriage31 and Thomson's lines beginning:

But happy they, the happiest of their kind,

Whom gentler stars unite,

are quoted in the same piece. Since quotations of this sort were the property of every Grub street scribbler on the hackneyed theme of matrimony,82 they prove very little. More significant is the fact that in the first catalogue of the Library Company,33 organized by Franklin, a rare catalogue of 1741, we find not only a *Complete Collection of the Works of Mr. John Milton,* in two volumes, but also a 1730 I *Paradise Lost, Paradise Regained,* and *Samson fAgonistes.* Again we must remind ourselves that in Cotton Mather's great and important library there is no edition of *Paradise Lost.* Increase Mather in

80" I used also sometimes," Franklin says in the *Autobiography,*

" a little prayer which I took from Thomson's Poems, viz:

'Father of light and life, thou Good Supreme!

O teach me what is good; teach me Thyself I

Save me from folly, vanity, and vice,

From every low pursuit; and fill my soul

With knowledge, conscious peace, and virtue pure;

Sacred, substantial, never-fading bliss I' "
Writings of Benjamin Franklin, ed. A. H. Smyth, Vol. I, p. 332.
"In *The Pennsylvania Gazette,* No. 326, February 25, 1734.
"For examples, see *The Weekly Segister,* September 30, 1732, and
The Grubstreet Journal, No. 305, October 30, 1735.
In the Pennsylvania Historical Society's collection.
Spectators, 8 vols.
Tattlers, 4 vols.
Guardians, 2 vols.
1664 had Milton's Defence of Smectymnuus34 and the *Defensio Populi Anglicani.*
The little catalogue of Franklin's Library Company, though not perhaps directly con-
nected with his newspaper or his periodical, has such a vital relation to his bookselling
and printing interests, that the literary section of it, at least, deserves a place here.
Besides the copies of Milton noted above, the catalogue notes:
"Written by some of the most ingenious Men of the Age, for the Promotion of
Virtue, Piety and good Manners."
Don Quixote. Original and Translation.
Steele's Dramatick "Works
The Ladies' Library36
Dryden
Waller
Cowley
Rowe
Pope
Voltaire
Arbuthnot
Bacon
Locke
Shaftesbury
Gay
Edmund Spencer
Works"! Dryden's Virgil
Xenophon
See *Proceedings of the American Antiquarian Society* for April, 1910, for a full ac-
count of the libraries of the Mathers by Mr. Julius Herbert Tuttle, of the Massachusetts
Historical Society.
"Probably Steele's.
Epictetus
Plutarch
Cicero
Plato
Horace
Swift
Congreve
Sallust

Juvenal

Persius

The Turkish Spy

Addison's *Miscellaneous Works, in Verse and Prose,* 3 vols.

Hudibras

Cato's Letters

To this library not only tradesmen like Breintnal and Franklin contributed, but important citizens of the town; and it is safe to conjecture that throughout the length of the Atlantic seaboard in 1740, there was not such a collection of pure literature accessible to common folk. Even the private ecclesiastical libraries of Massachusetts had no such volumes. Wealthy Virginian planters like Colonel William Byrd, as well as fairly prosperous citizens in all the towns could show their well-stocked "secretaries." But this meant that they were rich. enough to order from Europe.

In Franklin's case, books were constantly passing through his book shop and his printing press. Magazines from London, too, furnished him with literary tid-bits and gossip of all sorts. The *Gazette* is by no means lacking in news of the poetic world. "We hear his Majesty has been pleased to grant to Mr. Cibber the place of Poet Laureat," is an item of January 19, 1731, only two months late. Cibber's New Year ode is reprinted entire in the *Gazette* of May 19, 1737. Pope's epitaph on John Gay's monument at Westminster, containing the well-known lines,

Of manners gentle, of affections mild,

In wit a man, simplicity a child,

is quoted in the *Gazette,*36 doubtless from *The London Magazine* of five months before,37 where it is published in full. Sometimes a clever skit appearing in the London periodicals is used in the *Gazette* without acknowledgment, as if it were written by one of the regular staff, or a correspondent. For instance, Isaac Browne's *Pipe of Tobacco,* appearing in *The London Magazine* of November and December, 1735, is published in a supposed *Letter to Mr. Franklin,*38 describing the London wit who wrote the parody in response to a challenge. *The Pipe of Tobacco* is really a series of mock-heroic burlesques on the theme, *Tobacco.* One in "Mr. Pope's style," begins

Best Leaf, whose Aromatick Gales dispence,

To Templars Modesty, to Parsons sense.

Another follows imitating Young:

Criticks avaunt! Tobacco is my Theme; A third after "Mr. Phillips":

"No. 413, November 4, 1736.

" June, 1736.

"See *The Pennsylvania Gazette,* No. 400, August 2, 1736.

Pretty Tube of mighty Power,

Charmer of an idle hour,

Object of my hot desire,

Lips of Wax and Eye of Fire;

Last of all a burlesque of Thomson:

0 Thou matur'd by glad hesperian Suns,

Tobacco! Fountain pure of limpid Truth —

But far more significant than such stray pieces from London periodicals, are the advertisements of books actually for sale in Franklin's "New Printing- Office near the Market.'39 The very fact that books were for sale in a printing-office takes us back to "other times, other manners," before the specialization of business. Yet a printer of the eighteenth century conducted something not unlike a department store. The development is easy enough to understand, especially in the provinces. No man would be rash enough to conduct a bookstore alone, unless he were a philanthropist instead of a business I man. A printer, however, needed large supplies of / paper; naturally he might add an order of stationery for the retail trade without an appreciable risk, even if it were not sold. This would lead to blank books, legal forms and writing materials, for which the demand was steady and certain. Very cautiously Bibles and text-books could be added. At length an *I* invoice of ordinary stationer's goods would contain an odd volume or two, picked up accidentally, no one knows how, probably under the auctioneer's ham- i mer, or in a lot of second-hand supplies. To adver-

" See *The Pennsylvania Gazette,* February 16, 1731.

tise them in one's own paper would cost only the required space, and might lead to a sale. Hence such notices as "Scales, compasses, sealing wax, and *Religious Courtship"0* are not infrequent throughout the colonial press, though nowhere so unique or so interesting as in *The Pennsylvania Gazette.* Franklin, the born book-lover, took an unusual risk in his favorite commodity, regarding a book as a personal luxury,41 and a means of benevolence at the same time. If it did not sell, he could present it with considerable eclat to the Library Company. With all his shrewdness, Franklin was generous.

Yet even he has recorded the timid steps by which he became a bookseller. "I now42 open'd a little Stationer's shop," he says in the *Autobiography.43 "I* had in it blanks of all sorts, the correctest that ever appear'd among us, being assisted in that by my - friend Breintnal. I had also paper, parchment, chapmen's books, etc." Again, in the *Autobiography* he gives important, though careless testimony to the difficulty of the book-trade. " At the time I establish'd myself in Pennsylvania, there was not a good bookseller's shop in any of the colonies to the southward of Boston. In New York and Philad 'a the printers were indeed stationers; they sold only I paper, etc., almanacs, ballads, and a few common

"Vide supra, p. 94 and note 3.

""A book, indeed, sometimes debauch'd me from my work, but that was seldom, snug, and gave no scandal." *Autobiography,* in *Writings of Benjamin Franklin,* ed. A. H. Smyth, Vol. I, p. 308.

"About 1730.

"In *Writings of Benjamin Franklin,* ed. A. H. Smyth, Vol. I, p. 307.

44 Ibid., Vol. I, p. 321.

school-books. Those who lov'd reading were oblig'd to send for their books from England; the members of the Junto had each a few." Mr. Delano Goddard, in his interesting article on *The Press and Literature of the Provincial Period,6* says decisively, "There were no accessible collections of books in the country, and there was no book-buying class." He also thinks46 that the "remarkable literary revival of

Queen Anne's reign was little observed or felt here. The earliest catalogues of books make little mention of the writers who were at that time giving imperishable glory to our language."

Probably all these statements err a little on the dark side. No one will deny, of course, that good bookstores were lacking, according to modern ideas, or even according to Franklin's ideas. Yet we must not let ourselves forget that in a country where nearly all the influential culture is religious culture, secular j books of whatever sort, excepting school texts, will ' not be at a premium. This will have two important results. One is that a bookseller will naturally advertise his religious and theological treatises, put them in his show window to catch the public eye. Very well. It does not follow that if you stepped into his shop and asked for *The Beggar's Opera,* you would not find it. And secondly, where all secular literature, good or bad, takes its place among worldly delights, and fleshly vanities, we may expect to find it advertised in the most unexpected frivolous connections. This is exactly what we do find; it is

" In *Memorial History of Boston,* Vol. II, chap. XV, p. 412.

not safe to assume that an advertisement of headdresses and slippers will not have the *Tale of a Tub* tucked away in the middle of it. That is to say, hatters and clothiers sometimes imported books along with their other miscellaneous merchandise.

What could be more surprising than Peter Turner's advertisement47 of Superfine Scarlet Cloth, Hat Linings, *Tatlers, Spectators,* and *Barclay's Apology?* Turner retailed his goods near Market Street wharf,48 a favorable spot for merchandise from the incoming vessels. As a matter of fact, he probably never deliberately imported just the assortment which he finally took into his shop. Cargoes for America were fearfully and wonderfully made up of odd lods of merchandise jumbled together. On the other hand, when John Hyndshaw, the bookseller, advertised in the *Gazette,9* he confined his lists almost entirely to Bibles, Testaments, Psalters, Primers, Prayer Books and Texts. But we cannot suppose that he had nothing of secular interest in his shop, any more fairly than we could assume to-day that a store window flaming with best sellers necessarily indicates a shop in which Gibbon's *Decline and Fall* is not to be had.

Franklin's own early advertisement50 was perfectly conventional and commercial. In 1731 he advertised only " Jerman's and Godfrey's almanacs, Bibles, Testaments, Psalters, Psalm-Books, (in

" See *The Pennsylvania Gazette,* No. 534, March 1, 1738-39. "See *The American Mercury,* No. 1010, May 3, 1739, for Turner's advertisement. " March 18, 1731. *K* See *The Pennsylvania Gazette,* February 16, 1731.

large, heavy type) Accompt-Books, Pocket-Books, Bills of Lading bound and unbound, Common Blank Bonds for Money, Bonds with Judgment, Counter- bonds, Arbitration Bonds," and so on through all the legal forms in common use at the time. We next find a notice of "Archbishop Tillotson's Works com- pleat in 3 volumes, sold by the Printer hereof," and in the same notice, *The Traditions of the Clergy destructive of Religion; with an Enquiry into the Grounds and Reasons of such Traditions: A Sermon.61*

/ The little nucleus of a bookstore existed by 1731. But it must not be forgotten that Bradford also imported books; and when a new invoice came in, he was likely to advertise it in the *Mercury* under the heading, "Just imported," or "Lately imported from London." Probably neither Bradford nor Franklin printed a complete list even of the newest books, and certainly no complete list of all the volumes on sale. Nothing, however, could furnish a more significant contrast than a comparison of the book advertisements in the two papers. Parallel lists between 1730 and 1740 will show Bradford's conservatism and Franklin's ever growing attempt to make literature accessible.

The American Mercury The Pennsylvania Gazette
Catalogue of Books for Sale For Sale by Franklin.
by A. Bradford *Robinson Crusoe,* 2 Vols.,
Popery Anatomized advertised in the *Gazette*
Catechistical Guide to Sin- in 1734. *ners*
K See *The Pennsylvania Gazette,* March 23, 1732.
(Mercury, cont.) (Gazette, cont.)
The Popish Labyrinth
The Plain Man's Path-way
to Heaven Byfield's *Marrow of the*
Oracles Cunningham's *Warnings,*
Prayers and Hymns.
No. 626, Dec. 21, 1731.
Lately Imported from London
To be Sold by A. Bradford
Spectators
Tattlers
Guardians
Cato's Letters
The Whole Duty of Man
No. 882, Nov. 18, 1736.
[No other book advertisements in the *Mercury* up to 1740.]
Religious Courtship.
No. 415, Nov. 18, 1736, and No. 463, Oct. 20,1737.
Just Imported
To be Sold by B. Franklin
Crusoe's Life, 2 vols.
Bacon's *Essays*
Dryden's Virgil
Lock *Of Human Understanding*
Milton's *Paradise Lost*
Ovid's *Epistles*
Otway's *Plays*
Pembroke's *Arcadia*
Pope's Homer
Prior
Rowe's *Lucan*
Stanhope's *Epictetus*
Seneca's *Morals*

Tale of a Tub
Duck's *Poems*
Many others too tedious to mention.
No. 494, May 25, 1738.
"Glover's *Leonidas. Sense,* April 9, 1737.
Locke's *Works,* 3 vols.
Select Novels, 6 vols.
Rabelais, 4 vols.
Trap's Virgil, 3 vols.
Leonidas, a Heroick Poem52
Reviewed in the English weekly, *Common*
(Mercury, cont.) (Gazette, cont.)
Spectators, 8 vols.
Tatters, 4 vols.
Guardians, 2 vols.
The Independent Whig, 2
vols.
The Turkish Spy, 8 vols.
Pope's Homer, 6 vols.
Bacon's *Essays.*
Arbuthnot on *Aliments*
Dryden's *Fables*
Otway's *Plays*
Prior's *Poems,* 2 vols.
Howe's *Lucan,* 2 vols.
Seneca's *Morals.*
Craftsman, 14 vols.
Bunyan
Stanhope's *Epictetus*
Many other Sorts of Books,
too tedious to mention.
Jan. 11, 1738-39.

Would that 11e had not thought the other sorts of books too tedious to mention!
However, there is still another list before 1740, which partly compensates for the
omission. Into this last advertisement it is difficult not to believe that Franklin put
some of his irrepressible levity.

Books sold by B. Franklin
Bibles of several sorts.
The Independent Whig, 3 vols.
Tatlers, 4 vols.
The Tale of a Tub
Congreve's *Works*
The Family Instructor
The Art of Money-Catching
The Duty of Prayer

Cynthia, a Novel
The Eepublick of Letters
The Life of our Messed Saviour
The Garden of Love
The Ladies' Delight
Man's great Interest
History of Dr. John Faustus
London Jests and Cambridge Jests
The Travels of our blessed Saviour
Lives of the Apostles
Fair Rosamond
The Book of Knowledge
The Life and Death of Moll Flanders.
No. 582, Feb. 7, 17390.

So much for book advertisements before 1740; these, of course, represent direct importations of English books. American editions of any sort are much rarer. It is strange, that with all Franklin's genuine love of books, he should have cared so little to put standard English literature through his own press. Matters of transient importance, pamphlets of all sorts, a thousand expostulatory letters, apologies, answers, remarks, kept his press busy, as they did other colonial printing houses. The profit from them was immediate and certain. And Franklin's philanthropy never strayed too far from a sound business basis. It was one thing to order a shipment of good books from London, knowing that if he did not sell them, he had only expended something forhis library, or for the benevolence he was beginning to be in a position to afford; it was quite another to be left with an entire unsold edition of some classic on Ms hands. Moreover, his press was very busy with the affairs of the day. Naturally, if he projected reprints, they must wait.

"What he did actually publish is extremely interesting, and reminds us that, after all, Franklin was moral before he was literary; moral, that is, in his own particular utilitarian way. He left *Robinson Crusoe* for Robert Bell to publish in 1768, and *The Dreadful Visitation: In a Short Account of the Progress and Effects of the Plague* for Henry Miller in ' 1767, – and he himself published, in 1740, *The Family ' Instructor* in all its three parts, the first relating to fathers and children, the second to masters and servants, the third to husbands and wives.53 *The Religious Courtship* is the only other possible work of Defoe that he touched. And to these two reprints (if therewere two), he added Richardson's *Pamela f* in 1744. A certain provincial, vulgar note in Franklin's own moral code would draw him inevitably to Richardson's thrifty, successful little heroine.

Significant evidence of the impression which all these books made upon him is given us in the *Autobiography?* after Franklin's admiring remarks on his old favorite, Bunyan: "Honest John (Bunyan) was the first that I know of who mix'd narration and dialogue; a method of writing very engaging to the reader, who in the most interesting parts finds himself, as it were, brought into the company, and present at the discourse. De Foe in his *Cruso,* his *Moll Flanders, Religious Courtship, Family Instructor,* and other pieces, has imitated it with success; and Richardson has done the same in his

Pamela, etc." The very books which Franklin had either imported or reprinted. There is no mention of *Joseph Andrews,* in which the conversation is far more dramatically handled than in *Pamela.*

85 That is, Franklin reprinted Vol. I of 1715, not Vol. II of 1718. 51 See *Writings of Benjamin Franklin,* ed. A. H. Smyth, Vol. I, p. 251.

One or two more of Franklin's reprints touched literature. He was much interested in English translations of the Classics, and naturally so, since he was not a classical scholar himself, and hardly believed in a knowledge of the classical tongues for the ordinary man. A good translation, therefore, was a great public benefit, in his eyes. And to him belongs the honor of publishing the first translations from the Classics made on this side of the Atlantic. His friend, James Logan, translated the moral distichs of the unknown Dionysius Cato into English couplets, which Franklin published in 1735. This was absolutely the first classic to be both translated and printed in the colonies, but when Franklin came to publish Logan's version of the *De Senectute* nine years later, he either forgot the previous translation of Cato's distichs, or did not think it of importance as a classic, for his preface to the *De Senectute66* assumes that to be the "first Translation of a Classic in this Western World." Undoubtedly this was a matter of great pride with Franklin, for he boasts

"Preface to Logan's Translation of Cato Major, or his Discourse of Old Age. The Printer to the Header. Reprinted in *Writings of Benjamin Franklin,* ed. A. H. Smyth, Vol. II, p. 244.

a little of "the large and fair Character" of his type – for the especial benefit, he says, of those who are beginning to think of old age!

Bradford's press did not reach even the record of Franklin's. In 1747, he did reprint his admired Pope's *Essay on Man,* with *The Universal Prayer* added. That is all the standard literature he touched.

Both the *Gazette* and the *Mercury,* however, as well as other colonial newspapers, contain now and then stray notices and advertisements that throw light on the book-owning, book-loving public of the time. If libraries were few, lending was frequent. And a book was so important a possession that it was customary to advertise for the volumes lost, just as one might describe a watch in the "lost" column to-day. Particularly when the owner of a library died, his books were apt to be gathered together by his executors in every way possible before the inventory. These inventories themselves, where they are still in existence, form a fascinating subject of investigation, now in progress in various historical and colonial societies;56 but since very few of the actual lists were published in the newspapers, they are a little aside from the present subject. The preliminary notices, and the "lent" notices are full of interest, however.

The Hon. Charles Eead, sheriff, had a fine library, as well as a fine mansion to keep it in. When Andrew Bradford notified his readers57 of his removal

M See the recent publications of the Colonial and Historical Societies of Massachusetts, and the many articles in *The Virginia Magazine of History and Biography* and *The William and Mary College Quarterly.*

" See *The American Mercury,* No. 951, March 14, 1737-38.

from Second Street to Front Street, at the sign of the Bible, he made the locality clear beyond a doubt, by designating it as "near Charles Read's corner." We know, too, that Charles Read gave a copy of *Cato's Letters,* in four volumes, to Franklin's Library Company.68 So we are not surprised at the following notice in the columns of the *Gazette.69*

"Whereas the Library late of Charles Read, Esq., is very much dispers'd and many Sets of Books broken, particularly of the *Spectator, Tatler, Guardian, Conquest of Mexico, Athenian Oracle,* etc. . . . These are therefore to desire those who have any Books lately belonging to the said Charles Read, that . . . they would generously and gratefully return them."

James Logan, the translator, had one of the best libraries in the province. It was ever at Franklin's disposal, so we can imagine with what alacrity Franklin inserted and repeated Logan's notice:

"Jugemens des Savans, vol. 7 of a set of 17, lost out of a chaise on the way to Grermantown. Owner, J. Logan."

Franklin himself inserted a characteristic advertisement :80

"The Person that borrowed B. Franklin's Law- Book of this Province, is hereby desired to return it, he having forgot to whom he lent it."

That all the literature read in Philadelphia was religious or theological, could be amply disproved

"Noted in the Catalogue of 1741, Pennsylvania Historical Society. " No. 452, August 4, 1737. " No. 347, July 24, 1735.

if only through the repeated advertisements of "Lent, Machiavel's *Works,"61* and "Lent, second volume of *Select Trials for Murders, Robberies,* etc."62

Even Nicholas Eeddish, a saddler, who also retailed bar iron in Second Street, had his notice repeated three times in the *Gazette:63* "Lent, and forgot to whom, a large Geographical Dictionary."

The *Mercury's* notices are somewhat less interesting, since they usually give no particular titles. "William Dowell's Books lost in his lifetime are desired to be returned," and "Joseph Growden's Law Library to be sold" are not valuable indications of what was being read in the province. Once64 the second volume of Atterbury's sermons is advertised for.

In such out-of-the-way corners must we look to find evidences of a love of literature in the colonies. In Philadelphia, at least, we can show that it was being imitated, that it was for sale, that it was being reprinted to a certain extent, that it was to be had in the first public library, – and last of all that it was easy to borrow. Most of these facts were due to Benjamin Franklin, who advanced Philadelphia in so many ways above her neighbors. We shall cross his trail again.65 For the present, however, we take our leave of him.

" Nos. 472, 474, 475, 476.

MNos. 485-486.

No. 340, June 5, 1735, and following numbers.

"In *Mercury,* No. 1001, March 1, 173S-3&.

"Vide infra, chap. VIII.

5

SECTION 5

CHAPTER V

The Wab Between Bbadfobd's New Yobk Gazette And Zengeb's New Yobk Weekly Joubnal

William Bradford, editor of the first newspaper in New York, was the father of Andrew Bradford of Philadelphia. It is natural, therefore, that *The (New York Gazette* should be of an even more primitive type than *The American Mercury.* An examination of William Bradford's little weekly for the first seven years of its history shows that he aimed to publish a news sheet like Campbell*'s Boston News- Letter.* He was not attempting any advance upon the earlier method, and if the presence of a danger-, ous rival in the field had not at length roused the ' elder Bradford to unwonted activity, there would probably be little reason for including his *Gazette* in the present investigation.

The New York Gazette was established in the latter part of 1725. Incongruous items of foreign news, and the shipping entries of several colonial ports fill its columns from 1725 to 1730. Occasion- ally an advertisement of a runaway servant shows the comparatively close connection between printing offices in different colonies. For instance, we find in *The New York Gazette* of June 1, 1730: "Eun away from William

Parks, Printer at Annapolis in Maryland a Servant Man named John Grime. . . . Whoever brings him to his said Master at Annapolis,

or to Andrew Bradford in Philadelphia, or William Bradford in New York, shall have three Pounds Reward and reasonable charges." Such slight indications of mutual understanding between editorial offices are important for our purpose chiefly because , they strengthen the probability that one colonial 'newspaper could influence another; a probability which will have a decided bearing on a later chapter.1 In Bradford's *Gazette* of June 25, 1733, we have direct literary news from Philadelphia. The address of Franklin's Library Company to the Proprietor, "William Penn, is given in full in the New York weekly.

Stray essays, stories and verses from the English periodicals did find their way into the *Gazette,* even in these early years, but it was by the merest accident. Occasional literary material could be found in any colonial newspaper, however dry and bare. The story from *The Weekly Rehearsal,2* reprinted in the *Gazette* of February 4, 1734, the *Lesson for bad Husbands,* from *The Universal Spectator,3* reprinted in the *Gazette* of January 21, 1734, and the amusing verses from *The London Journal* extolling Gay's Fables,4 reprinted in the *Gazette* of July 8,1734, by themselves hardly constitute literary influence. And even though they are by no means the only instances of borrowed "Essays in prose or verse," in the early files of the *Gazette,* we are not justified in regarding a paper as literary in aim, unless the literary form appears frequently, and, at least to some extent, stimulates the native writers to imitation.

1 Vide infra, chapter VIII. January 7, 1733. August, 1733.

4January, 1733-34. The verses represent a mother training her children in the choice of literature:

This happy Mother met, one Day,
A Book of Fables writ by Gay
And told her Children, here's a Treasure,
A Fund of Wisdom and of Pleasure!

But there are very few original essays with a purely literary purpose in the *Gazette.* Even those that we do find have a strong tendency to point a moral rather than to adorn a tale. The correct discipline of children is the topic of several moral treatises,5 interesting chiefly for the different points of view expressed, either by actual citizens of New York, or through fictitious personalities. In view of the evident lack of imagination in the editorial office, there is some probability that these essays on discipline were written by actual correspondents. The first two treatises are anonymous, and treat of the discipline of children and youths. We are told that parents "love their little Ones, and it is their Duty, but they often, with them, cherish their Faults too; they must not be cross'd (forsooth!), they must be Permitted to have their wills in all things, be they

Such Morals! and so finely Writ I
Such Decency, good Sense, and Wit!

Her favorite son weeps at the concluding Fable, but his mother comforts him with the assurance that Queen Caroline will undoubtedly aid the unfortunate Gray, who deserves at least a thousand pounds a year. Queen Caroline, however, as a matter of fact, had not aided the poet. On her accession he was given only a small office, which he indignantly

. refused. At this time Gay had been dead two years.

5 See *The New York Gazette,* Nos. 403, 404 and 408.

never so wrong." This policy, the essayist reminds us, would be disastrous with a horse or dog! He next considers the vices of youth, in a strain even more serious. After several weeks, Thomas Stingo answers the two preceding essays with flippant remarks leading to the conclusion that "many (youths) will not leave trasing their Father's Foot-Steps." The general style of these essays, the Latin motto, and the formal introduction suggest a feeble attempt to follow the Addisonian model.

Certainly Bradford and his staff correspondents knew the *Spectator* well. When the reckless young journalist, John Peter Zenger, established *The New York Weekly Journal* in the latter part of 1733, and made it an organ of bitter opposition to the government, Bradford, the "King's Printer for the Province of New York," turned immediately to the pages of the *Spectator* for material to quote against his opponent. The letter to "Mr. Bradford" in the *Gazette* of January 28, 1734, must have been more or less directly inspired by him. Since this letter furnishes important evidence of the high regard and even veneration in which Addison was commonly held in the colonies, it deserves quoting.

Mr. Bradford,

Amongst the various Methods that Men of fine Genius have taken to convey their Sentiments to the World, none have been so deservedly successful as those Set of Papers published in England under the Title of the *Spectator,* and no wonder; for good Sense, good Manners, sprightly Wit, gentile general Satyr, a strict adherence to Truth, with aChristian like Intention of propagating Vertue, and rooting out Vice, being their Foundation, they have and will to all Ages support themselves even against Calumny itself. Amongst the Set of Gentlemen concern'd in those Papers I think Mr. Addison has always had the Preference. I am of no Party of Men, but as they act consistent with the Good of Society. Envy, Spleen, Clamour, and Falshood can never be introduc'd for the Benefit of any Community. I am sorry of late to have seen some printed Papers published in this Place, stuff'd with such Ribaldry: I heartily join with those that have a just Abhorrence of Calumny, and beg leave to publish my Dislike of it in the Words of that great and good Man, Mr. Addison. I am, Sir,

Yours, etc.

Then follows the well-known *Spectator* paper on "defamatory Papers and Pamphlets," reprinted entire in the *Gazette;* and this is only one instance among many, of the use of the *Spectator* to rebuke the enemy.

Meantime Zenger had been publishing *Cato's Let- ters* on the absurdity of the Divine Eight of Kings and governors,7 on the privilege of the individual to criticise the government,8 and other kindred ideals of a democratic state. Hardly a number of ther *Journal* from November to February of the year 1733-34 is without a quotation or a letter reprinted in full from the "Sentiments of (I had almost said, the Divine) English Cato."9 In this way were the admirers of Gordon and Trenchard's Letters accus-

Spectator, No. 451.

1 *Cato's Letters,* No. 131.

Ibid., No. 3&.

See *The New York Weekly Journal,* December 10, 1733.

tomed to speak of them. "The Divine English Cato" was a common expression on this side of the Atlantic, wherever the advocacy of popular government was most ardent.

This would seldom be the case, naturally, among xthe office-holders directly under the Governor. We do not find the *British Cato* quoted or even referred to in Bradford's *Gazette*. Bradford took the con- - servative, aristocratic point of view in government affairs, and Bradford's paper is scathingly described in the *Journal* of December 17, 1733, as "a Paper known to be under the Direction of the Government, in which the Printer of it is not suffered to insert anything but what his Superiors approve of, under the penalty of losing 50L per annum Salary and the Title of the King's Printer for the Province of New York." No doubt this is far from an unbiased statement of the case. Bradford was probably a genuine conservative, and a genuine enough supporter of Governor Cosby.

Zenger was reprinting not only *Cato's Letters,* but any other essays or verse that would strengthen or illustrate his point of view. Steele's *Englishman* is twice pressed into the service,10 Addison's. lines to Liberty are quoted,11 even Aesop's Fable of the sick lion who invited guests in order to eat them at his leisure, is related at length.12 Original essaysduring 1733-34 have the same controversial pur-TM; pose. Philo-Patriae explains in no ambiguous terms the duties of a "supream magistrate."13 The *Journal* of December 24, 1733, has an original essay on the unfortunate influences governing New York and New Jersey. An essay of January 21, 1733-34, is even more explicit in denouncing "bad Governors" as mischievous beasts.

"January 7 and January 14, 1733-34.

" January 28, 1733-34. Fourteen lines beginning

O Liberty, thou Goddess heavenly bright,

quoted from Addison's *Letter from Italy to the Sight Honourable Charles Lord Halifax,* 11. 119-132, inc. "January 14, 1733-34.

Indeed, Zenger went farther. With a grim, Swift- ian humor, and more than a suggestion of the Swift- ian coarseness, he published mock advertisements of strayed animals representing his political foes. Doubtless they are no more libelous than many cartoons of to-day, but in the cautious and timid colonial press they form a notable exception. We shall quote portions of two of these mock notices.

Advebtisement"

"A large Spaneil, of about Five Foot Five Inches High, has lately stray'd from his Kennell, with his Mouth full of fulsom Panegyricks, and in his Ramble dropt them in the New York Gazette; . . . whosoever will strip the said Panegyricks of all their Fulsomness, and send the Beast back to his Kennell, shall have the Thanks of all honest Men, and all reasonable Charges."

ADVERTISEMENT15

"A Monkey of the larger Sort, about 4 Foot high, has lately broke his chain and run into the country. . . . Having got a Warr Saddle, Pistols and Sword, this whimsicalCreature fancied himself a general; and taking a Paper in his Paw he muttered over it, what the far greatest Part of the Company understood not; but others who thought themselves wiser pretended to understand him; . . . but a Man appearing without a Button on his Hat, ... he fell into a violent chattering again."

a November 26, 1733.

" See *The New York Weekly Journal,* November 26, 1733.

Ibid., December 10, 1733.

These, and such as these, were the "printed Papers . . . stuff'd with . . . Eibaldry" of which the letter to "Mr. Bradford" in the *Gazette* of January 28, 1734, complained, and against which the *Spectator* was quoted. Even the *Journal* writers at once recognized the authority of Addison, and nothing could be a more striking proof of the universal veneration in which he was held than the quick response

j in the *Journal* of the following week.16 Addison's authority is not only upheld, but turned against

, Bradford, much as Andrew Bradford of Philadelphia had attempted to use Franklin's favorite author to rebuke Franklin's Deism. The *Journal's* answer is in the form of a letter or reply " to the Author of the Letter to Mr. Bradford, in his *Gazette* of January 28th last." But it is significant that the reply is sent to the *Journal,* not to the *Gazette.*

"With a great deal of Pleasure I have read yours, and heartily joyn with you in your Commendation of the *Spectator* and Mr. Addison/' the *Journal* writer begins, with suave politeness, "I am, and resolve to remain what you profess yourself to be, that is, *To "be of no Party of Men "but as they act consistent with the Good of Society; . . .* but think it odd that you rank *Clamour* in General, whether just or unjust, along with those low Vices (of falsehood, envy, and spleen).

" February 4, 1733-34.

"Methinks, Sir, before you had joined Clamour in General, with such Company, you should have shewn Sir Richard Steel's Error in the Letter reprinted in Zenger's Paper, No X.17 And should have well weighed, whether the ranking of Just Clamour amongst *Vices* be not introductory of the Doctrine of passive Obedience, and a Sapping the Foundation of our late Glorious Revolution. . . . And the rather for that many Inhabitants and Natives of this Place, who (as I do) acknowledge themselves to be only awful and distant admirers of Mr. Addison, do cast in their Mites in the best manner they can to the good of Zenger's Paper, as I'm informed. Addison, Steel, and the English Cato have been Men Almost Divine; we can hardly Err if we agree with them in Political Sentiments; and yet we ought not to give up our Reason to them Absolutely, because they were Men, and as such Lyable to Errors, *tho I know not of one Error in either of them."*

He then proceeds to turn the weapons of his opponents against them, by reminding them that Addison recommended exemplary punishments for "Authors that have supported their cause with Falsehood and Scandal."18 In brief, this writer for the *Journal* used Addison as another English Cato, and, as we have just seen, referred to them both as men almost divine, and practically free from error.

After hostilities had been declared in earnest, early in 1734, the use of literary authority became even more frequent on both sides. But always, as before, Zenger drew his arguments and ideas largely from *Cato's Letters,* while Bradford repeatedly re-

" January 7, 1733-34. Steele had asserted the right of rebellion on just cause. 18 *Spectator,* No. 451.

turned to Addison's papers on scandal and lying. At times the heat of the conflict warmed Bradford and his correspondents into something like wit, as ; when a letter to "Mr. Bradford"19 advocates the enrichment of the "somewhat blunt British tongue" by a new word for liar, – namely Zenger. If those who use this word frequently wish a little variety, they have only to say," Oh that is in my Lady Blue- mantle's Memoirs." Lest the readers of the *Gazette* should not understand the allusion, the letter explains: " For the reason of that Expression, please to read the 427 *Spectator, Vol.* VI, which should have been inserted here, but not having room, it will begin our next *Gazette,* to which we refer." And "our next *Gazette"20* has, according to the announcement, the four hundred and twenty-seventh *Spectator,* reprinted in full.

Ordinarily, however, we find no sallies of original wit in the *Gazette,* although there is plenty of invective. *Spectators* are usually introduced in a brief sentence or two, such as, "You are desired by a Friend of one of your Correspondents, to Print in your next *Gazette,* one of Mr. Addison's *Spectators,* as the properest Answer to Zenger's preceding *Journal."21* This leads to the four hundred and fifty-fifth *Spectator,* which is a plea for not answering your opponents! Or we find in a note to the editor of the *Gazette22 "I* received Mr. Zenger's Paper Nom. 139, which I find so gross TJngentlemanlike and false, that I think no better Answer can be made, than one of Mr. Steel's Lecubrations, *Spectator* Numb. 451." Sometimes a number of the *Spectator* is reprinted with no introductory word at all. In this way *Spectator* No. 594 appears in the *Gazette* of February 18, 1733-34. Even in citing other authors, Bradford and his friends liked to have the authority of Addison. "I am the more free to introduce the Authority of Clarendon," says one of Bradford's correspondents in the *Gazette* of February 11, 1733-34, "because it is following the Example of our favourite Mr. Addison, see the 439 *Spectator, Vol.* 6."

11 See *The New York Gazette,* No. 435, February 25, 1733-34.

20 Ibid., No. 436, March 4, 1733-34.

21 Ibid., No. 441, April 8, 1734. " Ibid., No. 558, July 18, 1736.

The article in Zenger's paper which Bradford's friends had found "so gross Un-gentleman like and false" was a bitter attack on the administration of Governor Cosby combined with personal criticism of Bradford, the Governor's adherent. In answer to the publication of "Mr. Steel's Lecubration" in the *Gazette* of July 18, 1736, Zenger again turns the *Spectator* against his enemies.23 He readily admits that "Defamation ... is a most base and horrid Crime," and more than hints that Bradford has been guilty of it. "But can relating the Truth be Defamation? ... I shall conclude this Paper with recommending to the few Approvers of the Conduct of Mr. Cosby and his Tools, the reading the *Spectator,* published by Mr. Bradford, and more particularly these Words of it. 'It is an uncontested Maxim, that they who approve an Action would certainly do it, if they could. . . . Ther's no Difference, says

" See *The New YorkJPeeMy Journal,* No. 142, July 26, 1736.

Cicero, between advising a Crime, and approving it when committed.'"

Now and then Zenger quotes Addison without any previous suggestion from Brad-ford,24 and one daring attack on Bradford,25 calling him a liar in no measured terms, is actually signed "Addison," and prefaced by a quotation from *Paradise Lost!* It will be observed, however, that both parties used the *Spectator* for controversial purposes, during the very years in which many other colonial papers were using it for the culture, or at least for the moral improvement of their readers. Instances of this latter use of Addison and Steele can be found both in *The New York Gazette* and in *The New York Weekly Journal;* but such instances are, comparatively speaking, rare.26

I In fact the writers for both papers seized upon frny literature that they could find to illustrate their political and personal opinions. One correspondent of the *Journal,* signing himself N. S., of "Hamstead, on Long-Island," not only uses *A Tale of a Tub* in an amusing way, but gives important, though incidental testimony, as to the books likely to be in the library of a New York gentleman in 1734. N. S. begins27 by informing Zenger that he hears much against the *Journal.* "It is libeling, it is damn'd Nonsense," and so on, and even he seems to place himself in the ranks of its enemies, until he goes onto explain, by a rather indirect method, what he really means. His testimony is important enough to deserve quoting.

See *The New York Weekly Journal,* No. 86, June 20, 1735. Ibid., No. 81, May 26, 1735.

a For examples, see *The New York Weekly Journal,* Nos. 80, 81, 82, 230, 231, and *The New York Gazette,* Nos. 480, 481.

" See *The New York Weekly Journal,* No. 18, March 4, 1733-34.

"My library is not large," he writes, "it consists of a Bible, Pool's *Annotations,* Calamy's *Sermons,* Dr. Clarke's and Locke's *Works,* Hugo Grotius, *The Tale of a Tub,* De Foe's *Jure Divino,* Jacob's *Law Dictionary,* Pryn's *Animadversions, The Compleat Justice,* Bunyan's *Pilgrim's Progress,* 2 Prayer Books, a Psalter, and one Primer. When I resolved to become an Author, I repaired to my Library, and the first Book I took up was *The Tale of a Tub,* and beginning at the Title Page, I there saw the Picture of a Vessel at Sea tossing, and a Whale alongside, the People on Board in great consternation, throwing Tubs overboard, to divert the Whale, fearing he might Swallow them up; I immediately thought that Picture a just Emblem, of your Writers, and those of the *Gazette;* the whale I took to be the *Journal* Writers, and the Ship the Gazetteers, and what I think justifies my Thought, is some of your late Performances: they clap some incoherent Piece, or other, into the *Gazette,* by way of Tub, and your Writers like the Whale catch at it, all which I think makes them highly blameable; for they might easily see the Tubs thrown for them, are purely Baits; now if they intend to gain their Points, that is, inculcate the Principles of Liberty so strongly, that none but those who are born blind can help seeing of them: mind not the Tubs and they will cease to throw them when they find you don't."

"Thus, Zenger, you may see what I intend,
Is still to keep you to the Point in Hand,
Keep close to that, in spight of all the Tubs
And then you'll meet with praise instead of Rubs."

The *Gazette* writers quickly tried to turn the tableson the Hempstead wit, by accepting his allegory, only making the tossing vessel a noble Ship of State, and the Whale a public enemy, ready to devour the *Gazette,* and "enjoy the Liberty of the Press" alone.28 "Then the Journalists are to meet with Eubs instead of Praise; for the People of this Province are not to be deluded with a, *Tale of a Tub."* As if to show how little the *Gazette* was to be deluded by such a tale, one of Bradford's staff has a long letter in the *Gazette* of the following week29 on false ambition and private designs, concluding with a bold comparison of Zenger's *Journal* to "Old Thersites, so aptly described in Pope's Homer." These lines of Pope seemed to the *Gazette* writer a very accurate description of Zenger:

Thersites only clamour'd, in the throng,

Loquacious, loud, and turbulent of tongue,

And by no shame, by no respect controul'd,

In scandal busy, in reproaches bold;

But chief, he glory'd with licentious style,

To lash the Great, and Rulers to revile.80

/ Original couplets in Pope's manner were the chosen vehicle of polite, formal compliment through- I out the colonies, while the native satiric verse more often followed Butler's *Hudibras.* Verses *On the Marriage of the Prince of Orange with the Princess Royal,* for example, which we find in the *Gazette* of June 24, 1734, along with the announcement that they are "The Product of an American Genius," – such verses consist of the usual florid addresses to liberty, "to the Enlivening Sun benign," and so on. The Popean couplets in the *Journal,31* too, *On Colonel Morris's going for England,* though somewhat simpler, and certainly more genuine32 in tone, belong to the same order of laudatory verse.

See *The New Yvrk Gazette,* No. 437, March 11, 1733-34, and Supplement.

Ibid., March 18, 1733-34. "Pope's Iliad, Bk. II, 11. 255-263.

Guard him, ye Gods, safe to the British Isle

Grant his just Cause may gain a Royal Smile

May he succeed in what he's gone to doe,

And save his Country from Approaching Woe.

On the other hand, when a certain *Gazette* correspondent, Z. D., wishes to pour contempt and ridicule upon the *Journal's* verses to its hero, he chooses *Hudibras* for his model, and even prefaces his own attempt in verse with a few lines from *Hudibras.33* Some of his introductory remarks in prose are not without force and point.

"As I can read," he begins, "I sometimes amuse myself with the *Gazette* and *Journals;* and find in some of the latter, that the Bemus'd Tribe have been very busie in praising, praying and Desiring the Protection of the Gods, for a certain Patriot or Heroe of their own making; I question his right to either of the Titles, but shall wave it, to take a little Notice of those so highly Celebrated Performances. And first, I find one of them is for Imploring the Protection of Neptune, and all the other Gods, on this Glorious Expedition; while the Second enforces and prays particularly to Apollo, to inspire his otherwise Empty

M No. 61, January 6, 1734-35.

" Two poems on Colonel Morris *'a* departure appear in this number of the *Journal,* the second poem being sent by J. 8. from Cape-May in New Jersey, as " the Performance of a rural muse."

" See *The New York Gazette,* No. 487, February 25, 1734-35.

Noddle with fine things in praise of his Heroe, and the grand Undertaking ... I wonder they had not given him Arion's Harp, and instructed him what tune to play on it, in order to bring those *Morris-Dancers* about him."

Then passing to the subject of his own verses, Z. D. offers the following brief and sententious apology for them. " 'Tis possible they (the *Journal* poets) may Laugh at them, but I'm even with them, in that, beforehand, – being assured, they cannot despise my doggrel more than I do their high Heroick Fustian. Perhaps they may call it a Tubb, and they are very welcome, Tubs being very proper to amuse and divert the Eage of their Insatiable Leviathan, which has so long been endeavouring to swallow up both Government and Law."

His "doggrel" is somewhat above the average of the verse in Northern colonial newspapers of our period. A few lines will furnish sufficient evidence of its quality.

Great Jove himself, must summon'd be,
And Neptune, sent in haste to Sea,
And ev'ry god in proper Station,
Assist them in Poetick Fashion,
Brave Patriots those! of Right and Laws,
And Guardian Angels of the Cause;
But know, ye Paltry Pedling Tools,
Ye praying, Rhiming, Factious Fools,
Know, if hereafter you again
Take Don Apollo's Name in vain,
To patronize such spurious Trash,
The Furies have prepar'd a Lash,
The Scourge of Paltry Poetasting.

The only effect of all this on the *Journal* scribblers was to elicit an ironical appreciation of Z. D.'s poetic gifts.[34] "That Author is intirely wrong, in my humble Opinion," writes a *Journal* correspondent, "to bury that fine Genius of his in this wooden Country; what an exalted Figure he would make in any Part of Europe! How much would he be admired by the Connoisseurs in Poetry!"

Nowhere in the colonies was the battle over the principles of representative government fought more fiercely at this period than in these New York papers. And although personal comments were made with peculiar freedom on both sides, yet the two opposing theories in regard to the responsibility of the ruling power to the people were developed in a long series of abstract discussions as well. Zenger based his ideas of liberty of the press, of govern- ment by the consent of the governed, of the privilege of juries, on *Cato's Letters,* while Bradford answered with arguments reinforced by Collier's *Moral Essays,* Hooker's *Ecclesiastical Polity,* and the Earl of Clarendon's *History of the Rebellion.* These arguments would seem odd to modern readers, since even conservative political opinion to-day would hardly accord with Bradford's point of view. To Bradford, indeed, and his correspondents, the idea that governors are only the executors and servants of the people's will was very dangerous – just a shallow appeal to popular ignorance.

As it happened, Zenger himself first suggested the authority of Clarendon to Bradford, by a

M See *The New York Weekly Journal,* No. 69, March 3, 1735.

letter in the *Journal36* on the undeserved sufferings of "Mr. Pryn, Dr. Bastwick and Mr. Burton in the Court of Star-Chamber" for the Puritan cause. Clearly their freedom of speech interested Zenger. But the *Gazette* writers immediately36 challenged his heroes, and accused Zenger of fabricating history. " These three honest Gentlemen's Behaviour," writes a correspondent of Bradford," he would recommend to his Eeaders for a Pattern of Innocence and Courage. God forbid! If the Earl of Clarendon, who is remarkable for his fine and impartial Character, may gain belief." He then quotes long passages from Clarendon's account of the three Puritan leaders. Zenger, not to be daunted by the awe-inspiring name of Clarendon, retorted with Oldmixon's charges against Atterbury and Smalridge, which virtually made them the authors of the passages in question. Again, the *Gazette* carried on the contest by insisting37 that there had been no interpolations in the history, and by reprinting a large portion of Atterbury's defence of himself. , 'U!

Zenger's open defiance of the Governor resulted in his arrest for libel on the seventeenth of Novem-

'ber, 1734. He was brought before the Justice on the twentieth, and committed to prison without bail to

, await his trial. The *Journal* continued uninterrupted, however, by these events, only taking a little more prudent course, in the expression of its ideas through well-known English essays, rather than through original discussions. We find a long series

"No. 14, February 4, 1733-34.

" See *The New York Gazette,* No. 433, February 11, 1733-34.

" See Nos. 436 and 440, March 4, 1733-34, and April 1, 1734.

of reprints from *Cato's Letters* in the spring and summer of 1735. Several times the fear of incurring the "Pains and Penalties of Lybeling" is sarcastically advanced as the reason for using an essay known to be "printed in England."38 The trial- took place early in August, 1735. The famous lawyer, Andrew Hamilton, from Philadelphia, defended j . Zenger, and the printer was acquitted. The *Journal* of August 18 gives an enthusiastic account of the "three Hurras of many Hundreds of People in the presence of the Court" at the verdict of Not Guilty. "About Forty of the Citizens entertained Mr. Hamilton at the Black Horse that day at Dinner," we are told in the same issue of the *Journal,* "and at his Departure ... he was saluted with the great Guns of several Ships."

The evidence for and against Zenger has been ably and fully discussed in a recent volume by Mr. Livingston Eutherford.39 The case of this bold New York printer was soon known in England, and used as a text for essays urging the liberty of the press in the *Craftsman* and *Common Sense.40* The book registries of both *The Gentleman's Magazine* and *The London Magazine* for January, 1738, include *The Tryal of John Peter Zenger, of New York,*

" See *The New York Weekly Journal,* No. 61, January 6, 1734-35, No. 84, June 16, 1735, and No. 85, June 23, 1735.

"John Peter Zenger, His Press, His Trial, and A Bibliography of Zenger Imprints, together with a Reprint of the First Edition of the Trial. By Livingston Butherford.

" *Common Sense,* No. 49, January 7, 1738, has an essay on *The great Importance of the Liberty of the Press,* and the *Craftsman,* No. 602, January 21, 1738, in a similar essay, reprints extracts from *Mr. Hamilton's Speeches at the Trial of John Peter Zenger.*

Printer, as well as *Remarks on the Tryal of John /-Peter Zenger.* But although the importance of i Zenger's case in the development of American polit- ical opinion could hardly be overestimated, the facts I of his trial have only an indirect bearing on the present investigation. They help to explain a certain change in the literary aspect of the *Journal]* after 1735.

Naturally, when Zenger's vindication was complete, when, after a time, he became the official printer for New Jersey, and a man of established reputation, his paper ceased to be an organ of violent political controversy. Not that hostilities ever ceased between the *Journal* and the *Gazette.* But the combatants slowly learned to content themselves with the firing of an occasional gun. Bradford went to sleep between the shots. Zenger developed his paper along a number of new lines.

First of all there is a distinct attempt to present public affairs in a coherent, organized way. Out of the mass of news items, a system begins to appear in the *Journal.* Even when there is no foreign news, we find something of real importance to the city, like the publication of the charter or the city laws. "As the Time affords but little News," writes Zenger in the *Journal* of February 20,1737-38, "and the City Laws seem to be in but few Hands, I thought it might not be amiss to publish them in the *Journal.*"

(Rarely in a colonial paper before 1740, can foreign affairs be followed so intelli- gently as in *The New York Weekly Journal.* Zenger seems to have selected from the English magazines and papers just) the group of situations and events which would most I vitally affect colonial interests. For instance, the' strained relations between England and Spain leading to Admiral Vernon's capture of Carthagena and Porto Bello meant more to British America than to England, and the desire to reinforce Admiral Vernon, for the purpose of finally wiping Spanish America off the map, was very strong in the colonies. Hence the convention between Great Britain and Spain, concluded in January, 1739, gave no satisfaction to the colonists, eager for the fray, and confident of complete victory. Zenger not only selected the clearest articles from the English magazines on the "present State of Affairs between Us and Spain,"41 but he published the convention, article by article, in two successive numbers of the *Journal.2* Bits of verse complimenting Vernon, criticisms of the English government's policy, are taken from English sources in a sequence logical enough to give a vivid and thorough account of Anglo-Spanish affairs. Essays on allied subjects of general interest to Americans, like the excellent description of the Musquito Indians in the *Craftsman* of November 11,1738, also appeared in the *Journal.* When dialogues between John Tar and Thomas Lobster on the victory at Porto Bello43 crept in, we already have the beginnings of the literary influence

41 See *The New York Weekly Journal,* No. 273, March 5, 1738-39, which contains an article of this sort from *The London Magazine* of November, 1738.

"Nos. 283 and 284, May 15, 1739, and May 21, 1739.

"See *The Craftsman,* March 21, 1740.

of the English periodicals. The most important reprints from the English periodicals of this period, in the *Journal,* are those of two entire numbers of Fielding's *Champion.* The reason for the first of these reprints is obvions, since a large part of the *Champion* of June 24,1740, is devoted to the exploits of "the brave Admiral Vernon." The second reprint from the *Champion,* however, is purely literary and illustrates the ease with which a newspaper of 1740 could pass from the literary tatment of current events, to literature itself.

The *Champion* was ostensibly published by Hercules Vinegar and his family. Through Hercules, Mrs. Joan, or Jack Vinegar, as mouthpieces, Fielding could give utterance to satire or nonsense, as he chose. The first *Champion* reprinted by the *Journal* has plenty of nonsense, combined with a warm defence of Admiral Vernon. In fact, the whole paper rings with the words patriot liberty, courage, Zenger's own favorite words. At a meeting of the Vinegar family, "on all Matters which properly belong to the Office of Censor of Great Britain," a petition to naturalize the Dutch word Skellum has been introduced. Skellum means everything that is bad; and "to utter one Syllable in Favour of them (evil-doers) shall henceforth be reputed Skellumy." In the list of skellums that follows, the item which undoubtedly helped to bring the *Champion* to New York is this: "Resolv'd, That any Person or Persons who attempt to whisper a Syllable against the brave Admiral Vernon, or to ridicule or lessen the Reputation of his late Success in America, is a Skellum, and shall so be reputed forever."

Moreover, this very number of the *Champion* ends with a song to Admiral Vernon, sent by "Brit- tanicus." Fielding's genius certainly did not lie in song, and this particular tribute to the Admiral ranks very little above the ordinary "poetical essay" in *The London Magazine* or *The Gentleman's Magazine.* "Brittanicus" merely scores the government roundly for not reinforcing the gallant officer,

Whose Virtue and Courage
If rightly sustain'd,
Had retriev'd our lost Fame,
And new Trophies had gain 'd;
Ov'r the whole Spanish Coast
Britain's Thunder had hurl'd,
And, like Neptune, gave Laws
To Columbo's new World.
This let fam'd Porto Bello,
And Chagre declare!
Those Earnests of Vengeance!
Those first Fruits of War!
Which, with six Ships now only,
He lay'd in the Dust,
And what Britain laments,
Is the Laughter of Spain.

These sentiments were sure to be heartily echoed in the colonies.

The next number of the *Champion* which Zenger reprinted44 consists of a dialogue between Harlequin and Punch, with the occasional excited entrance of their servant, Scaramouch, who brings terrifying messages from their creditors. This dialogue hasnothing to do with political affairs, and is therefore, introduced into the *Journal* merely for its own sake. Harlequin and Punch represent swindlers in high places, who have used the law for their own purposes. Evidently Zenger thought that the satire would be appreciated by his New York readers.

44 See *The New York Weekly Journal,* No. 368, December 22, 1740.

Thus by degrees Zenger began to draw from the English periodicals, as Franklin and Andrew Bradford had drawn from them even earlier. By using both the literary and the news sections of the magazines, the colonial editor could often provide himself with material for several weeks in succession. Zenger learned to avail himself liberally of this opportunity, and even William Bradford used it to some extent in the *Gazette.*

The selections in the *Journal* are more literary, however, as well as more numerous than those in the *Gazette.* Letters from *The Grubstreet Journal* on extravagant finery,45 several excellent numbers of *The Spy* describing Sunday afternoon tea-table gossip in London, and fashionable London life in general,46 essays from *The Gentleman's Magazine* on *The Vanity of affecting to be tho't younger than we are,47* or *The Desire of Matrimony in Old Women rebuked9* all found their way into *The New York Weekly Journal.* From *The Gentleman's Magazine,* too, came that series of papers in defence of *Gulliver's Travels,* which have an important connectionwith Samuel Johnson's *Debates in Lilliputia. Truth asserted, or a Demonstration that the Relations in Mr. Gulliver's Voyages are no Fictions* is the title of the first essay in the series.49 The *Debates in Lilliputia* began in June, 1738, and no doubt led to the defence of *Gulliver's Travels* in *Truth Asserted.* In any case, there is a possibility that if Zenger thought the defence of Gulliver's voyages worthy of reprinting, he may also have reprinted some of the Lilliputian debates in the numbers of his *Journal* not now extant.50 Unfortunately we have no proof of such a connection with Samuel Johnson.

" See *The New York Weekly Journal,* No. 172, February 28, 1736-37. "Ibid., Nos. 173, 174, and 175, March 7, March 14, and March 21, 1736-37.

" Ibid., No. 270, February 12, 1738-39. "Ibid., No. 266, January 15, 1738-39.

Original essays of a purely literary character are not numerous in the *Journal;* and yet the editorial staff felt the influence of the current English periodical to some extent. A long letter in the *Craftsman51* from Aminadab to Friend Caleb, "the Man called the Craftsman,"probably suggested the letter from Caleb Tenderheart to his friend, Nahab Din, in *The New York Weekly Journal.6* Caleb Tender- heart writes a solemn diatribe on the vanity, pride, and ignorance of a certain young miss, his cousin. After the letter, we have Nahab Din's comments. "I am very apt to think all that is therein contain'd is nothing but Truth, since I myself have often observed that the young Maidens of York and Flushing have not half the good Qualities they were bless'd with in the years 1710 and 1711."

"See *The Gentleman's Magazine* for February, 1739.

"The flies of *The New York Weekly Journal* in the New York Public Library are somewhat broken.

"No. 736, August 9, 1740. It was copied into *The New Yorle Weekly Journal,* No. 362, November 10, 1740.

No. 279, April 16, 1739.

Another attempt at writing the kind of sprightly essay common in the later English periodicals, and applying it to local conditions in New York and New Jersey, may be found in the letter from Peaceable53 on the "Spunger or Hanger-on." Peaceable complains that this unpleasing individual may be found "in every Corner of New Jersey. . . . The Town swarms with this sort of gentry; and a Man of Fortune cannot set his Foot into it, from his Voyage or Travels, but there are several of them come instantly humming and buzzing about him." Peaceable does not trouble himself much about syntax, but nevertheless he shows some ability to describe character, and point out the follies of his day. Original essays in the *Journal* are fairly well exemplified in these remarks of Nahab Din and Peaceable.

Zenger's taste in poetry was not of the highest order, as may be imagined, though it was certainly above reproach on the moral side. The Eeverend John Pomfret's Pindaric Essay on *A Prospect of Death* occupies the front page in two successive numbers of the *Journal*.6 It is introduced as a pleasant entertainment in a letter to "Mr. Zenger," which is worth quoting as evidence of the welcome afforded to any sort of literature by the colonial editor.

Mr. Zenger,

As the Season of the Year can afford you but little News, I thought that the following Lines of Mr. Pomfret would be no disagreeable Entertainment to your Readers; there-

" See *The New York Weekly Journal,* No. 388', May 11, 1741. " Nog. 164 and 165, December 27, 1736, and January 10, 1736-37.

fore I desire you to insert them, and you'll oblige one of your constant Readers,
Mort. Spect. sub.

Extempore Verses, by Stephen Duck, on the *Admission of his Son into Eton College,* also adorn the pages of the *Journal*.55 There are some original couplets, sent by Eachel Salem, on Chloe's absence, written by "a young gentleman, on the Departure of a deserving Young Lady from this City,"56 as well as a number of uninspired elegies. On the whole, there was little interest in poetry.

The moral tale, the moral dialogue, and the fable, on the other hand, never waned in popularity. Aesop's Fables are among the few secular books mentioned in the printers' advertisements, and in the *Journal* of December 13, 1736, we find the following letter to the editor:

Mr. Zenger,

In order to divert that Dulness under which you seem to labour, . . . insert the following Fable. It is taken from a collection of Sir L'Estrange. Yours, etc.

The moral dialogues of "the late ingenious Mrs. Eowe" against quadrille and ridicule are reprinted in full by Zenger,57 with a flattering introduction, describing them as "entertaining to All, and, I hope, profitable to Some of your Eeaders." / The book advertisements of both Bradford and

"No. 263, December 25, 1738.
" See *The New York Weekly Journal,* No. 242, July 3, 1738.
" Ibid., Noa. 382 and 384, March 30, 1741, and April 13, 1741.

/ Zenger are meager. Beyond an occasional notice of Bunyan's *Pilgrim's Progress,* Aesop's *Fables,* and *Religious Courtship,* they note only devotional manuals like *A Choice Drop of Honey out of the Rock, Christ,* or *The Joy full Deaths of several young*

/ *Children.* Sermons, of course, always abound.

Far more important than these meager book notices, are the advertisements of a pantomime entertainment given in New York early in 1739, and the notices of *The Beaux-Stratagem* early in 1741. /Theaters were common in Southern cities long before these dates, but Bradford and Zenger have the distinction of publishing some of the first, if not the first notices of theatrical entertainments actually presented north of Virginia. Through the month of February, 1739, both the *Gazette* and the *Journal* informed their readers that *The Adventures of Harlequin and Scaramouch* would be performed "in Mr. Holt's Long Room," where the Audience would also be shown "An Optick, wherein will be Represented, in Perspective, several of the most noted Cities and remarkable Places in Europe and America, with a New Prologue and Epilogue address'd to the Town." As the Epilogue was to be "spoken by Master Holt," we may infer that the whole of this varied performance represented private enterprise. The pantomime was similar to that advertised in Charleston four years before, if not identical with it. Therefore the subject will be more conveniently treated in a later chapter.58

The *Journal's* advertisements of *The BeauxStratagem* early in February, 1741, refer to a public performance in the "new Theatre in the Broad Way," and indicate that Farquhar's comedy was as popular in New York as it had been earlier in Williamsburg.59

58 Vide *infra.* Chap. VTII.

Taken as a whole, the literary material of *The New York Weekly Journal,* and, in lesser degree, of *The New York Gazette,* is unusually significant. That a violent political quarrel in a provincial town of 1734 should rouse the participants to the use of Addison, Steele and the British Cato as models for their controversial essays, to the use of *A Tale of a Tub* for their bitterest satire, to the use of *Hudibras* as a model for their verse, proves beyond a doubt that English secular literature often influenced the colonies within a generation of its original publication. In the further development which Zenger 's paper underwent, we often find English essays of only two months previous, either reprinted or used as models for original work in the *Journal.*

"Vide *infra,* Chap. VII.

6

SECTION 6

CHAPTER VI

The Mabyland G-azette

Hitherto a rare good fortune has enabled us to rely on complete, or nearly complete files of eighteenth-century newspapers. The Massachusetts Historical Society lacks comparatively few issues of *The New England C our ant,* while its file of *The New England Weekly Journal* combined with the file in the Athenaeum Library furnishes a sequence almost as orderly as one could ask for in a newspaper office to-day. Only a paper now and then is missing from the volumes of the *Mercury* after 1729, and *The Pennsylvania Gazette* complete is in the possession of the Pennsylvania Historical Society.

By using the New York Public Library's collection along with those of the New York Historical Society and the New York Society Library, an excellent set of New York papers can be pieced together. For a historical investigation, of course, even the loss of a few issues may take on a grave importance. For a literary analysis it is not so. Although something of immense interest may be gone from our account, the literary characteristics of a paper remain fairly constant, and, given any considerable stretch of time, are sure to repeat themselves. But if we have only fragments to go upon, even literary analysis becomes very difficult.. This is especially true in the case of *The Maryland*

Gazette, established contemporaneously with *The*
New England Weekly Journal, and two years before
Franklin's *Gazette.*

As the case stands at present, the Maryland Historical Society's rigid and extensive search throughout the country has brought to light only scattering numbers of *The Maryland Gazette* before 1750. Its own file from December 10, 1728, to July 22, 1729, can be supplemented by two numbers of June and October, 1729, in the New York Public Library, which also has ten numbers of 1730, six of 1733, and nine of 1734. These are all the extant papers until the Maryland Historical Society's fairly complete file from 1745 to 1749 takes up the tale. The Massachusetts Historical Society has four scattering numbers of October and November, 1748, in addition to a few numbers after 1750. More than ten interesting years, therefore, important for our purpose, are entirely a blank.

However, there are one or two significant facts which put the treatment of the earlier years on a somewhat firmer footing. The publisher and editor of the old *Maryland Gazette* became the first proprietor and editor of a Virginia paper, the rather famous *Virginia Gazette,* in 1736. Of this the Virginia Historical Society has a beautifully preserved file up to 1740.1 Naturally, then, the editor of the two papers gave somewhat the same general character to both, though of course the Virginia enterprise represents his maturer work. Presumably the

1 Vide, infra, chapter VII, for a full discussion of *The Virginia Gazette.*

early missing numbers of *The Maryland Gazette* partook of the general literary tone of the Virginia paper. And this conclusion is borne out by an examination of the extant numbers of *The Maryland Gazette* up to 1735. After that we can draw no (inferences from the character of the Virginia weekly, jsince the Maryland paper passed out of the hands of | its first editor when he was about to make his new (venture in Virginia.

And who was this editor? The name of William OParks is not widely known, perhaps for the reason that tradition has left such meager details of his life. Nothing personal, characteristic, remains to tell us what manner of man he was. The few known facts are very significant, however. He was an Englishman, born in Grosport, England, and emigrated to Maryland to establish his *Gazette* there in 1727. Hence he may fairly be called one of the pioneer colonial editors, the first, as it happened, to be born and reared in England. And this fact must have had an important bearing on his work. He published *The Maryland Gazette* in Annapolis, for eight years, until 1735. But at least two years before that date, he opened a printing office in Williamsburg, the old capital of Virginia. His advertisements of 1733 and 1734 in *The Maryland Gazette* tell us that certain books were "printed and sold by William Parks, at his Printing-Offices in *Williamsburg and Annapolis.*" The Virginia State Library has a copy of the Laws of Virginia, bearing his imprint, and the date, 1733. This means that he had won official recognition. The Maryland assembly, too, passed an act, April 12,1733, providing "for the speedy and effectual Publication of the Laws of this Province; and for the Encouragement of William Parks, of the City of Annapolis, Printer."2

So we see that Parks conducted just such a triple) business establishment as Franklin's. He soldi books, he printed books, and he printed and edited a newspaper. The importations from London were quite casual, however, until he established a regularly well-supplied store in 1742, at his office in Wil- liamsburg. He seems to have lived in Virginia after 1735, and to have become thoroughly identified with his adopted land. Sarah Shelton, Patrick Henry's first wife, was very probably a granddaughter of William Parks.3

Naturally, Parks must have had a later and more first-hand knowledge of contem- porary English life than the ordinary provincial editor. Franklin, it is true, was in England for eighteen months before he wrote the *Busy-Body* papers, but although he met a number of distinguished persons, he dissipated his time, on the whole. Very likely William Parks was a young journeyman in London when Ambrose Phillips's *Freethinker* was coming out twice a week,4 and possibly also when Aaron Hill's *Plain Dealer* was enlightening the town.5 Beyond a doubt heknew them both. The first thing to meet the eye in the first extant number of *The Maryland Gazette* is an essay periodical called *The Plain Dealer,* of which the material is taken from Phillips's eightieth *Freethinker.*

3See *The Maryland Gazette,* No. 19 of the new series, April 13, 1733.

8 For a discussion of this point, see an interesting article in *The William and Mary College Quarterly,* Vol. VII, pp. 9-17, on *Old Virginia Editors.*

That is, from March 24, 1718, to September 28, 1719.

From March 23, 1724, to May 7, 1725. Reprinted in 1734.

Of course there is no means of knowing that Parks or his unknown correspondent borrowed the title of his essay series from Aaron Hill's *Plain Dealer.* The name is so typical of early eighteenth-century writing that it was probably to be found in many a source not now accessible. More significant than such a profitless inquiry is the fact that for the first time an American paper gave a distinct title like *The Plain Dealer, The Censor, The Freethinker,* to its periodical essays. *The Busy-Body,* we remember, began several months later.6 The literary efforts of Proteus Echo in *The New England Weekly Journal7* had no specific title. Moreover, all the earlier groups of essays are more distinctly modeled on the *Spectator.* That is to say, they were a little behind the fashion. Periodical writing in England had undergone a number of changes and developments in ten years. And although echoes of the newer papers can be heard in even the earliest American essays, the new style definitely appears for the first time in *The Maryland Gazette.*

A new fashion often merely exaggerates some aspect of the old. This was emphat- ically true in the periodicals following Addison and Steele. Very little can be found in them that does not hark back

Early in 1729. ' Of 1727-1728.

to the *Spectator* or the *Tatler.* But whereas fable, allegory, legend and fairy tale played a subordinate part in the classical British essays, they were frequent in the later periodicals along with a changed tone of philosophical discussion, and, curiously enough, with a great advance in the dramatic handling of conversation. No doubt the essay and the novel were beginning to play upon each other. This last aspect, however, does not appear in the extant numbers of *The Plain-Dealer,* and may be more profitably considered in examining a brilliant series of essays in *The Virginia Gazette,9* unexampled in this particular on this side of the Atlantic before 1750.

As to the other developments referred to, they are all represented in the few extant numbers of *The Plain Dealer* and furnish one more proof that the eighteenth century should not be summed up as "the age of prose and reason." Fables in verse and prose obtained an amazing popularity, not only the fanciful, original variety of Gay and Smart, but popular collections of ancient fables like *The Fabu- lator, or the Hall of Aesop.* Toland edited Aesop's fables in 1704 for Anthony Collins. Sir Roger L'Estrange's collection was known in New York. And all the eighteenth-century periodicals drew on them for their lighter papers. As to fairy tales and popular legends, no medieval audience ever received them more greedily. The one vital difference between the medieval fairy tale and that of the eighteenth century is in the moral treatment. The original version had a moral – perhaps. Certainly the wicked stepmother or mother-in-law meets her doom. But the eighteenth-century tale is all moral, from beginning to end, a mere embroidery for a text on contentment, or a warning against the snares of beauty.9 Even the mother-in-law's fate is forgotten, so long as the heroine's character becomes beatific through discipline.

8 See chapter VII for a full discussion.

To be more specific, just such a series of fairy stories and legends from the East may be found in Ambrose Phillips's *Freethinker.10* Phillips was assisted in his undertaking by Bishop Boulter, Richard West, Chancellor of Ireland, George Stubbs, Gilbert Burnet, and Henry Steevens. Their solemn philosophical discourses are interrupted11 by a series of *Winter Evening Tales.* Phillips did not forget the fair sex, and laid great stress on pleasing them. For had not Phillips himself written for the *Spectator?* One of these *Winter Evening Tales12* is no other than Chaucer's *Man of Law's Tale* under a new guise, – that world-old tale of the cruel mother- in-law and the beautiful young bride, whom she succeeds in separating from her husband. The story goes back through the Constance saga to remote Eastern origins, but nowhere on its long road had it taken this unique form. Instead of the happyreunion, and the summary punishment of the scheming mother, the imprisoned bride is given one chance of escape by the benignant fairy who visits her. She may return to her shepherdess life, this time with an ugly face, but with a contented heart! This is the tale which is taken bodily into *The Plain Dealer13* in *The Maryland Gazette,* introduced by six lines from Dryden's Juvenal on man's ignorance of his own good.

8For example, see *The Prophetic See,* p. 131 of *A Collection of Fugitive Fables.* Florella is warned by the bee against trusting in beauty.

10 *The Freethinker* began March 24, 1718, and ended with its one hundred and fifty-ninth paper, September 28, 1719.

11 See Nos. 80, 84, 92, 109, 110 for instances. "In *Freethinker* No. 80.

Look round the habitable World how few

Know their own Good! or knowing it pursue!

How void of Reason are our Hopes and Fears!

What in the Conduct of our Life appears

So well design'd, so luckily begun,

But when we have our Wish, we wish undone?

Thus a good old popular story is made to fit Dryden's moralizing couplets. Dryden, indeed, and Pope as well, furnished the text of many a pious tale, many a commonplace sermon-essay, not only in England, but in the colonies.

Allegory, vision, dream literature of all sorts, are nearly as common in an eighteenth-century periodical as in a fourteenth-century homily. The allegorical characters frequently have even the same names, though of course the eighteenth-century figure of Eeason or Virtue or Love is not developed with the rich and quaint physical imagery of the earlier type. No mystic numbers,14 no crown ofpearls,16 no gem-stone Maidenhood,16 no blue robes for Loyalty17 bring varied beauty to the cold lay figures of eighteenth-century abstractions. The landscape which forms the setting for these lay figures is often not unlike the conventional May morning of medieval allegory, although treated more formally and at the same time more sentimentally than the latter.

a Plain Dealer, No. 4, *Maryland Gazette,* December 10, 1728. " See *Sir Gawain and the Green Knight,* et passim, in medieval literature.

The dream or vision of virtue and vice in the eighth number of *The Plain Dealer18* begins with the wooing of a maid in a spring landscape of flowered meadow, and proceeds to give the warnings and exhortations of Virtue and Vice as they individually appear to the lover. Virtue, as usual, means reason or self- control. This whole allegory is undeniably tedious. The introductory sentences promise well, but emphatically do not fulfill their promise. "There is nothing more common," says the Plain Dealer, "than to Nod over a Standish, and to write out several Sheets of Paper (as it were) in One's Sleep, while the Author imagines himself broad awake. On the contrary, Our *real Slumber* may sometimes contribute to our Instruction." Alas, he was deceived if he thought that his did. We prefer him nodding over his standish.

Speculations on government were popular not only in party papers and pamphlets, but in all periodicals, especially after the publication of *Cato's Letters.* The theory of constitutional liberties was threshed out from both conservative and liberal points of view. *The Plain Dealer19* takes a rather conservative middle ground, emphasizing the danger of designing leaders, which he illustrates by the Civil Wars in "our Mother Country." He advocates the preservation of "as many of the Antient Forms of Administration, as possible" if a government is to be remodeled, and observes without a hint of a possible reference to the colonies, that a great commonwealth, or republic, is impracticable. The article concludes with a hearty eulogium on the late Revolution, as "not only the Happiest but also the most wisely conducted affair that was ever executed by Man." After all, the chief value of this specula- i tion on government lies in its references to "our j Mother Country" and "our Parent-Country" which/ prove that *The Plain Dealer* is beyond a doubt/ American, however it may have borrowed individual! ideas, lines of argument, or tales.

" See *The Pearl,* a fourteenth-century poem of uncertain authorship.

" See the *Love-Bune of* Thomas de Hales, an allegorical poem of the fourteenth century.

1' See the *AssembU de Dames,* in *Chaucerian and Other Pieces,* ed. Skeat.

"See *The Maryland Gazette,* No. 70, January 14, 1728-1729.

Perhaps more astonishing than any other echo from England is the Deistic tendency of four numbers of *The Plain Dealer.* One would have thought that the general piety of any colonial community, whether Church of England or dissenting, would have made the slightest approach to Deism perilously offensive. In fact we know that it did, in Franklin's case;20 even though he had really lost interest in Deism before his return to Philadelphia.

"No. 10, *Maryland Gazette,* No. 74, February 11, 1728-29.

"Vide supra, chapters III and IV.

That is to say, he never wrote or acted in defence of it after his early "wicked" tract on liberty and necessity. Philosophically he remained a Deist, it is true, but actually he developed a kind of pragmatism or humanitarianism of his own. Certainly he never wrote any articles for his *Gazette,* openly advising free enquiry on all hands.

i *The Plain Dealer* deliberately defends philosophical doubting21 as the only way to a firm and reasonable faith, saying22 that "it is highly unreasonable and very insiduous to deter Men yet more from a fair Enquiry ... by grave Representations of the Danger of it; thus furnishing an Excuse for contented Ignorance and Presumption; Strengthening thereby the Treachery of our Prejudices with a false Colour of Sanctity and Zeal." He recommends "a manly freedom of thought." Yet he adds a modification which leaves the bewildered modern reader with the dazed sense that he has been told to swim without going near the water. "The great Truths of Religion, Morality and Virtue," says the Plain Dealer,23 "are easily apprehended by the ordinary mind." Further, he explains, there is no need to regard the "Refinements in these several Topicks, which have been introduced into the World by Speculative Men." Just how a free enquiry is to be conducted without touching on the great truths of religion, morality and virtue is as mysterious as any speculative refinement could be.

11 *Plain Dealer,* Nos. 3, 5, &.

In a *Letter to the Plain Dealer,* No. 9, *Maryland Gazette,* No. 71, January 21, 1728-29.

" *Plain Dealer,* No. 5, *Maryland Gazette,* No. 66, December 17, 1728.

But it is a mystery very characteristic of Deism, especially early Deism in England. Shaftesbury24 pulls himself together again and again with the assurance that his principles are in perfect accord with " our holy religion." In fact every idea of the *Plain Dealer* on philosophic doubt shows the influence of the Deistic speculation in England. "This, my Lord," says Shaftesbury, in his *Letter concerning Enthusiasm25* addressed to Somers, "is the best security against all superstition; to remember that there is nothing in God but what is godlike; and that he is either not at all, or truly and perfectly good. But when we are afraid to use our reason freely, even on that very question, 'whether he really be, or not,' we then actually presume him bad, and flatly contradict that pretended character of goodness and greatness; whilst we discover this mistrust of his temper, and fear his anger and resentment, in the case of this freedom of inquiry. . . . For what merit can there be in believing God, or his providence, upon frivolous and weak grounds? What virtue in assuming an opinion contrary to the appearance of things, and resolving to hear nothing which may be said against it? Excellent character of the God of truth! that he should be offended at us for having refused to put the lie upon our understanding, as much as in us lay, and be satisfied with us for having believed at a venture, and against our reason, what might have been the great-

M Throughout the *Characteristics,* but especially in the *Miscellaneous Beflections.*
"See *Characteristics of Men, Manners, Opinions, Times,* ed. John M. Robertson,
Vol. I, p. 25.

est falsehood in the world, for anything we could bring as a proof or evidence to
the contrary!" / By enthusiasm, of course, Shaftesbury meant fanaticism. Such was
its common significance, especially among Churchmen, and such will be its ordinary
meaning in any eighteenth-century allusion. To call a person an enthusiast meant
calling him an evangelist and something more. To have "an en- thusiastick fit" was to
have a fit of raving. The distinction will be an important one for our later chapters.

The Plain Dealer uses the word in precisely this sense in a passage very suggestive
of Shaftesbury.26 "Eeligion has three great Adversaries, Atheism, Superstition, and
Enthusiasm," the *Plain Dealer* says. A treatment of superstition follows, characteriz-
ing Christian superstitions as worse than others, even as the Christian religion in its
purity is the best of all.

No doubt *The Plain Dealer* would yield much literacy material if we had more than
these ten numbers to examine. We do not even know that there ever were more than
ten. The series is abruptly cut off so far as the extant files of *The Maryland Gazette*
show. Yet other essays and verse of various sorts may be found in the scattering
numbers up to 1735.

Besides the usual reprints of articles from current English papers and pamphlets,27
there areseveral English items of lively interest. One of the earliest theatrical notices
to reach an American paper28 informs the inhabitants of Maryland on May 26, 1730,
that on the 27th of January last (in London, of course) "at the Anniversary Feast of
the Ancient and Honourable Society of Free and Accepted Masons, after Dinner, the
Grand Master bespoke the Tragedy of The Sequel of King Henry IV, with the Humours
of Sir John Falstaff, etc. to be Acted on the Twelfth of February following, at the
Theatre Royal in Drury Lane, for the Entertainment of the Society . . . and ordered
a new Prologue and Epilogue to be made upon the Occasion, with proper Alterations
in the Play to introduce the Apprentice's and Master's Song; all which was perform'd
with great Applause last Thursday, the Brethren in the Pit and Boxes joining in the
Chorus." Both the prologue and the epilogue of this ill-assorted entertainment are
given in *The Maryland Gazette;* dull enough couplets offering a general apology for
Masons. No doubt all this fanfare was a bit of advertisement for the Ancient and
Honourable Society of Masons.

" Plain Dealer, No. 7, *Maryland Gazette,* No. 69, January 7,1728-29.

21 Such as the long sermon on tea drinking in No. 162, Oct. 20, 1730, introduced
as follows: "In hopes it may prove diverting, if not useful to some of our Readers; we
give them the following Letter from An English Paper."

A delightful item from Bath29 takes us to the scene of English pride and fashion
in the season: "Mr. Congreve, the celebrated Poet, was overturn'd in his Chariot by
the Horses running back down theHill as he was going to the Races, but he received
no hurt, having been immediately let Blood. Never was known a greater Concourse
of Quality here than at this Season, but many of them will be going away next Week."
How vividly this puts "Mr. Con- greve" in his own appropriate setting! One has the
feeling that it must have been manufactured for the very purpose.

88 Doubtless the Virginia and South Carolina newspapers would have had such notices even earlier had they been in existence. *The South Carolina Gazette* was not established until 1731; *The Virginia Gazette* not until 1736.

"Item of Sept. 28, 1728, inserted in *The Maryland Gazette,* No. 73, February 4, 1728-29.

One piece taken boldly from the "Pamphelet entitled *The Intelligencer,"* published in Dublin in 1728 and 1729, assumes an importance far greater than the literary value of the essay itself, which is an ordinary eighteenth-century treatment of the old theme of Prometheus and his journeymen moulding their clay images. By itself this would be only one more indication of the popularity of the essay-fable. When we recall, however, that this little Dublin weekly was conducted by Dr. Thomas Sheridan and Dean Swift, the matter assumes quite a different aspect. If Parks read the first number, a general introduction to the *Intelligencer,* the third number, a defence of *The Beggar's Opera,* the nineteenth, on Irish grievances, he was reading Swift directly. Certain papers in *The Virginia GazetteTM* go far to strengthen the probability that either Parks or his correspondents knew the *Intelligencer* well. Like so many of the little weeklies between 1720 and 1730, it had only the brief existence of a year. On March 6, 1729, Swift wrote to Pope that Dr. Sheridan "made but sorry work of the *Intelligencer."*

Ireland and Irish affairs were evidently of interest to Maryland and Virginia readers. The *Gazette* celebrated Saint Patrick's Day, 1730,31 by publishing in full the verses of Somerset English, " sacred to Mirth and Good-Nature" on Saint Patrick and the serpents,

10 Vide infra, chapter VII.

whose Names I'll not rehearse,
Lest they should shed their Poisons o'er my Verse.

The whole poem is a plea for good-will between
England and her nearest neighbors:

Why should a true-born Son of English Breed,
Despise his Brother dwelling o'er the Tweed?
Or why not deign with cheerful Face to smile,
On him who dwells in near Hybernia's Isle?

Besides other commonplace English verse, and some rather good doggerel like these lines on the Spaniards,32

" Jack Spaniard should know,
and speedily too,
He's no more at Sea than a Go6se, Sir,"

native verse takes a rather prominent place in the *Gazette,* if we may judge by the scattering extant numbers, and by *The Virginia Gazette.* There are the usual stupid elegies,33 and complimentary poems, but, in addition, two or three interesting attempts to reflect the life of the new world. One of these indicates the close relationship between Williamsburg and Annapolis, which eventually led William Parks

" See *The Maryland Gazette,* No. 131. 82 Ibid., No. 81, April 1, 1729.

"Such as the elegy on Miss Elizabeth Young, in couplets, October 20, 1730, No. 162.

to open a Virginia office. No doubt he was already considering his new venture when the two poems from William and Mary College were published in his Maryland paper in 1729.34 The college was obliged to pay two complimentary Latin poems to the Governor of Virginia every fifth of November as quit rent for its land. President Blair's verses on *The Suppression of the late Rebellion,* and Professor Blackamore's35 on *The Mountain Expedition into western Virginia,* were translated into Popean heroic couplets by the Rev. George Seagood, and sent to *The Maryland Gazette* by Ecclesiasticus,

Swhoever he may have been. The important fact to be noted is that through all their formal imitation of Pope's epic manner, they were attempting to describe new conditions of life in a new world. As a matter of fact, the difficult mountain exploration had made a great impression, as the latest travelling exploits are always sure to do.

Another "Copy of Verses" shows an amusing translation of eighteenth-century ideals of poverty and retirement into the terms of native life in Jamaica. The verses are called *The Aged Creole: or the Way to Long Life in Jamaica.* A Copy of Verses, Occasioned by a Conversation with an Ancient Person of that Island.36 References to the race problem and other local facts establish clearly enough the general Western origin of the verses. The eights and sixes of their metrical form, too, were doubtless intended to reflect the rustic simplicity of

"No. 93, June 24, 1729.

"Professor of Humanities at William and Mary College.

"In *The Maryland Gazette,* No. 133, March 31, 1730.

the ancient Creole, whose ideas are so elaborate. He resigns ambitions that he could never have heard of in his native state, in favor of the simple cot invoked by every eighteenth-century poet sooner or later.

" Tell me, Old Man, with stooping Head,
With Snowy White o'er-run;
Tell me, what Life you here have led,
So long i' the Burning Sun."
Answ. "Free from Ambition is my Mind,
I know my lowly State
I humbly yield to what I find,
Nor spurn the Laws of Fate.
Of Rum I keep a moderate Cask,
And eat the Food I love.
With troubl'd Mind I ne're was caught,
For Loss of Land or Gold;
I ne're was vex'd for Skooner bought,
Or Duke of Chandos sold.
On what I have my Mind I fix
Nor envy Neighbour's Fare;
I never long'd for Coach and Six,
Or rob'd the Orphan Heir.
You say, The Climate is the Cause,
By Heats and Colds, you fall;

You die not, Sir, by Nature's Laws,
Ambition Mils you all."

No doubt all this is very absurd. But surely in a remote country, in an unpoetic age, it is worth mentioning, as an attempt at verse form other than the elegy and the hymn.

In the mere relating of news a colonial paper sometimes shows art of an interesting kind, especially in letters between individuals in the different provinces. A letter from a distance meant almost more than we can conceive. Naturally the recipient often shared its news items or its descriptions with the public. Such a letter could be easily written in the editor's chair, of course, and given an imaginary date, place, and signature. There is no means of proving that the *Extract of a Letter from a Gentleman in South Carolina, to a Gentleman in Philadelphia,* dated July 1, 1734, and inserted in *The Maryland Gazette37* is genuine. In any case, it contains a most Defoe-like narrative of a bloody mutiny led by four mulattoes on a schooner from Havannah and Harbour-Island. The story has all Defoe's precision of detail; we are told the exact number on board, the particular circumstances of each passenger, the exact day after sailing on which every thrilling event occurred. The villains all met their just fate in one way or another. The narrative is more rapid, of course, than Defoe's, as the letter is brief, comparatively speaking. But certainly nothing could be more like his cold, plain way of telling horrors. The schooner belonged to a " Spanish Gentleman of the Havannah" who "marry'd about 8 Months ago to a clever young Lady."

This is not the place to speak of *The Maryland Gazette's* full reports38 of Governor Burnet's com-

"No. 73, new series, August 2, 1734.

"See No. Ill, October 28, 1729, and Nos. 9 and 10, new series, February 2 and February 9, 1732-33.

plicated arguments with his Massachusetts legislature over grants of money and the proposed issue of Bills of Credit without asking His Majesty's consent lest it should establish a precedent of dependence on the crown. The deep significance, the influence of such full reports in a peaceful province, we leave to the future historian who will sometime trace the growth toward nationality in its earlier stages. The voluminous articles on the tobacco market, on "restraint of trade," on a fixed price, and on a tobacco trust, – these, too, we must leave to the investigator who will write the industrial history of Maryland. Even Benjamin Franklin's *Modest Enquiry into the Nature and Necessity of a Paper- Currency,* "lately publish'd in Pennsylvania," and "so nearly adapted to the Circumstances of this Province" that it was published in full in *The Maryland Gazette, TM* concerns us little, except as a proof of communication between the provinces.

Another aspect of the *Gazette* is very important, however, for our purpose. As early as 1728 Parks was advertising books for sale at his printing office. At first, and indeed, chiefly, for many years, he noted merely devotional or else very practical treatises. He did not open a regular book shop until 1742, in Williamsburg. He began, in fact, just as Franklin and Bradford had begun. His early notices40 simply informed his little public that at his printing office they could be supplied with the Acts of the Assembly, John Warner's Almanac, and Dulany's *Eights*

" No. 97, July 22, 1729.

" See *The Maryland Gazette,* No. 66, December 17, 1728.

of the Inhabitants of Maryland. Soon afterward, Henry DarnalPs *Letter to the Inhabitants of Maryland on the Transactions of the Merchants in London, for the Advancement of the Price of Tobacco,* was announced as a new publication by Parks.41 Manuals of devotion and doctrinal treatises were just as prominent as in the Northern states, only they represent the devotion and doctrine of the Church of England. Some of these Parks himself reprinted. As early as May 6,1729,42 he advertised his own reprint of *The Week's Preparation toward a worthy receiving of the Lord's Supper,* "after the "Warning of the Church for the Celebration of the Holy Communion," combined with *The Church of England Man's Private Devotions,* and an *Explanation of the Feasts and Fasts, as they are observed in the Church of England.* These, he says, were "printed on a good Letter and Paper: and all Three bound up together, and sold by W. Parks, Printer in Annapolis. Price 2s. 6d. And considerable Allowance to those that buy a Quantity." He evidently expected large orders from churches. By 1729, then, he was extending his Annapolis business, but there is no mention of a Williamsburg office.

This book of devotion is advertised again and again, but very soon becomes one of a considerable list, largely importations. In fact the advertisement of October 20,1730,43 has the headline "Lately imported by William Parks, from London." Theinteresting list which follows is very much like Franklin's early notices, except that one innocent item in Parks's account may have unsuspected literary significance.

41 See *The Maryland Gazette,* No. 70, January 14, 1728-29. "Ibid., No. 86. "Ibid., No. 162.

Tate and Brady's Psalms bound up alone
Testaments
Psalters
Spelling Books
Primers
Hornbooks
Books of Devotion, as,
Drelincourt on Death
Taylor's *Holy Living and Dying*
Duty of Man
Divine Entertainments
Nelson's *Fasts and Feasts*
Week's Preparation for the Sacrament, etc.
Grammars and Construing Books
Large and small Copy Books, with Copies ready
wrote in several curious Hands for Youth to
learn to write by.

Truly, if Maryland gentlemen depended on this catalogue for their books (and there is not the slightest probability that they did) their culture in pure letters would not be extraordinary. Drelincourt on Death, oddly enough, furnishes the only possibility of this sort, with the exception of Taylor's *Holy Living and Dying.* Drelincourt's treatise on the fear of death had been translated by D'Assigny, and published in England in

1675, under the title *The Christian's Defence against the Fear of Death, with several Directions how to prepare ourselves to die well.* Charles Drelincourt was a minister of theCalvinist church in Paris in the seventeenth century. To the fourth English edition of his book was added Defoe's *Apparition of Mrs. Veal.* Since the *Apparition* was written in 1706, the edition that Parks had for sale in 1730 may have included Defoe's report of the case of Mrs. Veal. In many roundabout ways like these there can be no doubt that Defoe was being read and enjoyed in America.

The fear of Deism in Maryland and Virginia was evidently strong enough to warrant a reprint by William Parks of Charles Leslie's famous tract against Deism. "Lately Published," we read in *The Maryland Gazette* of May 24, 1734,44 *"A Short and Easy Method with the Deists.* Wherein the Certainty of the Christian Eeligion is demonstrated by infallible Proof, from Four Eules, which are incompatible to any Imposture that ever yet has been, or that can Possibly be. In a Letter to a Friend. To which is added, *A Letter from the Reverend Mr. Leslie, to a Deist, upon his Conversion, by reading this Book.* The Fifth Edition. Printed and sold by William Parks, at his Printing-OfSces in Williams- burg, and Annapolis, 1733." This is explicit and definite. Parks reprinted the pamphlet himself. It was first published in London, in the year 1698. The *Letter to a Deist upon his Conversion5* was written by Leslie to Charles Grildon, who had been converted by the *Method.* This *Letter* was often reprinted in subsequent editions of the *Method.* Hence Parks reprinted both in his edition.

"No. 64. Repeated September 27 and November 22 of the same year.

"First published in Gildon's *Deist's Manual*, 1705.

So great was the Southerner's love for a bit of verse to set off even a most practical subject, that Parks, in advertising46 his reprint of *Every Man Ms own Doctor: Or, The Poor Planter's Physician,"* added a quotation from *Paradise Lost* on death, to emphasize the need of his book:

But many Shapes
Of Death, and many are the Ways that lead
To his grim Cave, all dismal, yet to Sense
More horrible at th' Entrance than within.
Some, as thou saw'st, by violent Strokes shall dye,
By Fire, Blood, and Famine, by Intemperance more
In Meats and Drinks, which on the Earth shall bring
Diseases dire.
Paradise Lost, Bk. XI.

High argument for the *Poor Planter's Physician;* fortunately for our purpose, too, it establishes Parks's familiarity with Milton, as well as that of the community. No doubt he had copies of *Paradise Lost* for sale at this time. His advertisements do not show it, however, probably for the reason that he was more interested in noting recent publications in the *Gazette.*

After August 2, 1734, there is no extant number of the *Gazette* until May 10,1745. Eleven years had made a great difference in most colonial newspapers. Political and economical discussions had become / ever more absorbing and more pressing. News was I

" In *The Maryland Gazette,* No. 73, August 2, 1734.

" " Prescribing Plain and easy Means for Persons to cure themselves of all, or most of the Distempers, incident to this Climate and with very little Charge, the Medicines being chiefly of the Growth and Production of this Country." Ibid.

) more accessible, and intercommunication more fre- ' quent. Current English magazines supplied an inexhaustible fund if all else failed, so that it gradually became unnecessary to recur to the classical essayist in the dull season. Above all, the first *I* American monthlies had begun to draw out the native talent. Young scribblers would naturally send their verses to *The American Magazine and Historical Chronicle8* if they were conveniently near Boston.   That other periodicals of the same sort (in addition to the early Philadelphia magazines) were projected, at least, before 1750, is evident from one of the most interesting contributions to the later numbers of *The Mart/land Gazette.*

A correspondent calling himself Philo-Musus sent some lines49 which he had intended for *The American Magazine* several months previous, – but since that design was now at an end,50 he enclosed the verses to Mr. Green. Thus we have good evidence of the American origin of the verses of Philo-Musus, which represent an outburst of indignation at Colley Cibber's well-known epitaph on Pope, published in *The Gentleman's Magazine* for June, 1744. Cibber's epitaph began with these two couplets:

Our pious Praise on Tomb-Stones runs so high,

Eeaders might think, that none but Good Men die!

If Graves held only such, Pope, like his Verse,

Had still been breathing, and escap 'd the Hearse.

"Established in Boston, in 1743.

"See *The Maryland Gazette,* November 8, 1745, No. 3 of a new series begun by Jonas Green, postmaster, "at his Printing-Office in Charles-Street."

Not *The American Magazine and Historical Chronicle,* for that was continued through 1746. *The American Magazine* referred to was probably only a project.

The remainder of the epitaph was equally complimentary. Philo-Musus, after a few spirited remarks, answers the epitaph in no mean couplets of his own. "Anyone the least acquainted with Mr. Pope's moral Character," says Philo-Musus, "will at first Sight see the barefaced Injustice of it, that it is evidently the Effects of an impotent Malice, exerted in the most ungenerous Manner, which nothing less than a Cibberian Front could have had the Assurance to brazen out. – A grateful Eegard for our English Homer's Memory, occasioned this, as well as what follows:"

Verses occasioned by Mr. Colley Gibber's Epitaph

on Mr. Pope, in The Gentleman's Magazine

for June, 1744

What Kake now doubts he has a Soul to save,

When graceless Colley preaches o'er a Grave?

Pope's Verse he could not damn, in Part or Whole;

But, like a hot-brain'd Bigot – damns his Soul;

To shew this Age (the next shall never know it)

He was as good a Christian – as a Poet.

Wretch! do'st thou triumph o'er thaf sacred Urn,

Where all the Virtuous, all the Learned mourn ?
Yet must thou live ? Late Times shall know, that once
An English Laureat was a sprightly Dunce.
Ungrateful Monster! thank those lasting Strains,
That save your Carcass, tho' it be in Chains.
Let thy vile Muse take its low grov'ling Plight,
And scream or gabble to the Sons of Night;
Or fawning, sooth some Lord's polluted Ear
With smutty Jest or irreligious Sneer;
Whilst all the Good and Just, – an awful Throng,
Lament the Muse who moraliz'd his Song.

Here is evidence of a fairly close, perfectly contemporary knowledge and imitation of English literary form. Philo-musus, whoever he may have been, knew even the current literary gossip of London; while his close study of the Dunciad appears in every line of his own verse. On the whole, one begins to suspect that many Americans were eager to read, to criticise, and to imitate the English literature of their own day.

Sometimes it happened that an event of great literary interest was not treated as such, but passed over lightly as a matter of political news. Usually, however, this would occur only when English papers had been equally blind. The letters, messages and addresses from the Hague in connection with Chesterfield's recall from his diplomatic mission there, furnish a significant case in point. They are all given in full, from the letter of their High Mightinesses to the "King of Great Britain" expressing their regret at his recall, to Chesterfield's own graceful and even tender address of farewell to the Deputies of the States General ;51 yet neither the Virginia nor the Maryland paper52 put forward these items as literary. They were giving the political news of a great diplomat and statesman. But that is exactly what the English papers were doing. Chesterfield, in fact, was known in 1745 chiefly as an English peer who patronized letters. His own literary fame was a matter of much later date, due to his

" See *The Maryland Gazette, Nob.* 19 and 20, August 30 and September 6, 1745.

M *The Maryland Gazette* took many of its London items from *The Virginia Gazette.*

private correspondence. Some inkling of his grace and charm his own immediate contemporaries, even in the colonies, must have had, nevertheless, for the little poem called *Contradiction,* appearing in *The Maryland Gazette* March 11,1746, proclaims the great anomaly of all,

When Chesterfield shall write or speak amiss.

Of course the older fashion of commonplace essays on pride, envy, malice and so forth, by no means entirely died out. Nor did elaborate quotations and extracts from Addison and Pope ever fail of their authority. Sometimes the quotations "were anything but apt in themselves. In the *Gazette* for April 13, 1748, Britannus complains that certain recent papers have used Addison and Pope foolishly, quoting them in the discussion of district courts! These are the exceptions, however. A current article on Turkey or a poem on the capture of Cape Breton, from *The Gentleman's Magazine,* even an essay from Boston's new American miscellany, Polly Baker's famous speech, from *The Pennsylvania Gazette,* English character pieces coming by way of the Virginia and South Carolina weeklies, – all these are characteristic of the later *Maryland Gazette.* So common had intercommunication between the colonies become, that we even find an amusing dispute between the *Gazette* and *The New York Weekly Post Boy* sustained several weeks, in the fall of 1746. Tom Type in the *Post Boy* accused Maryland of Catholic sympathies, because she did not contribute to the Cape Breton expedition. Timothy Antitypepromptly answered in *The Maryland Gazette* that poverty was the only cause of Maryland's failure. If you are poor, retorted Thomas Type, it is because your staple is not properly regulated!

Scattering as our examination of *The Maryland Gazette* has necessarily been, the extant numbers yield no small results. The periodical essay in an advanced form, much tolerable verse in direct imitation of current English forms, a great regard for Pope and Addison, – Milton as well – are all strikingly evident in its fragmentary pages.

7

SECTION 7

CHAPTER VII

The Vibginia G-azette

As we turn southward to the heart of the Old / Dominion, we enter a society whose interest in pure j letters was more natural, more permanent, and more I unrestricted than that of any other section of British America. Not so enterprising, perhaps; we hear ! of no brilliant young apprentices doing without luncheon to read, or busily planning new projects for the general culture of the community. The Virginian took all these things easily and gracefully as his birthright. Col. Henry Fitzhugh, for instance, whose father left him a study full of books in his will of 1700,1 had no particular reason to be ardently interested in a subscription library. When we remember, too, that he was matriculated at Christ Church, Oxford, in 1722, the situation becomes even clearer. Not only did the custom of educating sons at Oxford or Cambridge linger in Virginia, but native boys who went to William and Mary often met there professors who had been trained abroad, or had lived abroad. Literary London was far nearer Williamsburg than Boston.

Books of a secular nature could have been found in the ordinary Virginia household. The interestingresearches of President Lyon Gardiner Tyler, of William and Mary College, and Mr. William G. Stanard, of the Virginia Historical Society, have unearthed from the old county records of wills and inventories of estates, valuable evidence of such volumes even in comparatively poor families.2 Christopher Robinson of Urbanna, whose estate netted only about two hundred and fifty pounds, had, according to the inventory of March 28, 1727,3 sixteen books, and in another item " a parcell of old books." Frequently the expressions " all my books" and "books, per a catalogue" in wills and inventories indicate libraries of no small size. As early as 1669, Col. John Carter divided, by will, his library, which he described as "all my books," between his sons; "son John" to have five-sixths, "son Robert," one sixth, and his wife, as a special bequest, *David's Tears,* Byfield's treatise, and the *Whole Duty of Man.* Robert Beverley's books, recorded in the inventory of his estate, in 1734,5 included not only an ample classical and religious library, but also volumes of Locke, Temple, Bacon, Shaftsbury, Clarendon, *Spectators* (8 vols.), *Tatlers* (4 vols.), Ambrose Phillips, Milton's *Paradise Lost,* Garth's *Dispensary,* Pope's Homer, Pope's other poems, *Hudibras,* Pomfret's poems, More's *Utopia,* Aesop's *Fables,* a volume of tragedies, and *The Beggar's Opera.*

1Recorded in the Stafford County Records, dated 1700; see *The Virginia Magazine of History and Biography,* Vol. II, pp. 277: "My Study of Books (I leave) to William and Henry."

2This evidence has been published in many volumes of *The Virginia Magazine of History and Biography.*

8See *The Virginia Magazine of History and Biography,* Vol. Ill, p. 4.

4 Ibid., Vol. II, p. 235.

In the Spotsylvania County Court records. See *The Virginia Magazine of History and Biography,* Vol. Ill, pp. 388-391.

After the Eestoration, plays, balls and pastorals / enlivened the town life in old Williamsburg. As ! President Tyler has shown, in his book on Williamsburg,6 the first recorded notice of a play7 performed in any part of the present United States is in the Accomack County8 records for 1665. Several persons had been brought before the court for acting a play called *Ye Bare and Ye Cubb,* and this old record explains that they were obliged to enact it over again, in costume, before the court. The result was exactly what might have been expected in a liberal community. The play was judged innocuous, the players were discharged, and the informant had to pay the costs! This was in the days of Sir William Berkeley's administration. Though his name hardly suggests liberality of any sort, he was in his own way a patron of art, especially dramatic art. His fondness for the stage was well known, and when he visited London for a year9 he saw his own tragi-comedy, *The Lost Lady,* acted at the theater. The indefatigable Pepys saw it also, and has recorded his own rather unfavorable impression of the play, as well as his later moderate liking.10 Thus Sir William, with the plaudits of London playhouses in his ears, could hardly have failed to encourage the drama in Virginia, at least when his all too vigorous colony allowed him enough

Williamsburg, the Old Colonial Capital. By Lyon Gardiner Tyler, LL. D., President of the College of William and Mary, Williamsburg, Virginia. Whittet and Shepperson, publishers.

1 So far as known at present.

' Accomack County, Virginia.

' In 1661.

10 See *Diary,* January 19 and 28, 1661.

peace to do so. Certainly the custom grew up of performing a play before the Governor on the King's birthday, and other festivals.11 The actors in these comedies or pastorals were often "scholars of William and Mary College."12

After 1716 one could have seen professional actors in a public theater in Williamsburg. A local merchant, William Levingston, built a theater13 for Charles and Mary Stagg, actors, who were to manage a company from England. Levingston distinctly agreed to provide actors, scenery and music out of England, "for the enacting of comedies and tragedies in said city" of Williamsburg. While he was about it he built a bowling alley alongside, so that when, a few years later,14 Eev. Hugh Jones described Williamsburg, he noted, evidently with pride that "not far from hence, *(i. e.* from the church and the court house) is a large area for a market-place, near which is a playhouse and a good bowling green." After Stagg died, his wife held dancing "assemblies," otherwise balls, earning her living by her moderate fees.

Hence it is not surprising to read in one of the first advertisements of *The Virginia Gazette:16*

11 Governor Spotswood, for instance, recorded a play acted before him on His Majesty's birthday, 1718. Apparently it was not an exceptional or unusual celebration.

"A "Pastoral Colloquy" was recited in 1702 by "scholars of William and Mary College," before the Governor at Williamsburg.

"The contract is recorded at Torktown, dated July 11, 1716; in November, 1716, Levingston bought the land for the theater, church and the court house. See Tyler's *Williamsburg,* chapter VIII.

1722.

a September 10, 1736, No. 6.

"This evening will be performed at the Theatre, by the Young Gentlemen of the College, the Tragedy of *Cato;* and on Monday, Wednesday, and Friday next will be acted the following Comedies by the Gentlemen and Ladies of this Country, viz. *The Busy-Body, The Recruiting Officer,* and *The Beaux- Stratagem."* A similar item in the *Gazette* of the following week16 adds to the evidence that plays were not uncommon in Williamsburg. "Next Monday Night," we read, "will be performed *The Drummer; or, The Haunted House,* by the young Gentlemen of the College."

Plays were not uncommon then, after 1700. And - 1700 is a conservative date, in view of Sir William Berkeley's fondness for plays. But after 1750 there were regular professional engagements every winter, extending even to Norfolk, Petersburg, ' Hobbes' Hole and Fredericksburg. With these performances, interesting as they are, we have little to do, except to remark in passing that *Richard III, The Merchant of Venice* and *Othello* opened seasons of considerable prestige in 1751 and 1752. In one particular, tradition has been at fault. "On the first Friday in September, 1752," says President Tyler,17 "they opened the season with *The Merchant of Venice.* The prologue,18 spoken by Mr. Eigby, is said to have been the first ever spoken in America, and was composed on shipboard by Mr. Singleton, another of the company." But seventeen years

M September 17, 1736, No. 7.

11 See *Williamsburg, the Old Colonial Capital,* p. 229. M Given in full in *William and Mary College Quarterly,* Vol. XIII, p. 9.

before, a prologue had been composed in Charleston, and spoken there at a presentation of Otway's *Orphan,* January 24, 1735. The fact that the first prologue does not belong to Virginia, however, detracts little from her well-earned place as the first seat of the drama in America.

For the earlier records of that drama we are obliged to depend largely upon chance notices in diaries or letters, deeds of sale or other court documents. Interesting indeed it would be if we had newspaper advertisements of plays to guide us all the way. Virginia, so brilliantly in advance of her

neighbors in the arts and graces of life, had no newspaper until 1736, nine years after the first paper in Maryland, seven years after the first in New York, seventeen years after the first in Pennsylvania, twenty- two after the first in Massachusetts, and nearly five years after the first in South Carolina. Various reasons have been assigned" for this long-continued lack in Virginia. For one thing, there were the very practical difficulties in securing a license, since an early, short-lived experience with the printing press had taught the authorities its danger. For another thing, the very fact that the Virginia planter kept in close touch with London and Oxford affairs made

(it easier and more natural for him to send for English papers, than to promote a native enterprise. Town business, too, had no great hold upon his interest. At length the initiative came from an outsider, when William Parks set up his little shop and printing press in the small wooden building on Duke of Gloucester street which was standing until 1896. The post-office and book store, as usual, were combined with the printing office.

The bearing of this somewhat long introduction to *The Virginia Gazette* will be seen at once on turning to its first pages. The earlier numbers of the paper all devote a large part of the first page to an essay- serial called *The Monitor.* It is sprightly, witty, dramatic in method, full of the opera, the theater, tea-table gossip, and slander, playful slurs on the fashions over games of piquet, town beaux in"tu-j pee" wigs, and other aspects of London life, to the extent that the whole series has hitherto been con-j sidered merely a colonial reprint of an English per- j iodical. But these papers have never been really examined, and an analysis of them in the light of the ordinary social regime in Williamsburg at thatdate19 ! leads to a conclusion in favor of their Virginian origin. Indeed proof would hardly be too strong a ! word, except for a barely possible chance that Parks may have tinkered over some unknown English weekly.

Tradition is silent as to the existence of a Monitor in London, in 1736. The name itself is not uncommon. Anonymous letters often had signatures like *Th, e Seasonable Monitor.*20 There seems to have been also a periodical called *The Silent Monitor* fifteen or twenty years previous, but as it is not extant, no conclusions can be drawn from it.21

1736-37.

" Such was the signature of a political letter in the *Craftsman,* No. 541, November 13, 1736.

"Defoe's political paper, *The Monitor,* of 1714, (attribution of Professor Trent), could have had no influence on these essays.

Moreover, it is intrinsically very unlikely that this unknown paper furnished any hints for the Virginia *Monitor,* or that Parks would have possessed a complete file to use serially week by week. Indeed, this last consideration is one of the cardinal points in favor of a colonial origin. Stray papers could be copied, and often were taken bodily into colonial weeklies. But that a whole file of a periodical so abreast with contemporary modes of essay writing could have reached the office of the *Gazette* in time for publication through the fall and winter of 1736 is incredible. For another thing, *The Monitor* will bear comparison with *The Universal Spectator, The Craftsman, The Grubstreet Journal, Common Sense,* the best, in short, of the English weeklies in that decade. Therefore, it is again incredible that never once from 1731 to 1737 should it be mentioned, inserted, or quoted from in the two great rival monthly magazines, *The London Magazine* and *The Gentleman's Magazine.* One of them surely would have used it, if only to surprise the other. Most notable articles in the weeklies found their way into the monthly magazines; often an almost complete series may be followed in them. The very excellent files of both monthlies in this country[22] have been searched. There is no hint of *The Monitor.* But how natural if it was written three thousand miles away, in a country suggesting convicts to many Londoners!

In fact the matter is practically ruled out of court

" For example, the files in the Library of Congress, Virginia State Library, Columbia University Library, New York and Boston Public Libraries.

by the references to James River,[23] York River,[24] "this colony,"[26] "the first ship in York River,"[28] "my first coming into these Parts"[27] (when inhabitants were few), and other external indications. After the eighteenth number of *The Monitor* had appeared, Zoilus, an unknown critic, attacked it mercilessly in the columns of the *Gazette.* Now it is inconceivable that Parks imported both the periodical and the running commentaries of its critic. On the other hand, if Zoilus represents the "home talent," he would hardly be as contemptuous toward a known English paper. *The Monitor* is beyond all reasonable doubt a Virginian performance, adding no small prestige to our colonial literature.

Important confirmation of all this could be found, perhaps, in the first five numbers of *The Monitor* not now extant. The Virginia Historical Society's file begins with number six.[28] There we first meet the Monitor himself, lolling in his elbow-chair, contriving some method to give fair Letitia Tattle a view of his long nose. While he is absorbed in such pleasing meditation, three taps at the door of his outward chamber announce the arrival of a figure which scares his man Dominic into believing he has seen the Devil. Upwards of six feet tall, with a swarthy complexion, and "a large Bottle-Nose," the mysterious figure advances. "The Dress was aMan's Hat, a Woman's short Cloak, that hung loose down to the Waste. . . . From the Waste downwards, was a large Pair of Trowsers fit for a Burgher-Master."[29] In this combination of riding-habit and harem skirt, she informs the Monitor that she is a woman of fashion K "I was born and bred in France, and the dress you see me in, was French, originally, but now modeliz 'd."

" See *Monitor No. 14, Virginia Gazette,* November 19, 1736.

"Ibid.

M Ibid., No. 17, December 31, 1736.

"Ibid.

Ibid., No. 18, January 21, 1736-37.

See *The Virginia Gazette,* No. 6, September 10, 1736.

The Monitor, somewhat disgusted at this harangue, bids her be brief, as he is busy. She immediately proceeds to recommend her six daughters for posts on the monitorial staff. " There's my eldest Daughter, Miss Leer, . . . will draw a Circle about her immediately wherever she goes. . . . Then my second, Miss Sly; she has not one bit of French in her, she's as Secret as Death. . . . My third Daughter, Miss Fidget; she's here, and there, and everywhere; she never misses a Tea-Table, if there be Ten within Compass of her Visits in a Day. There she hears Slander, Backbiting and Scandal, which may turn out to some use. As to my Fourth Daughter, Amo- ret, she's a Fine Girl." So the description goes on. Phillis, number five, is " forever receiving or answering of Billet-doux, and Scraps of Poetry which may not be amiss." Euphemia, the youngest, is " courted by Sir Politick Wou 'd-be; he can inform her how Affairs stand in ... (but no matter.) " The Monitor finally engages these promising young reporters, after administering to them the oath of the Free Masons with bolted doors!

Now of course the unknown author of these essays

"An undoubted slur on the Dutch influence.

did not in any case originate the conception of a fair bevy of news-gatherers presiding over different departments of high society. The idea had been a favorite one in the essay-periodicals for several years previous. It was more dramatic than the older *Spectator* letter, for the ladies generally made their report to the editor in the form of sustained witty dialogue rather than grave disquisition. The editor then adds moral reflections much in Addison's general manner. Now and then dialogue in these later periodicals rises to high comedy level for a passage or two. Always it is the vehicle for light, social satire chiefly directed to women, though the beaux in "tupee" wigs have their share.

The Monitor's club certainly had a prototype in the Fiddle-faddle Club, the ladies of which described it to Mr. Bavius, the lofty editor of *The Grubstreet Journal.* TM The description was copied into *The London Magazine* for May, 1733, and thus would have been easy to procure in Virginia. Seven ladies made up the Fiddle-faddle Club, Lady Tiptoe, Lady Fanciful, Lady Lazy, who "often borrows a Hand to stir her Tea," Caecilia Thoughtless, Miss Love- Mode, Miss At-all, and Coquetilla. They met regularly twice a week to settle the fashions, and discuss beaux in general and in particular.

A little too late to serve as model for *The Monitor,* yet significant as showing the contemporary popularity of the main conception was Ned Friendly's letter to *The Craftsman, Of News Writers,31* calling

" See *Grubstreet Journal,* No. 176, May 10, 1733. "See *The Craftsman,* No. 546, December 18, 1736. Also copied into *The London Magazine* for December, 1736.

attention to a club of merry ladies. "I am likewise apprized that there is a club of merry Ladies, in this Town, who make it their Business to surprize the World with extraordinary Pieces of Intelligence. They meet, it seems, once a Week; every Lady brings in her Story, and that which is the farthest removed from Truth, and yet most likely to pass as such, is voted the current Article of the Week. The fair Author is immediately ordered to take the Chair, and the whole Society are obliged, by the Rules of the Club, to circulate it amongst their particular Acquaintance. The common Collectors of News are apt to catch a little too greedily at such ingenious Reports; and thus they become generally believed; till the Club meets again, and propagates some other Rumour, in the same Manner." / A still more interesting coincidence lies in the 1 resemblance between *The Monitor's* general plan ' and the plan of Sheridan and Swift's *Intelligencer.* We have the best of proof that Parks and his correspondents in Maryland and Virginia knew this little Dublin pamphlet.32 Swift himself wrote the first number, which outlines a program not indeed so near in detail to *The Monitor's* as that of the Fiddle- faddle Club, but sufficiently close to have afforded many hints and suggestions. We are, therefore, probably on the track of Swift's direct influence here. "There is a society lately established," he says, in *The Intelligencer,* "who, at great expense, have erected an office of intelligence, from which

"Vide supra, p. 164. Of this no doubt Parks had a more or less complete file.

they are to receive weekly information of all important events and singularities which, this famous metropolis can furnish. Strict injunctions are given to have the truest information; in order to which, certain qualified persons are employed to attend upon duty at their several posts; some at the playhouse, others in churches; some at balls, assemblies, coffee-houses, and meetings for quadrille; some at the several courts of justice, both spiritual and temporal ; some at the college, some upon my lord mayor and aldermen in their public affairs, . . . only the barracks and parliament-houses are excepted, because we have yet found no enfant perdus bold enough to venture their persons at either. Out of these and some other store-houses we hope to gather materials enough to inform, or direct, or correct, or vex the town." No Swiftian touches like these last two sentences will be found in *The Monitor.* Indeed the resemblance would hardly be worth noting, were it not that *The Intelligencer* was read in Virginia. Countless instances of the same reporting plan could be cited in the periodicals from 1728 to 1740, including Fielding's *Champion,*,33 where Captain Hercules Vinegar and his family contribute the news.

The eighteenth-century dread of masculinity in women was no less than that of our own days. We have seen how the Monitor's man Dominic thought he had seen a devil when that monstrous creature, a Woman of Fashion, walked in with her man's hat

" *The Champion.* Published three times a week from November 15, 1739, to June 19, 1740, 94 numbers in all. This was too late, of course, to affect *The Monitor.*

and huge trousers. *The Universal Spectator* had voiced an equal horror four years before34 in a clever censure on the ladies, signed H. Bluntly. This, too, had been copied into *The London Magazine* for July, 1732, so it could easily have been seen in Williamsburg. *The Universal Spectator* ranks as one of the cleverest periodicals of the period. It was founded by Defoe's son-in-law, Henry Baker, in 1728, and usually succeeded fairly well in living up to its illustrious name. Bluntly's article is dramatic and forcible. English ladies "this Summer intended to ride astride," he says, "at the instigation of 'des Dames Francoises,' but for political reasons have not. ... In return the English Amazons have introduced Romping among the French, and advise the

Dutch ladies to the thorough neglect of Family affairs. In Days of Yore, for a Lady to be dress'd like a Woman, to speak and act like a Woman, was thought decent; but now the Case is much alter'd. ... I went once to visit Stradella, and found her . . . with her Hands behind her, whistling and trying in how many Paces she could measure the Room. She turn'd upon her Heel, and extending her Right Hand, gave me a friendly Shake, and saluted me with 'How do'st old Hal?",' He bemoans the loss of reserve among the fair ones. Mr. Maidly and Bob Brawny have been proposed to. "Is it not, dear Spec, a melancholy reflection that (the members of the opposite sex are) women at twelve, men at eighteen, and girls at fifty or sixty?" So we see that there werfe plenty of clever sources

" No. 197, July 15, 1732.

from which *The Monitor* could have received important hints. Probably a comparatively large number of people in Williamsburg subscribed to *The London Magazine.* Beyond a doubt, Parks had it in his office regularly.

The next number of *The Monitor*36 explains more fully that the ladies are to report every week in Remarks, Letters, Poems, Billet-doux – what not. The restless Miss Fidget naturally enters first. "Miss Fidget with abundance of Briskness and Alacrity, told me that if my Monitorial Worship was at Leisure, she would lay before me a very notorious Remark which she had made upon her Sister Females, since she had engaged herself in my Service." Again the fashions, this time in the more feminine guise of hoops and high shoulder effects. Helena gives the remark of a lady who exclaims in conversa- ti6n with her, "Pray, Madam, did you observe Miss Airy in Company last Sunday? Lord! Lord! what a frightful figure she made." The Monitor's reflections at the close of Miss Fidget's remarks endorse her criticisms heartily, adding a slur to the effect that very soon a hump-back will be accounted no piece of deformity.

Of course the other ladies fretted a little under Miss Fidget's "Assiduity to be the first in my Favor." They must needs protest to the Monitor,36 Miss Leer demanding first place on the score of being eldest, and so on. At length Miss Fidget decorously asks pardon, says she will stand correctedif she is too forward. The matter is then happily adjusted by a strict division of labor among the fair contestants. The Monitor will accept Miss Leer as "Sifter, in the Service of the Club, Miss Sly, for Observation, Miss Fidget, for Scandal, Miss Amoret, for Discoveries, Miss Phillis, for Love Affairs, and Miss Euphemia, for Politics." What an excellent text for a sermon on envy and jealousy, is this little tempest in a tea-pot! The Monitor does not lose the opportunity; and again we remind ourselves that the cleverest, most dramatic themes in the eighteenth-century periodicals are never far from the moral treatise. "Si vis me flere, dolendum est" closes the reflections on jealousy.

"No. 7, September 17, 1736.

Monitor No. 8, October 1, 1736.

We next37 hear from the observant Arabella Sly on a point of propriety in manners. She has attended the theater, has seen *The Beaux-Stratagem,* and was so "highly delighted at Love's Catechism" that she giggled. At this indiscretion Miss Tan- crede gave her "a most terrible Hunch with her Elbow" and warned her to cover her face with her fan. Arabella asks the Monitor if propriety demands that one should always hide behind a fan at a humorous scene? This leads to an essay by the Monitor on the folly of Prudishness. "Honest Jack Pamflino informs me," he says, "that in the year 1718, he made his address to a Prude." The courtship was disastrous. Now at first sight it seems highly improbable that Arabella Sly's indiscretion at the theater could have been inspired by anything in Williamsburg. But Farquhar's comedies, *The*

" *Monitor* No. 9, October 15, 1736.

Beaux-Stratagem and *The Recruiting Officer* had been given three weeks before at the theater in Williamsburg by "the Gentlemen and Ladies of this Country." The coincidence is strikingly significant as an indication of the Virginian authorship of *The Monitor.*

The next number38 is a rather dull vindication of music. The young reporters are for the moment disregarded while the Monitor listens to a dispute among three gentlemen about the benefits of music. He himself believes that it is more than mere pleas- use of the ear, – that it is "the Operation of the Mind upon those materials that gives the Delight." Commonplace essays of this sort occur in every eighteenth-century periodical; they are less frequent in *The Monitor* than in many.

A "Reverend Gentleman" who signs himself " J" now39 interrupts with a compli-mentary letter to the Monitor, praising his bold rebukes of folly, and admitting with gentle condescension that the press is "a natural and necessary Auxiliary to the Pulpit." Candidly and generously he says that the subjects for ridicule are "even more abundant in our Sex," and invites him to animadvert more impartially upon both sexes, without fear of any sort. "Let the stricken Deer go weep."

Following the letter from the reverend correspondent is a mock advertisement of Miss Amoret, one of the fair reporters of the Monitor, who indignantly calls upon the gallant in a "tupee" wig who ogledher at the theater, to explain himself. " This public notice was doubtless a great joke directed against the town dude, whoever he was," says President Tyler,40 evidently not connecting the advertisement very closely with *The Monitor.* Nevertheless, his remark may very well serve as one more clear indication of native talent at work in the colony, as well as an illuminating suggestion in itself. No doubt Williamsburg had a town dude who haunted the theater and flirted with fair dames.

Monitor No. 10, October 22, 1736. "Ibid., No. 11, October 29, 1736. See his book, *Williamsburg, the Old Colonial Capital,* p. 226.

The twelfth *Monitor* has a lively letter from Zach- ary Downright on the opera. He has been to London, has heard Signora Cazzoni and Signora Faustina, and would as soon listen to his father and mother quarrel in a fugue. He even quotes *Hudibras* to relieve his feelings.

And folly as it grows in years

The more extravagant appears.

He noted that everybody applauded at the opera, though he was convinced that they were all as ignorant of music and Italian as he himself was. The Monitor blames him for his lack of appreciation, ascribing it to inattentiveness and dulness. Satires on the absurdly ignorant audiences at the opera were very common in English papers. It is just conceivable, of course, that here Parks copied from some obscure weekly. Undoubtedly Zachary Down- right's letter reflects London experiences and no other. Yet the very fact that he speaks of *going* to London, combined with the fact that going to London meant nothing extraordinary to a Virginian, points rather to a colonial imitation of English satire. An instance of this latter may be found in *The London Magazine's* Polite Conversation, in which one of the ladies speaks of the Adagio as " so quick and nimble."41

At length one of the Monitor's assistants comes on the scene again.42 Penelope Leer, this time, writes a letter describing a certain Miss Fain- would's lovers; a doctor, a lawyer, and a parson. Miss Painwould herself preferred the doctor. Her mother favored the lawyer, who "had promis'd to recover an Estate that was never in the Family." The unfortunate parson had long since been dismissed for his "ill Habit, (uncommon to the Profession,") of reading too much. Evidently he took his repulse to heart, for some rather gloomy verses on the deceitfulness of pleasure were found in his room. Miss Leer transcribes them, and the Monitor shakes his wise head over them and over the folly of being in love, which he associates with smallpox.

The next number43 returns to the *Tatter* for its model, though it represents a form of wit as popular then as it is repellent now. In the two hundred and sixteenth *Tatler* may be found the will of a Virtuoso who leaves to his wife a dried cocatrice, a skeleton, a drawer of shells, a box of butterflies, and other biological specimens. So in *The Monitor,* various rarities from the collection of Jack Near-

" Quoted in *The Virginia Gazette,* No. 65, October 28, 1737.

a *Monitor* No. 13, November 12, 1736.

" Ibid., No. 14, November 19, 1736.

 August 26, 1710.

sight are noted for sale, such as the drum of a mouse's ear, the pleura and lungs of a moschetto, a scull-cap made from a possum, neatly dressed, and so on. The whole article would be too trivial to dwell upon, were it not that just here in the most unexpected way we have a confirmation of *The Monitor's* colonial origin. In the inventory of Jack Nearsight's estate are *Lines on a Spider:*

Artist, who underneath the Table,

Thy curious Texture hast display'd

followed by *A Satyr upon the Freshes of James- River,* and *A Panegyrick upon the Oisters of TorJc- River.* Whatever local hits or allusions were intended here, hardly matter now. The important facts are the genuine references to James Eiver and York Eiver, – particularly York Eiver oysters. They were not topics of conversation in London.

The lively Miss Fidget has been silent for some time. True to her function, however, she comes forward with base slander in the fifteenth *Monitor.45* It is not called slander, in so many words. Only the sly use of Miss Helena Fidget's personality to relate it, informs the reader what he may expect and find. As the ridicule centers about *The Monitor,* itself, this subtle insinuation is very effective. The letter is extremely dramatic, – a good example of the changed method in periodical essay writing since the days of the *Spectator.* Miss Fidget begins, then, with a game of piquet at Miss Commode's.46 Miss Flounce, Miss Tippet, Mr. Coupee, and Mr.

" November 26, 1736.

" The commode was a head dress.

Bergamot were also guests. The passion for naming characters after some pronounced quality or fashion was at its height. Names like Miss Edging, Miss Courtly, the Duchess of Frippery, Miss Love- rule, abound everywhere. Here the names indicate a very fashionable salon. Among other things, the conversation turns to the Monitor. "0 Lud," says Mr. Bergamot, "don't name the stupid Toad."

"Well," answers Miss Flounce, "I thank God, I, nor any of my Family, can either read or write; but I take him in, to make Thread-Papers for my Servants."

"True," adds Mr. Coupee, "the sending Children to School is only practis'd among the Vulgar. The Men of Quality in England, (especially in this Age,) rarely send them anywhere 'till they are fit to travel. Some of them, indeed, have Tutors for their Sons in their own Houses; but that is more for the Grandeur of the Thing, than any real Service."

Of course the whole letter of Helena Fidget becomes a text for the unhappiness of a want of education, and the selfish idleness of wealthy leisure. But the letter itself is ingenious and clever.

The Monitor next47 returns to his meditative strain. As he is riding out on the highway one day, he sees a pack of ill-joined hounds dash by. He immediately moralizes over the incongruities between them, the keen and the idle yoked together, as well as other contrasting pairs. Upon being invited to dinner with the master of the hounds, he observes that the guests present a spectacle just as incongruous. He even ventures to share his thought with the host, who sagely remarks that this is life itself, – a bewildering contrast. The Monitor strongly urges keeping one's temper in these circumstances, and accommodating oneself to all companies, agreeable or otherwise!

a Monitor No. 16, December 10, 1736.

Very late in the series,48 we have the Monitor's account of his own life. The classical essay periodicals had always begun in this way, with a history of the imaginary editor's life, usually in humorous vein, yet keeping a certain dignity withal. The story of the Monitor's life belongs to the extravagant, fantastic development of a later taste. The later periodicals all reveled in Arabian Nights' entertainments, transformations, feats of magic, second sight, and, if nothing better offered, witch trials. We must not forget that one of the most fanciful continuations of Chaucer's *Squire's Tale* was done in the earlier half of the eighteenth century.49 So it is entirely in the natural order of things that the Monitor should travel in the East, should be transformed to a Danish dog, then to an ape, and so on. While he is an ape, he assists as Trainbearer at high Mass! After this sly hit at the Eoman Catholic church, he proceeds to relate his escape from the Vatican in the shape of a bear, and his melancholy arrival at Hockley in the Hole, "the antient Amphi-

Monitor No. 17, December 31, 1736.

"In *The Canterbury Tales of Chaucer, Modernis'd by several Hands.* Published by George Ogle, London, 1741. *The Squire's Tale* ' in this edition was written by Boyse, Ogle and Sterling. Sterling's contribution has been retold in *Tales of the Canterbury Pilgrims,* by F. J. Carton, pp. 219-230.

theatre of London." In other words, he was baited by the dogs, and after a tolerable resistance, submitted. His last groan "occasioned a general Shout; but Dr. Faustus being present, bow'd his Magic Wand, repeating the words of Shakespeare:

By my rough Magic I have oft
bedim'd
The Noon-tide Sun. . . .
Graves at my command
Have wak'd their Sleepers, op'd and let
them forth.

And I instantly ressum'd my first Body, to the great Surprise of the Spectators."
After serving the famous Doctor for seven years, "I took shipping for this Colony, in
order to spend the Remainder of my Days." Hence, he arrived in Virginia, and hence
another incidental proof of colonial origin for the whole series of papers.

The Monitor still boasts of his wizard qualifications in the new world. "My House
stands in the midst of a Wood," he says. And his man Dominic has posted "the Hand
that has two Thumbs" on the cross roads for the guidance of travellers. "I unfold
Mysteries equal to any Person or Persons, that have been heretofore in this Colony, or
any other of His Majesty's Dominions, viz.,

Who is like to die a Maid.

Who not.

I name the first Ship in York River.

I name the Ship that's first loaded.

Who will have the largest Consignments, etc."The fact that all this magic hardly
accords with the previous high judicial tone of a rebuker of folly, would not trouble
either writer or reader.

The eighteenth *Monitor60* contains another indication of pioneer, colonial existence
(even though in joke) in a letter from Timothy Forecast, of Forecast Hall. " Sir, "he
begins," I think myself oblig 'd to acquaint your Worship, that at my first coming into
these Parts, our Inhabitants were few, and for some years after the County was seated,
we were most grievously infested with Wolves and Bears, to the great Perplexity of
myself and Neighbors, . . . But now we labour under a much worse Calamity. . . .
'Tis call'd, (as our Parson informs us) a Tale Bearer. ..." This he thinks may even be
an evil spirit, since " 'tis at all Times upon the March, Day and Night." The parson's
moral couplets against scandal and tale-bearing are thus introduced as a charm. But
they could hardly have had much effect, even on the mildest of evil spirits. / In brief,
The Monitor was running down, was beginning to depend on exaggeration, artificial
stimulus, instead of humorous observations of real life. The reader rather welcomes
the criticism of a certain Zoilus, when it appears in the same number of *The Virginia
Gazette* in which the eighteenth *Monitor* was published. Who Zoilus may have been,
or what criticism he represented, it would be profitless to speculate about. Zoilus was
a favorite name for a critic to assume, derived ultimately, of course, from the ancient
Zoilus's criticism of Homer. The

January 21, 1736-37.

bantering, hectoring critic especially liked to assume it. For instance, *The Grubstreet Journal* of April 6, 1732, has a clever paper signed Zoilus, ridiculing Dr.
Bentley's edition of Milton's *Paradise Lost* by mock emendations in Bentley's very
manner. Milton's line

Millions of spiritual creatures walk the earth51 becomes

Several angels walk upon the earth.

and there are many other ridiculous mock imitations of the learned doctor.52

A similar Zoilus, then, whoever he may have been, writes to Mr. Parks, of *The Virginia Gazette:*

Sir,

I should take it as a Favor, if you'll give the following Song a Place in your next Paper. It is a Kevenge, long since due to good Sense and fine Writing; which have been used in a most barbarous and inhuman Manner by the Monitor. . . .

Your constant Reader and Subscriber,

Zoilus.

51 *Paradise Lost,* Bk. IV, 1. 677.

M"Bavius," the editor of *The Grubstreet Journal,* was a severe critic of Bentley, as an editor of Milton, and published in *The Grubstreet Journal* a series of *Animadversions upon Dr. Bentley's Preface to Paradise Lost.* He concludes the *Animadversions* by saying: "For a person, who, tho' allowed to be a very learned Critic, was never imagined to be a Poet, to publish his extemporary, crude and indigested criticisms, upon the compleatest Poem in the English Tongue; to pretend to alter and correct it in every page; to strike out a great many Verses and to put in several of his own; this justly raises the wonder, Scorn, and Indignation of all that hear it. This is to treat the Heroic Poem of the great Milton like the Exercise of a school-boy; and infinitely exceeds the Audaciousness of Zoilus in his Animadversions upon Homer."

The song that follows is set to the tune of Dorset's sentimental ballad *To all ye Ladies now on Land,63* a great favorite at the time. *The London Magazine* for July, 1733, has among its poetical attempts, *Richmond: A Ballad,* to the same tune, and *The London Magazine* for January, 1735, likewise indicates this identical tune for *The Constant Lover in Metamorphoses,* a song, or sentimental ballad, beginning

Dear Phillis by great jove I swear

So it was the fashion to use it as a musical setting for timely verses. No doubt Zoilus had seen the new ballads in *The London Magazine,* or others precisely similar when he composed his scathing lines on the Monitor which we quote in part:

The Monitor Admonished

A new Song

(To the tune of, *To all ye Ladies now at Land*)

I, who long since did draw my Pen

To injur'd Wit's Defence,

Amnowalass! compell'd again

To succour common Sense;

For sure it never suffer'd more;

Than lately by the Monitor.

With a fa la

 To all ye Ladies now on land

We men at sea endite

We'd have you now to understand

How hard it is to write.

Our paper, pens and ink and we,

Go up and down upon the sea
with a fa la. (Both music and words are published in Walter Crane's Pan *Pipes.)*
This Monitor pretends to preach
In sacred Wisdom's Schools; /
But I'll a useful Lesson teach
Worth all his silly Rules;
By which he'll mend what's gone before;
And this is, Never to write more.
With a fa la
I'm sorry that 'tis still my Fate
Ungrateful Truths to tell;
But since, that he's a Dunce of late
The World does not conceal,
'Tis Pity, to himself alone
This weighty Truth should be unknown.
With a fa la

This stinging rebuke, with its curious resemblance in phrase to almost all the epigrammatic English poets of the day, was perhaps just enough if applied to *The Monitor's* recent extravagances, but certainly would be overwhelmingly unjust applied to any of the earlier papers. Even now he showed that he had enough of the old fire to make a spirited reply both in prose and verse in his next number.54

"It is very certain," he begins, "that there is not a more infectious Disease than that of Writing: And as my Admonisher Zoilus observes, 'twou'd be a glorious undertaking to clear the World of those Vermin, call'd Scribblers, *Save One!* for it has been long observ'd that writing is quite useless, and the Spirit of it maintain'd only by men of the Super- idiot Class." He proposes therefore "a Bill, in every Parish Church, to pray for the continuance of

" *Monitor* No. 19, January 28, 1736-37.

the hard weather to starve them all out *'Save One,'* or make them useful in other directions, as physicians do distempers." He announces that he too will write a song, and steal nothing from Zoilus but his tune – "Nothing can make me ill natur'd, at this Juncture," he declares, "but the want of Wood, and a chearful Glass."

The Monitor to Zoilus
If useful Lessons you can Teach
Pray let them be concise;
No matter whose they are you preach
We will not criticise.
Do but observe the Rule laid down
Hold forth, – *But let it be your own.*
With a fa la.
The Dogs you lately saw in Print
Were silly Dogs indeed;
Zoilus, my Friend, take back your Hint,
And probe them 'till they bleed;
Since they have given such Offence,

Pray spare but One, – The Dog of Sense.
With a fa la.

Zoilus had, in one stanza of his poem, hinted that the Monitor included himself in his category of ill- paired dogs, representing human kind.

Himself he plac'd a Sad-Dog there
With a fa la.

The Monitor, then, by asking mercy only for the Dog of Sense, and proposing prayers in every parish for the continuance of the hard weather to starve all thescribblers but one, obviously returns the thrust against "vermin scribblers."

In his next number55 he very wisely leaves personal discussion and broadside for a pleasant, soothing little essay on good nature, reminding his readers and incidentally his enemy that "The great Lord Chancellor Clarendon, in one of his Speeches to the Parliament, soon after the Restoration, when he would recommend to the Nation Unanimity and Peace, after their long continu'd Contentions, earnestly desires them, as a Means thereto, to make use of Good Nature towards one another, which he tells them is so peculiar to the English Nation, that the very Word itself will not bear a Translation into any other language."

But Zoilus will not let him rest in this peaceful retreat under cover of the great Lord Clarendon. In the same issue of *The Virginia Gazette* which has the Monitor's plea for good nature, we find another stinging and somewhat witty attack from the pen of his foe. Zoilus does not hesitate to bolster his own wit with lavish quotations from English satire, however, and intersperses lines from Congreve and Dryden, references to the *Rehearsal,* and other reminiscences, to increase his general effect. His motto from Juvenal, of course, is merely the commonplace heading of the ordinary eighteenth-century essay. "There is no Tribe of Mortals so incorrigible as your Mortal-Writers," he begins rather smartly, passing on immediately to the proposition that *The Monitor* has really been dead five or six

M Monitor No. 20, February 4, 1736-37.

months; that is, during the entire period of its supposed existence. He has nothing but the sharpest condemnation, naturally, for this spectre stalking about under a sham pretense of being alive. In his utter contempt, he quotes Congreve's "excellent Epistle to Lord Cobham:"

Baboons and apes ridiculous we find;
For what? For ill resembling Human Kind.
None are, for being what they are, in Fault,
But for not being, what they would be thought.

Then he continues in his own particular vein of rather heavy satire: " There was published, in your *Gazette* of last Friday, a certain unmeaning, shapeless Monster, called a *Monitor;* and as far as I could penetrate into its Design, (for it was very mysterious) it was intended as an Answer to my last." But in this answer Zoilus thinks that the Monitor has surpassed even his own notorious silliness. Dry- den's famous couplet on Shadwell is used at this point to add venom to his shaft:

Others to some faint Meaning make Pretence;
But . . . never deviates into Sense.

Zoilus goes so far as to say that the Monitor should have his works translated into English, – witness his first sentence,56 which his critic regards as unpardon- ably obscure, since, "like Bays in *The Rehearsal,* he opens the Scene with a Whisper." Above all, Zoilus shows that the Monitor's hint of plagiary rankled. The Monitor had said, we remember,

"On "those Vermin, call'd Scribblers," *Monitor* No. 19, January 28, 1736-37.

Do but observe the Rule laid down,

Hold forth. . . . But let it be your own.

Zoilus insists that to accuse Mm of plagiary is ridiculous, when the Monitor himself had "slily purloined from a Song-Book" his lines on the spider's artistry under the table. As usual, he cannot resist ending with a mocking song to his enemy, who is rather wittily characterized in these terms:

Resolv'd, like a Hero, to bear all the Brunt;

But says nothing in his, or his Party's Defence;

Since he only there pleads for the Dog of good Sense.

Derry down

But perhaps the cleverest satire of Zoilus is contained in the mock notice immedi- ately after the song. We quote a portion of it.

Advertisement

" To all Gentlemen and Ladies, who delight in the Noble and Princely Diversion of Hunting: This is to give Notice, That a Dunce will be hunted every other Friday, in the Gazette, 'til he is fairly run down. He is an Animal of a most peculiar and singular Nature; being very long-winded and pertinacious; and is known to afford excellent Sport, having tired more People, than all the Foxes that ever Yorkshire produced. . . . His only weapon is a Gray-Goose Quill through which he can distill a poisonous Juice, which has deprived several Persons of all Manner of Patience.

"And, that he may be hunted to some Tune, Musick shall attend the Company to the Field; and after the Chase is over, the Gentlemen and Ladies shall be diverted with a Song. So, God save the King."

But it is the Monitor who writes the new song,57 and also quotes the rather apt epigram, frankly acknowledged as a loan from *The Gentleman's Magazine:*

Has Codrus, in his Critic Pride

Approv'd of Works yet known?

Yes, Sir, what none approv'd beside,

Of Works, that were his own.

He also has the next word in his last essay, the twenty-second,58 a very typical example of the eighteenth-century vision-allegory. Criptonimus writes to the Monitor, begging him to use his supernatural powers in the interpretation of a strange dream, which he describes in some detail. The dream showed Criptonimus a man sitting under a tree disputing by himself. He had with him a few books, *The Pearl of Eloquence, A Help to Discourse, The Spiritual Mouse-Trap, or The Painful Speaking Trumpet to his Deaf Auditory.* Presently "a Lady appear'd; her Mien was tatter'd – her Garment Patch- work, compos'd of Verse and Prose." But the strange being under the tree addressed her in enthusiastic couplets, as his genius, promising to restore her power and beauty. The Monitor has no difficulty in deciphering the meaning of the dream. By the stars, he says, the first letter of his character is the last in the alphabet. The reader, of course, has suspected as much at the mention of the solitary disputant reading *The Spiritual Mouse-Trap, or The Painful Speaking Trumpet to his Deaf Auditory.*

" February 11, 1736-37. *a* February 25, 1736-37.

Zoilus is clearly enough the painful speaking trumpet to a deaf auditory. The identity is put beyond doubt when we read that "this carping Creature would have invok'd the Muses." But he was given instead "the Goddess of Dulness, to attend him, the said Carping Creature, upon all Occasions. This Sir, was the Lady you saw appear with that tatter'd Mien. . . . Given at my House, this twenty-fifth of February."

So the Monitor makes his final bow, and leaves the stage; whether because Zoilus had actually succeeded in his plan of "running him down" or because he himself had tired of the game, it is impossible to say. Three weeks later59 Zoilus sends his last criticism to *The Virginia Gazette,* and the brief literary skirmish is over. This last attack of Zoilus rather deserves to be called carping criticism. It is concerned chiefly with the Monitor's trifling inexactness of phrase, here and there, and need not detain us. The principal thing of importance to note in all this play and counterplay is the ease and naturalness with which they could both fit words to the lilt of an old song. Compared to the attempts of Mather Byles, the verses in *The Virginia Gazette, j* not only the verses under consideration, but others scattered through its files, are almost poetry. There is even some knowledge of contemporary English literary criticism. Zoilus knew Congreve, Dryden, Pope, Buckingham's satiric verse as well as *The Rehearsal,* all from the particular point of view of ! their critical ideas.

" March 18, 1736-37.

To pass a final judgment on *The Monitor* as colonial literature would be a difficult and complicated matter. But taking all the noteworthy production throughout British America up to 1737 as a guide, we find the only rivals in the writings of the Mather dynasty in Massachusetts, the essays that we have previously considered in other journals, Franklin's prefaces to *Poor Richard,* Colonel William Byrd's *History of the Dividing Line,* and some stray poems and letters here and there. Cotton Mather's *Magnalia Christi* did not even pretend to be literature, though at times it had a severe art of its own. Much colonial writing, especially the sermons, treatises and histories of the ecclesiastics, hitherto treated as literature largely because of the supposed dearth of anything else, would fall into other classifications under any strict judgment. Even if we leave all these out of consideration for the moment, and take only the small amount of creative work that would remain, we could not claim for *The Monitor* so high a place as that of Franklin's best prefaces to *Poor Richard* or Colonel Byrd's best sallies, or some other pieces of various sorts produced in the colonies. But it is fairly certain that a selection of the liveliest numbers of *The Monitor* would make Franklin's *Busy-Body* seem pale and lifeless. Patience,60 in her busy little shop, complaining of tedious, impertinent callers, is the only figure of the *Busy-Body* series worthy to be placed alongside of the *Monitor's* woman of fashion and her daughters Arabella Sly, Helena Fidget,

See *Busy-Body,* No. 4.

Amoret, and Penelope Leer. The *Busy-Body,* of course, being formed upon an earlier model, does not even attempt the sort of witty, fashionable dialogue found in the letters of the *Monitor's* young reporters. And indeed there is nothing just like it to be found in the colonies in 1736, unless directly copied from English sources. *The Virginia Gazette,* then, contains several pieces of light social : satire, unique in kind, and surpassed by very few/ other colonial writings up to 1737.

As to the author of *The Monitor,* speculation would probably be profitless. The most important fact for our present purpose is that a considerable number of Virginians might have written it. Aside from Parks himself, a not very likely candidate, "William and Mary College was continually sending out "scribbling collegians." These young fellows were the very ones who delighted in acting, sometimes contrary to the desire of the authorities, and who would be likely to attend the public theater. We must not forget that old Williamsburg had its theater, its bowling alley, its balls and assemblies, its games of Piquet. It was as much a miniature London as it could be made. The Professors of the College, too, often wrote occasional verse of some merit. In one instance, at least, one of them produced a rather remarkable little volume of poems in varied metrical forms. Over and over again they are advertised in *The Virginia Gazette* from the time of their first publication on October 22, 1736. In the *Gazette* of that date, we read: " This Day is publish'd, Poems on several Occasions, never beforeprinted. By a Gentleman of Virginia. Price stitch'd 15V A copy of this rare little book has been seen by the present writer in the Boston Athenaeum, among George Washington's private books, largely owned now by the Athenaeum Library. It has his autograph signature on the flyleaf, G. Washington. A Virginian gentleman of to-day owns a copy with a signature indicating the author of the poems, a professor at William and Mary.61

Since these poems, with their *known* Virginian origin, were advertised so often in the *Gazette,* and since they furnish an excellent illustration of the writing that could be done and was being done in Virginia at a time exactly contemporaneous with *The Monitor,* it will scarcely be aside from our present purpose to say a few words more about them. They are full to overflowing of references to London, Twickenham, Oxford, Windsor. They are full of experiments in meter, from Miltonic verse to four accent rhymed stanzas to Sylvia. They show an immense interest in the recent development of the London stage, and a strong resentment at the intrusions of Harlequin and his merry acrobats. The poet looks back with regret to the days when "Shakespear, Row, and all those Sons of Fame" held the stage.

Next Harlequin, ingenious Antique, came;
With Kick facetious, or with witty Grin,
"A private letter in the possession of Mr. William G. Stanard, of the Virginia Historical Society, is the source of this information.
He rais'd our Laughter . . . but expos'd our Brain.
In vain Mercutio jests, poor Juliet mourns in vain.
Phough! Who can bear th' intolerable Strain!
Where strong and manly Sense disturbs our Ease,
And Passions, too affecting e'er to please.
To burning Houses, Monsters and Grimace,
To flying Bottles, wands and Waving Seas,
To cheated Cuckolds, and the bold Rogere,

Illustrious Hero! pendent in the Air;

To these we fly, and leave those Sons of Spleen,

The Fools of Sense, to doat on Shakespear's Scene.

Truly, when a known "gentleman of Virginia" can have such an appreciation of London life as this, there is no matter of surprise in the chance London scenes of *The Monitor.*

These poems have no bigoted view of human pleasures, in general. We fear they would have made the New England divines look for some immediate curse from Heaven:

True Joys are few; then boldly fill,

The racy Juice will heal Despair.

Then let the ruddy God advance,

And some beauteous lovesome She;

With Mirth, and Joke, and Quirp, and Dance;

These alone have Joys for me.

Obviously, the Monitor could easily have been conceived in the same atmosphere of belief in the vivid realities of life.

The translations and adaptations from the classics in the little volume we have been speaking of, were, of course, to be expected. They occur naturallyenough among any eighteenth-century poems. The Latin verses produced for one occasion or another at William and Mary College may not have been more numerous than usual in a college, but it is very certain that far more than usual were translated and inserted in *The Virginia Gazette.* They vary from complimentary formalities addressed to the Governor of the Colony62 to elegies of more or less merit, such as the ode to the memory of Sir John Eandolph, probably by a professor of William and Mary, though possibly written by the Eector of Bruton.63 No doubt the frequent lines in imitation of Horace or Anacreon came less directly from the college.

But more interesting than imitations of the classics are the absolutely genuine lyrics sprinkled through the *Gazette* at intervals. When a poem is headed "By a young Gentleman of Virginia," we may be fairly sure that it was composed at home, in the colony, often by some college student. Most significant of these little lyrics, is one which in all probability came from the pen of Colonel William Byrd. If this is so, it will indeed add little to his fame, yet it will form an interesting addition to his writings as we know them.

In the *Gazette* for May 5, 1738, is a letter to Mr. Parks, as follows:

See *The Virginia Gazette,* No. 18, December 3, 1736, where the Honorable William Gooch is addressed in an imitation of Horace, Book 4, Ode 15.

" Both Latin and English are given in the *Gazette,* No. 36, April 8, 1737.

Mr. Parks:

Please to insert the following Performance of a Youth of my Acquaintance, in your *Gazette,* and You'll oblige,

your constant Reader,

W. B.

Not only does the signature, W. B., seem significant, here, but the title is followed by a little explanatory note which puts us on Colonel Byrd's track at once. The poem is called *The Discovery,* by a Youth of the Frontiers. Now we know that Colonel Byrd was interested in the frontiers along the Blue Eidge. He wrote a pamphlet "booming" the frontier lands. And this pamphlet was even translated into German for the benefit of the Swiss settlers. So the little poem called *The Discovery* is very probably his. "The youth of my acquaintance" who, he tells us, composed it, need not be taken too seriously. Colonel Byrd would perhaps not care to be known as the author of such gallantly youthful lines as these:

In vain, I strove my Love to hide,
In vain, th' apparent Truth deny'd,
My Blushes told my Tongue, it ly'd.
Whether my Breast's involv'd with Cares,
At her approach a Calm appears,
Or if my Heart with gloomy Grief
Is clouded o'er, she brings Relief;
Her charming Eyes n; w Joys distil,
And my fond Soul with Raptures fill.

That the *Gazette* knew Colonel Byrd and his family well is amply proved by the "Acrostick upon

Miss Evelyn Byrd, lately deceased" printed in the
Gazette, December 9, 1737. This beautiful girl had
died because of her father's opposition to a love-
match, as the story goes, and in a pencil note in the
margin of the *Gazette* we read that the acrostic was
also her epitaph. The odd lines have an almost flippant ring to-day:

Ever constant to her Friend
Vigilant in Truth's Defence,
Entertaining to her End,
Life! Brimful of Eloquence.
Youth in Person; Age in sense,
Nature gave her Store immense.

This epitaph is interesting for its associations merely. But there are a few lyrics of real merit in the *Gazette,* such as the "Verses occasioned by a young Lady's singing to the Spinnet. By a young Gentleman in Virginia."64 We give the opening couplets:

Sweetness and Strength in Silvia's Voice unite,
The God that gave it, gave it for Delight;
Orpheus, who drew, by Musick, Woods along,
Must yield to Silvia's entertaining Song.

Another, not quite so good; is written *To a Lady, on
a Screen of Her Working. TM* We are told that "the
following Lines were wrote by a Gentleman of Virginia." After describing the flowered screen in all
its glory, he closes with the wish:

Refreshing Green, from age preserve those Eyes
By which You flourish in immortal Dies.

" See *The Virginia Gazette,* No. 44, June 3, 1737.

" Ibid., No. 19, December 10, 1736.

Many other bits of verse, epigrams, trials of wit, love songs to Chloe or Fidelia, no doubt represent the native talent. When we come to the borrowing from English sources, the number of reprints soon grows bewilderingly large. Not only fairly important occasional poems like Cibber's odes,65a Pope's inscription on Gay's monument,65" or a new prologue to be spoken at a revival of *King John* at Drury Lane65c are copied in full into *The Virginia Gazette,* but all sorts of absurd squibs, jokes and light vers de societe come directly from the poetical section of) the London magazines. Any chance page of a *Virginia Gazette* that one may turn to, is likely to be broken with verse of one kind or another.

So far as actual affairs abroad were concerned, Irish interests held a very high place in the *Gazette.* Dean Swift is often quoted at length, usually as the champion of oppressed Ireland, rather than as a poet or man of letters. After the religious disabilities of 1704 had been established beyond hope of change, Virginia had attracted many Scotch-Irish Presbyterians from Ulster County in the North of Ireland. By 1730 they drifted through the Shenan- doah Valley in large numbers, and Governor Gooch was kept busy dispensing grants to the valley lands. It is very natural, therefore, that Parks should copy Irish items into his *Gazette,* which he expected to circulate through the country districts.

The first of these items is from *The Political State* for June, 1736,66 and describes the petition of the Dublin Guild against lowering the coin. Dean Swift is mentioned with just the dignity belonging to his office, and to his advocacy of Irish interests, and no more. "On the 24th of April last," we are told, "there was a Grand Meeting of the Guild at Dublin, where above a Hundred and Fifty eminent Merchants were present. The occasion of their Meeting was to draw up a Petition, to his Grace the Lord Lieutenant and Council, against lowering their Gold Coin. . . . Among the rest, the Rev. and Worthy Dr. Swift, Dean of St. Patrick's, appeared as a Member of the Guild, and as he has always behav'd with a proper Zeal and Concern, when he thought the Interest of his Country at Stake, he made a Speech upon this Occasion." A report of the speech follows in *The Virginia Gazette.* It is an eloquent plea for the poor as the the real losers by the fall of money. The Dean insists that Bishops and Justices will be as well off as before.

" See *The Virginia Gazette,* No. 35, April 1, 1737.

"b Ibid., No. 11, October 15, 1736.

" Ibid., No. 44, June 3, 1737.

"Inserted in *The Virginia Gazette,* No. 12, October 22, 1736.

The same argument appears in a more flippant and amusing form in some popular verses which Parks copied into the *Gazette,* April 28, 1738, under the title, *Ay and No. A Tale from Dublin, done into Verse.*

At Dublin's high Feast sat Primate and Dean,

Both Dress'd like Divines, with Band and Pace clean.

Quoth Hugh of Armagh, the Mob is grown bold.

Ay, ay, quoth the Dean, the Cause is old Gold.

No, no, quoth the Prime ... if Causes we sift,

This Mischief arises from witty Dean Swift.
The smart one replied, there's no Wit in the Case;
And nothing of that e'er troubl'd your Grace.
'Tis Matter of Weight and a mere Money Job;
But the lower the Coin, the higher the Mob.
Go tell your Friend Bob, and other great Folk,
That sinking the Coin is a dangerous Joke.
The Irish, dear joys, have enough Common Sense,
To treat Gold reduc'd like "Wood's Copper Pence.
'Tis pity a Prelate should die without Law;
But if I say the Word . . . Take care of Armagh.

Swift's own birthday poem to himself was copied into the *Gazette07* from *The London Magazine* for December, 1736. And it is just possible that Virginians took a special interest in Dean Swift from the vague plan of about twenty years before, that he should be appointed Bishop of Virginia, with a sort of Metropolitan authority over the Colonial clergy. The idea was probably a suggestion of his friend Colonel Hunter, on his own appointment as Governor of Virginia in 1708. Naturally he would have liked his distinguished friend's company in the new world. But the suggestion never took root, and Colonel Hunter was himself captured by the French on his voyage across the Atlantic. His commission was saved from the enemy, later, and its remarkably fine script is now preserved in the rooms of the Virginia Historical Society.

But the great Dean is by no means the only Irish personality of interest to readers of *The Virginia Gazette*. We have seen that they were acquainted with Dr. Thomas Sheridan's *Intelligencer*. After his death the obituary appreciation from Dublin was copied into the *Gazette,68* along with a humorous

"No. 32, March 11, 1736-37.

" No. 130, January 26, 1738-39.

epitaph. The serious little prose essay describes him in the well-known fashion as "a most sincere Friend, a delightful Companion, and the best Schoolmaster in Europe"; also as the "best natured Man in the World." None of *his* scholars, we are told, was ever an atheist or a free-thinker.

In *The Virginia Gazette,* as in most other colonial papers, entire essays or acts of plays, and even whole plays were reprinted serially when the original publication could be imported in convenient form, in one volume. Such would not be the case of course, with the current English weeklies. But /a little dramatic satire like Dodsley's *Toy Shop* [could be very easily cut up into several parts to fill 1 the front page of successive Gazettes. Parks began the *Toy Shop* on April 15, 1737, and in the next number of his *Gazette* informed his readers that the i conclusion must be deferred for lack of room. Lit- 'erature was only resorted to when the news failed. In the following number, however,69 the *Toy Shop* takes three entire pages out of four. It had been published in *The South Carolina Gazette* in four instalments more than a year before,70 so whether Parks copied it from the Charleston weekly, or whether he imported it directly from London, it is impossible to say; probably from London, however. *The Prompter71* had rightly characterized the piece as "without any theatrical merit whatsoever," though it had been acted at Covent Garden. The colonial press reprinted it merely as moral satire.

68 See *The Virginia Gazette,* No. 39, April 29, 1737.

TC See *The South Carolina Gazette,* Nos. 104, 107, 108, 109.

" The English periodical of that name, No. 29, February 18, 1735.

In the case of Addison's *Cato* there was immense interest in the actual theatrical performance in both Williamsburg and Charleston, yet the moral and literary aspects made perhaps an equally profound impression. In *The Virginia Gazette* of November 19, 1736, we find a portion of the fifth act of *Cato* reprinted under the title of *Cato and his Genius,* beginning with the words of the Genius:

Awful Hero, Cato, rise!

Addison, in fact, had never lost his hold anywhere in the colonies. The essay on the *Spectator* model' constantly appeared along with the later modes. *The Virginia Gazette* has its full share of moralizing on death, marriage, true happiness, envy, malice and discontent, whether in the form of the fictitious letter to the editor, or merely by way of the week's editorial. The Addisonian letter is, however, not the best kind of contribution to be found in the *Gazette,* as we have seen, though there are several fairly good instances of it in 1737 and 1738.

Philo-Gunaicus sends some" unpolish 'd Thoughts" on the proper behavior of women,72 advising them in the old familiar way to be modest in their apparel, not wearing every fashionable trinket. Above all they had better not try to manage their husbands. Two weeks later,73 comes a spirited reply from Andromache, hinting that perhaps idle coxcombs deserve animadversions as well as frivolous ladies. "A good Husband makes a good Wife," she remarks pointedly, and continues: " There are several

"See *The Virginia Gazette,* No. 42, May 20, 1737. n Ibid., No. 44, June 3, 1737.

Ladies of my acquaintance who have read the *Spectator* on the same Subject, and for the Most Part admir'd yours as incomparable Peices, but since this Gentleman has appear'd in Print, those Letters, for anything I know, may be lay'd aside as trifling and vain; in short, I'm inclin'd to pitty poor Mr. Addison, and Steel, when I observe a Genius so much exceeding theirs. I, hope such Thoughts as these will encourage Mr. G. – to oblige us with more of his Performances." This, of course, is strong enough evidence that Philo-Gunaicus had been attempting the Addisonian essay.

A better example, combined with some local color, is furnished by Tom Tell Truth's letter to Mr. Parks74 on the vicious practice of opening the English mail. His essay begins in regular Addisonian style with a motto from Cicero's De Natura Deorum, but soon attains a vitality of its own. "The other Day calling at a Public House," he begins, "a Box of Letters came from on Board a Ship lately arrived from England; . . . having no Concern myself (from the Misfortune of out-living my Friends) I took my Place in a Corner of the Room, when of a sudden a Person snatches up a Letter, reads the

Superscription, To . 'Egad,' says he, 'I must
Know the Contents of this,' – and made off."

Even more direct evidence of the continued influence of Addisonian prose occurs as late as 1739 when the one hundred and second number of the *Guardian* is taken bodily into the *Gazette,'5* with an

" See *The Virginia Gazette,* No. 88, AprU 7, 1738. "No. 158, August 10, 1739.

introduction in which the reader is told that the *Guardians, Tatlers,* and *Spectators* are inexhaustible treasures for the promotion of learning, and the suppression of vice.

In a general way several controversial papers of 1738 on the tobacco inspection conform to the *Spectator* model, although the discussion has really too sharp an edge for anything like Addisonian urbanity. There is the outward form of the essay under fictitious signatures, and there is a mere semblance of pleasantry in the bitter ridicule. Timothy Touch- Truth advocates76 a strict inspection of tobacco and the actual production of less in order to maintain a Mgher price in the London market. This policy was known as the "stint." Morforeo replies77 with & ridiculous life history of Mr. Timothy Touch- Truth, who, he says, was born in the Cripplegate district of London, of honest parents, but ran away from school after learning "to write and cypher." At twenty-one he set up for a great politician and projector, and is at present writing a new system of algebra. "He made the first Model of a Chaise that would run with one Wheel"; and since he believes that all the disadvantages in traffic consist in bulky goods, "proposes that the Gauge of a Tobacco Hogshead should be reduced to the Size of a Butter- Firkin."

Touch-Truth's answer78 is rather mild and condescending in tone. The low esteem which he has for the praise of this world, he says, makes Mr. Morforeo's piece rather "delightful than vexatious," since he has made himself ridiculous rather than his foe. Touch-Truth proceeds to perpetrate some wretched doggerel which certainly puts him in a more absurd position than it does Morforeo. Then he becomes serious, and defends his course as meant to "raise up those fainting Spirits, who have long laboured under the weight of their misfortunes." He believes thoroughly in his method of changing the inspection.

78 Ibid., No. 105, August 4, 1738.
77 Ibid., No. 106, August 11, 1738.
78 Ibid., No. 114, October 6, 1738.

Morforeo, not to be daunted, insists79 that Touch- Truth could not have written his last production, for Dr. Annodyne had forbidden him to touch pen to paper, on account of his serious illness in the head. The present writer (of Touch-Truth's last paper) "is a Stranger to the Sense of what he has wrote, and to Mr. Touch-Truth as well, tho' he imitates his obscure Style pretty well." The colonists must not be stirred to a dislike of existing laws. At length the whole bantering controversy is ended by a sensible letter from "a planter" against the stint advocated by Touch-Truth.

The Virginia Historical Society's excellent file of the *Gazette* extends only to 1740. There follows a gap of ten years for which no single copy is known to exist. After 1750 the New York Public Library takes up the tale with a fairly complete file of the years 1751 and 1752. And scattering files of still later date are to be found in Virginia. All these lie outside our period. But it happens that the literary character of Virginia's weekly was well enough

TM See *The Virginia Gazette,* No. 116, October 20, 1738.

established for other newspapers between 1740 and 1750, and even the first American magazines, to quote from it. *The Boston Weekly News-Letter,* of no literary pretensions whatever, quotes a story of Sir William Temple80 from *The Virginia Gazette* as late as 1747.

The first number of Franklin's monthly, *The General Magazine and Historical Chronicle for all the British Plantations in America,81* introduces its literary section under the heading *Essays on various Subjects, from the News-Papers published in the Colonies.* Just here we have an important bit of; evidence that newspapers were expected to offer essays and other literary material to the public. The first newspaper which Franklin culls from for his new magazine is *The Virginia Gazette.* So in this incidental and hitherto unnoted way, we have a few selections of later date from Parks's paper. The first one shows the continued interest in translations from the classics, as well as the Addisonian form of introduction.

Mr. Parks,

Beading 'tother Day, for my Amusement, in Ovid's *Bemedy of Love, I* happen'd to come across a Passage therein, where the Author, (speaking of himself in the first Person) relates a very Singular Cure that befel him in the Course of his Amours; and from his own experience of its Success, recommends it to his Love-sick Readers. I must confess I was so taken with the Oddness of his Method, that I could not help attempting a Translation, or at least an Imitation of the Passage in English, which Ihere send you, together with the Original, to be inserted in your next *Gazette,* if you think it merits a Place there.

See *The Boston Weekly News-Letter,* August 13, 1747. 81 Published in Philadelphia in January, 1741.

Yours,

The translation follows. Again in the May number of *The General Magazine,* among the Poetical Essays, we find quoted in full from *The Virginia Gazette,* a *Translation of Mr. Addison's Latin Poem on a Picture of the Resurrection, in Magdalen College Chappel at Oxford.*

The wond'rous Draught, the Pencil's daring Stroke,
The rising Dead, the Judge's awful Look,
The Spectre's ghastly Form, and pallid Face,
Dread Pomp to view, and difficult to trace;
Unfold, my Muse, with more than mortal Flame;
The Theme is sacred, be the Verse the same.

Great as the contemporary admiration for Addison's prose undoubtedly was, his own generation ranked him rather as a poet. It is not at all uncommon to find him grouped with Shakespere and Milton.

The next colonial monthly, *The American Magazine and Historical Chronicle,* established in Boston in 1743, takes verses from *The Virginia Gazette* of July 26, 1744, into the August number of the magazine, 1744. These verses on the Paper-Mill, inscribed to Mr. Parks, are certainly of Virginian origin, though the fictitious signature, J. Dumble- ton, gives no clue to their authorship. They have been copied into *The Virginia Magazine of History and Biography82* from *The American Magazine,* thusreturning in a somewhat roundabout way to their native soil. By scattered hints and chance quotations in other journals, then, we can infer that *The Virginia Gazette* lost nothing of its general literary flavor from 1740 to 1750.

a Vol. VII, p. 442.

The extant files, as we have seen, furnish a variety of excellent prose, and tolerable verse. Much of the prose could stand comparison with the best pieces of *The Pennsylvania Gazette,* while it would be a poor compliment to the verse in *The Virginia Gazette* even to compare it with that in any other early colonial weekly, except the Charleston paper. Surely these facts are enough to dispel that faintly inquisitive lift of the eyebrow with which literary historians have often greeted any reference to Southern literature.

8

SECTION 8

CHAPTER VIII

The South Cabolina Gazette

It has long been known that Benjamin Franklin's journalistic enterprises were not confined to the province of Pennsylvania. He frequently furnished the capital for able young journeymen to equip printing houses in distant towns. Thomas White- marsh, for instance, a compositor whom Franklin had known in London, came to Philadelphia and proved his ability in Franklin's business to such an extent that Franklin decided to send him to Charleston. Here he was to establish a printing house, and, if possible, a newspaper. Franklin noted in his journal that Whitemarsh "arrived in Charlestown the 29th of September, 1731, at night, so our Partnership there begins October 1, 1731." The first number of *The South Carolina Gazette* was issued on January 8, 17&.-32.

These facts have often been commented upon as evidence of Franklin's foresight and enterprise in business. What seems to have escaped notice is the literary influence which could be inferred from the facts, and which an examination of *The South Carolina Gazette* fully establishes. Franklin's fellow- compositor in London, his able assistant in Philadelphia at the time of Franklin's best imitative writing, must have imbibed his employer's enthusiasms. And we should expect to find Whitemarsh imitatingFranklin; that is to say, imitating his imitation of Addison. This is precisely what we do find.

Even after *The South Carolina Gazette* had passed into the hands of Louis Timothee, a French refugee, the cordial business relations with Franklin were not severed. Louis Timothee, or Timothy, as he was' soon called, had a son, Peter Timothy, who carried on the paper and left it in his turn to a son, Benjamin Franklin Timothy. From 1792 to 1800, Benjamin Franklin Timothy edited the *Gazette,* showing both in name and work, the influence of Benjamin Franklin on American journalism.

It will not be surprising, then, to find in, the first number of *The South Carolina Gazette,* an Addi- sonian editorial inviting communications, "whether in Prose or Verse," every Saturday, for the purpose of "interspersing the Dulce with the Utile." One condition is imposed, however, on all correspondents. They must carefully "avoid giving Offence, either publick, or private; and particularly, . . . forbear all Controversies, both in Church and State."

It is probable that Whitemarsh himself, or some member of his staff, wrote the letter of the following week,1 signed Martia. We can hardly suppose that, any Charleston writer would have responded in a manner so like Franklin's, to the invitation of the first number. Many of Franklin's best early pieces were avowedly letters from members of the fair sex. It was his favorite device for expressing his homely wisdom. And this letter from Martia in the South

1 See *The South Carolina Gazette,* No. 2, January 15, 1731-32.

Carolina weekly is an attempt at something of the same sort. Nor is the *Spectal or* forgotten. Martia's first sentences give direct evidence that Whitemarsh intended to imitate Addison. "I suppose," she is made to say, "you don't expect your Correspondents to give you their respective characters at full length, in the manner of that you'd fain pass upon us for your own." She proceeds, however, to tell us that she is a young lady of sixteen, before she begins her essay on *Levity in Conversation.* Very sensibly she then urges that this will never bring a man reputation. Her motive in writing, she acknowledges, may seem obscure, but "your Wonder, Sir, must cease, when I tell you, that one of these Sparks is my Brother, and that another of 'em stands so fair in my opinion, that I can see no other Blemish in his Conduct, than what has been here hinted at."

The following week2 a facetious reply was published in a letter from Battle to Miss Martia's Papa. Rattle is convinced that some warning is necessary. "Faith, old Gentleman, you have got a very pretty forward Lass for a Daughter. ... A hopeful Girl, upon my Word!" He advises Papa "not to let my little Angel stir abroad unmask'd." Since he perceives, however, that the poor girl has a mind to a husband, he may possibly become "sedate or tame enough to be made her loving Dear for Life." The attempt to create character and situation is evident in letters of this sort.

The same number of the *Gazette* has an entertaining apology for scribblers. Perhaps the idea ofliterary essays in a weekly gazette had been ridiculed by aristocratic gentlemen of Charleston, but more probably the accusation which serves as a text is merely a humorous fiction. After the motto from Terence in due form, the essayist proceeds to inform us that gentlemen " of polite Taste" have been making fun of scribblers as "idle Fellows, driven plaguy hard for a Dinner." The writer denies this accusation, and brings a counter charge against gaming, the "idle Sport" of the rich.

2January 22, 1731-32.

With number four of the *Gazette,* begins a remark- , able series of reprints of entire numbers of the) , *Spectator.* In no other newspaper of the period are such reprints so continuous. Whitemarsh must have had a full set of the *Spectator* in his office to; draw from at a moment's notice. Usually a correspondent is supposed to send the selection, which emanated in all probability from the editorial office. In the case of the introductory letter of Honestus, in number four, we have direct evidence that the *Gazette* was attempting to imitate as well as to cir- culate the *Spectator.* The brief, note of Honestus runs as follows:

Sir,

Not being so expert a Scribbler as those you are concern'd with, I pretend not to send you the Efforts of my own Pen, yet I expect you to insert what follows, which I have taken from a Writer whom I wou'd advise your good Friends to endeavour (if they can) to imitate; if 'tis so bad with 'em that they can't possibly get the better of their cacoethes scribendi.

Honestus.

Then follows the essay on the tradesman's reputation, taken verbatim from the *Spectator,3* and reprinted in full. The constant interest in affairs of the business world is worth noting in this little South Carolina weekly.

But now Martia appears4 again, promising contritely to be less bold in future. And her apology is quickly followed by a warning against scandal and personal censure from Publicola. Publicola admits, however, that censure is the tribute which all men must pay for being conspicuous. "This is a Maxim of so long standing and advanced by so good an Author, that I doubt not but you're acquainted with it," he says. The maxim is Swift's. But no doubt it came to Publicola by way of the *Spectator,* who quotes the saying.5 The editor gravely and decorously acknowledges Publicola's letter, and adds: "Like our fair Correspondent,6 ... we shall be glad to be instructed how to behave when (as Johnny Gay says,)

' If you mention Vice or Bribe,

'Tis so pat to all the Tribe,

Bach cries – that was levell'd at me.'"

This familiarity with Gay is only the first instance of the free use of the eighteenth-century poets in the Charleston weekly.

All the essays and letters that we have now examined occur in the first four numbers of the*Gazette.* Certainly the amount of literary material to the issue is extraordinarily large, even for a ; colonial newspaper of this period. The quality (our present concern is with the prose only) is not much above the average eighteenth-century imitation of Addison, except, possibly, in the liveliness of some character sketches.

' *Spectator,* No. 218.

4 See *The South Carolina Gazette,* No. 4, January 29, 1731-32. '*Spectator,* No. 101. " 'Censure,' says a late ingenious Author, 'is the tax a man pays to the public for being eminent.' " Martia.

In number five Honestus resumes his selections from the "same excellent writer." This time he chooses the *Spectator's* remarks on idleness.7 Lucretia sends a letter on vice the following week,8 quoting Honestus' "own favorite author's" version of the seventh chapter of Proverbs, "being the Description of a Harlot." Lucretia took Addison's lines from the *Spectator.9*

Mary Meanwell's letter is one of the best in the *Gazette.10* Her very name is familiar to us in the *Spectator,11* and her character of bigoted, ill-natured devotee bears a strong resemblance to Addison's portrayal of the same character.12 We quote a portion of Mary Meanwell's letter.

"To The Gentlemen News-wbiters In Chables Town.

Gentlemen,

I am one of that uncouth Sort of Females, which your forward young Flirts call – an old Maid. Yet, you must know, I am not much turn'd of Forty neither. ... I have endeavoured to be profitable as to the next world, andattend divine Worship regularly. Which now affords me the Occasion of troubling you with This, to let you know that notwithstanding the profitable Hints that have been heretofore given the World, by that great Predecessor of Yours, the *Spectator,* there is still subsisting the same Offence to Us who wou'd fain be attentive to our Duty in Places appointed for that Purpose, as in his Days. ... I have the Misfortune to sit in the next Pew to a parcel of Girls and young Fellows, who are, three Parts of the Service, Giggling and Prating."

ISpectator, No. 316.

February 12, 1731-32.

'*Spectator,* No. 410.

"No. 8, February 26, 1731-32.

II No. 208.

"In *Spectator,* No. 354.

After thus delicately introducing the *Spectator* as a predecessor, the editor modestly disclaims attempting to succeed the *Spectator* in a brief editorial postscript to Mary Meanwell's letter. He even fears that "we may be look'd upon as Medlers in other Men's Business; we not pretending to the Abilities or Authority of Him, whom the Lady (in too high a Strain of Compliment to us) calls our Predecessor." Of course the modest disclaimer only draws more attention to Addison.

The following number 13 presents a lesson for the fair sex, from the *Spectator,* with a brief introductory notice addressed To the *Author* of the *Gazette.* The word author is in itself a noteworthy indication of what the *Gazette* was attempting to do. The notice begins:

"Sir,

As the Character of Emilia, which I have taken the Pains to transcribe, may be of general Service to all the Fair Sex, for their Imitation, ... I cou'd wish you wou'd give it a Place in your Paper. ... I need not tell you from whence I have taken it."

"No. 9. March 4, 1731-32.

The three hundred and second *Spectator* follows the introductory remarks. In this number of the *Spectator* we have the characters of Emilia and Honoria, – light and darkness – contrasted.

But it is unnecessary to multiply instances of quotations or reprints from the *Spectator.* All through the earlier years of the *Gazette,* we constantly meet with "some useful Hints from great Authority,"14 or a "Letter and Report which I have borrowed from a Writer you seem to be pretty well acquainted with,"16 or again, the "Thoughts of one of the politest Authors of the Age, on this Subject."16 Frequently Addison is mentioned. "My Quotation, as you justly observ'd, was from the ingenious Mr. Addison."17 In one interesting instance18 the reprint of a Spectator paper19 is combined with an introductory essay of which a large part is copied word for word from Bradford's *Mercury* of October 9, 1735. Thus we have incidental confirmation of the fact that a close relation existed between newspaper editors of Charleston and those of Philadelphia. Whitemarsh began the introductory paragraph under discussion in *The South Carolina Gazette* by remarking to his readers:

"For want of Foreign News, when I insert what I think may be useful to Mankind in general, I don't think it material from what Parts such Pieces come; tho' to satisfythe more curious, the following is of the late Mr. Addison, the justness of whose Sentiments – "

" See *The South Carolina Gazette,* No. 10, March 11, 1731-32.

Ibid., No. 12, March 25, 1732.

"Ibid., No. 44, November 18, 1732.

"Ibid., No. 114, April 3, 1736.

a Ibid., No. 112, March 20, 1735-36.

" *Spectator,* No. 441.

The unacknowledged quotation from the *Mercury* begins with "the justness of whose Sentiments" and continues to the end of the paragraph, including the reference to Addison's superiority to Toland. "We have. already given the paragraph from the *Mercury* in a previous chapter.20

The unbroken file of *The South Carolina Gazette* in the possession of the Charleston Library Society shows us that so late as 1746 and 1750, extracts from Addison were still used by newspaper editors. In the *Gazette* of January 11, 1746, we read: "The following extract from Mr. Addison's *Remarks on several Parts of Italy, I* hope will be favourably received by my Readers at This Time. That ingenious Author, in his remarks on Switzerland (P. 286, 287, 288) says – ." Then follows the long quotation. And in 1750, the last year which the present investigation will cover, the *Gazette* of April 9 reprints the four hundred and fifty-sixth *Spectator.*

Meanwhile the ordinary essay in imitation of the Addisonian model continues throughout the period. We shall not pause over the numerous treatments of hackneyed topics like pride, death, the power of silence, and so on.21 There are a few original essays, 'however, which demand separate notice. Among them is the sprightly letter from Penelope Aspen,22 accusing the essayists of trying to engross all thetalk to themselves: "What!" she exclaims, "debar us from those sweet Topicks of Conversation, Dress, and Fashions, and the dear delightful Satisfaction of railing at our Neighbors? Fie upon ye, even Addison himself, were he here, dared not to have said so much."

"Vide supra, chapter III, p. 87.

K See Nos. 23, 25, 26, 34, for examples.

a See *The South Carolina Gazette,* No. 24, June 17, 1732.

But perhaps more noteworthy in some respects than individual papers is the series of essays purporting to come from the members of a certain Meddlers' Club. Probably the editorial staff was primarily responsible for the Meddlers' Club papers, since they show the influence of Franklin's *Busy-Body,* as well as that of the Spectator Club. Yet, in reality, they offer nothing but a burlesque on all serious essay writing, until the series is abruptly cut short after the third number by the irate letter of Diogenes Rusticus. We have only three *Meddlers* to examine, then, and since they are undoubtedly of Carolinian origin, they deserve a place in any examination of the native literature in early periodicals.

After a humorous address to "Mr. Lewis Timothy," the first essay purporting to come from the Meddlers' Club23 proceeds to describe the club in this mocking vein:

"Among the innumerable and various Clubs, both in Europe and America, many of whom the famous *Spectator* and *Tatler* give an Account of, I know of none by the name of the Meddlers' Club. This name I believe is new, and an Original. ... It is not long since, that a parcel of young illiterate Fellows assembled together and erected a

" See *The South Carolina Gazette,* No. 81, August 16, 1735.

Club of the name above mentioned, one of whom I have the happiness to be. We consist of six Persons only, and desire, if you have nothing else of greater moment, to insert this in your *Gazette.* . . . And although the highest of our Wit does not come up to that of a Waterman's Boy, . . . yet we have forsooth set up for Reformers, ... or Meddlers of Nobody's business, or to speak plainer, of everybody's: For we have set that refined maxim of Nobody's meaning everybody; though we shall in particular avoid all personal Reflections, and don't doubt but our Countrymen will be as well pleased to see the Attempts of Carolinians, tho' weak, as to see foreign Pieces of more refined Sense, since our Intentions are good, tho' our Capacities small."

Franklin, we remember, in the first number of the *Busy-Body,* had said: "what is every Body's Business is Nobody's Business; and the Business is done accordingly. I, therefore, upon mature Deliberation, think fit to take Nobody's Business wholly into my own Hands." Evidently the unknown writer of the first *Meddler* had Franklin's, idea in mind. The very meaning of the word is not far from the meaning of busy-body.

The description of the club members is a kind of travesty on the Addisonian model.

"Imprimis. . . . Jack, would be Taller: for tho' he is the least person among us, yet according to the old Proverb, of little head great Wit, we have, and I hope not unjustly, thought that a little Body must have most Sense. His Talent consists chiefly in contradicting others, and (he) thinks he knows more than all the Club; for which reason I have placed him first.

"Item, the second is Tom Snigger – his Talent consists most in telling Stories, and because nobody else will, laughs at them himself.

"Item, the third is Dick Haughty: he thinks merit nowhere but in fine Clothes, but is otherwise a very agreeable person."

The fourth member, Will Generous, and the fifth, Ralph Hippo, are equally absurd characters, and sixth and last comes Bob Careless, "the most careless Fellow breathing," on whom the other members imposed the task of writing the first *Meddler,* "because," Bob tells us, "it was in opposition to my Temper, and in all I have said, you may see how carelessly I have displayed our several Talents." With all these extraordinary endowments, we are not surprised that the club, as Bob Careless puts it, will be able "to divert nobody into a better Opinion" of it; "for we have resolved not to meddle with Church or State Affairs, but to learn morality ourselves (which we want, God knows) satyrize our Friends and speak well of our Enemies!" After a paragraph more of this sort of wit, Bob Careless brings the first *Meddler* to a close, signing his own name "by order of the Club."

Will Generous next sends an account of the Club's last proceedings.24 In this account the characters are fairly well sustained. Jack-would-be-taller says he wonders that most people should pretend to know all the matter contained in a book upon reading the title. Especially, he believes, if the book be written by a poor man, they will call it a heap of

M *Meddler* No. 2, *South Carolina Gazette,* No. 82, August 23, 1735.

nonsense; and, in general, prefer light jests to refined morality.

" 'Tis true," answers Tom Snigger, "yet 'tis better to be merry than sad." For his part, he can tell the author of any piece by the humor in it, and the complexions of the characters!

But Dick Haughty immediately questions his friend Snigger's ability to discern much by complexions, for clothes alter complexions so materially that a man in rags has a more melancholy aspect than a fine, well-dressed beau. " You 're much in the right," agrees Ralph Hippo. So the conversation continues. On the whole, the second paper sustains fairly well the characterization of the first.

The third *Meddler* gives us a genuine glimpse into old " Charlestown." Apparently its promenade by the sea was fully as much enjoyed then as now, for Jack-would-be-taller writes an amusing animadversion on *The Vice of the Bay.*25 "The Vice that was debated on this Evening," Jack tells us, in his account of a meeting of the club " altho' 'tis plain to the whole Town, yet is so little minded, or else so customary that 'tis unobserved to be one, is the Vice of the Bay."

"Says Dick Haughty, I can't help taking Notice of the great Concourse of People of both Sexes that assembles on the Bay almost every Evening: And I think as we are Meddlers, that that is a Topic worthy of our Observation; for in my Opinion, it is a custom that will never resound to the Honour of Carolina, and tends to promote Vice and Irreligion in many Degrees. And tho' it may be objected

Meddler No. 3, *South Carolina Gazette,* No. 83, August 30, 1735.

that the Heat of the Climate will not permit them to walk in the Day, and it can't but conduce to their Health to walk and take the Air; yet I think there are many more fitting places to walk on than the Bay: For have we not many fine Greens near the Town much better accommodated for Air, than a place which continually has all the nauseous Smells of Tarr, Pitch, Brimstone and what not, and where every Jack Tarr has the Liberty to view and remark the most celebrated Beauties of Charles Town ? . . . " Your Observation is right, reply 'd Will Generous, for I have heard that in Great Britain the Ladies and Gentlemen choose the Parks and such like Places to walk and take the Air in, but I never heard of any Places making use of the Wharfs for such Purpose, except this, and in my humble Opinion I think the Greens a much better Place than the Bay."

The true secret of the objection to the promenade by the sea appears to be that" Cupid has shot more Darts on the Bay than in all Carolina," and in the development of this idea, the essay becomes a mere vulgar harangue against "Sea sparks." But the opening paragraphs, which we have quoted, show the beginnings of social satire with a clear attempt at local color, and it is almost a matter for regret that the letter from Diogenes Rusticus, in the following number of the *Gazette, TM* brings the Meddler Club papers to an abrupt and immediate close. The criticism of the disgusted Rusticus is fair enough; the absurdity of the *Meddlers* could hardly be exaggerated, though in their defence it must be said that in all probability they were intended as burlesque. Rusticus takes "Every Fool is Meddling"27

"No. 84, September 6, 1735. Proverbs XX, verse 3.

for the text of a vigorous denunciation which incidentally reveals the difficulties of the early colonial editor's situation. The opening sentences of Rusti- cus 's letter deserve quoting.

"To Mb. Lewis Timothy, Printeb nsr Charles-town.

Sir,

Observing for some time past, for want of something either foreign, or some more sprightly Genius among ourselves to fill the first part of your Papers, that you have been forced to compleat your Sheet with anything that comes to hand, I (who am your Subscriber and a Carolinian) thought I might as well for once see something from myself in your Paper, at a time when it has been lately fill'd with so nnedifying and impertinent stuff, from a Club rightly by themselves termed Meddlers. ... I am sorry that they think so much of their own parts, that they would make the World believe they were Carolinians, when their Performance is so void of Sense, and their Design (if I may so call it) but sprung from the spurious Issue of a boosy-bottle. We your Subscribers in this part had as lief you would relate the celebrated History of Jack the Giant Killer, or Tom Thumb's Exploits, which would bring to remembrance the Innocency of our childish Years, when such Trifles were relished."

Probably very few of the essays hitherto considered were written by Carolinians, though White- marsh and Timothy may have had a few Charleston friends. But when we turn to the drama in Charleston, as it is represented in the *Gazette,* we find beyond a doubt the prologues and epilogues of Carolinian wits. Charleston had its theatrical season as a matter of course, and plays were given in twotheaters, the Dock Street Theater and the Queen Street Theater, as well as occasionally in the Court Boom. The plays themselves were probably in every instance either English or adaptations from the French, but the prologues and epilogues written for London performances naturally did not altogether suit the conditions in the new world. We find, then, in the *Gazette* of February 8, 1734-35, what is probably the first recorded instance of a prologue written in the colonies, describing colonial conditions, for a colonial audience. The occasion was a presentation of Otway's *Orphan* on January 24, 1734-35, and the prologue dwells at length on the changes from the wilderness which Columbus found, to the "smiling plenty" of the new world in 1735. The material prosperity seemed great enough to warrant a still further advance.

Hence we presume to usher in those Arts

Which oft have warm'd the best and bravest Hearts.

A different prologue, for a performance of the *Orphan* on February 7, is also given in full in the same number of the *Gazette*. This second prologue is important for several reasons. It shows the apologetic attitude which lovers of drama, even, in Charleston, felt compelled to assume. Boston was farther from Charleston than it is now, but not so far that it had no influence upon the South. All these prologues insist on the moral value of "what Addison and Shakespear wrote," as well as of the *Miser*, and the *Orphan*, whose

Tender Scenes Have mov'd the fairest Nymphs and bravest Swains.

Two weeks later28 an epilogue to the *Orphan*, "spoken after the Entertainment at Charlestown" is reprinted in full in the *Gazette*. And this epilogue combines an apology for the drama, with a stinging allusion to the Salem witchcraft. New England had begun to feel the witch trials as a disgrace by 1735, so that this amusing Charleston epilogue by no means failed of its point. In addition the epilogue contains valuable information as to the plays most often presented in Charleston. We quote the more important passages.

Epilogue to the Orphan

From the old World in Miniature we shew

Her choicest Pleasures to regale the new

For your Delight and Use has Otway wrote,

And pow'rful Music tunes her warbling Throat.

Thence from their Graves pale Ghosts arising slow

Shall clear the injur'd, and the guilty show.

From nobler Themes shall loftier Scenes appear,

And Cato urge what Senators may hear;

Or Congreve 's Drama shake the laughing Dome,

With wit unmatch'd by Athens or by Rome.

The little Term that Heaven to Mortals spares

Is daily clouded with prolonging Cares;

Nor real Virtue blames the pleasing Strife,

To blend Amusement with the Shades of Life;

Wise, innocent, serene, she smiles at Base,

Nor hanging Witches, nor abjuring Plays.

"February 22, 1734-35.

From these lines we may safely infer that *Hamlet* and Addison's *Cato* were often acted in Charleston. The mention of "what Addison and Shakespear wrote" in the second prologue to the *Orphan* also shows how natural was the association of Shakesperian tragedy with *Cato*, and strengthens the supposition that the "pale Ghosts arising slow" to "clear the injur'd and the guilty show" indicate *Hamlet*. The next couplet in the epilogue,

From nobler Themes shall loftier Scenes appear,

And Cato urge what Senators may hear

expresses nothing more than a commonplace dramatic criticism of the day. Certainly on this side of the Atlantic *Cato* was hailed not only as "nobler" and "loftier" than Shakesperian tragedy, but as a moral work of epoch-making greatness.

Discussions of the ethical problems involved in the tragedy were especially popular. S. C. sends an epilogue to *Cato* to the *Gazette,29* – an epilogue which we can well believe "was wrote by a young man . . . about 17 years of Age, for his own amusement." He gravely decides that Cato's suicide "was brave, nay generous, in a Heathen's view," though "our better Light forbids the impious Crime." The epilogue begins jauntily enough, however:

Well, Sirs, what think ye now of Cato's fate?

Pray was his Exit pitiful, or great?

Caesar and he had quite a different Notion

Cato lov'd Rome, but Caesar lov'd Promotion.

M September 5, 1743.

On the whole, we cannot blame the editor, Timothy, for his note at the close of this epilogue: "In order to oblige S. C. I have inserted the above Lines, but desire, when that Gentleman shall send any more, he will please to correct them."

The fact that neither *Hamlet* nor *Coto* happens to be noted in the theatrical advertisements of the *Gazette* of this period is no proof whatever that they were not often presented in Charleston. The *Gazette* was published weekly, not daily, and managers of plays advertised in its columns only when it was especially convenient or profitable. For instance, only the last performance of *The London Merchant* is announced in the *Gazette.* In the issue of March 13, 1735-36, we read:

At the New Theatre in Queen Street

will be acted on Tuesday next

for the last time,

The London Merchant, or the

History of George Barnwell

with a Farce, called *The Devil*

to pay, or, the Wives Metamorphos'd.

Chance notices like this obviously do not afford complete information as to all the plays given. Farquhar's *Recruiting Officer* was certainly a favorite. The *Gazette* of January 31, 1735-36, announces that "on Thursday, the 12th of February will be open'd the New Theatre in Dock Street, in which will be perform'd The Comedy called The Recruiting Officer." The next year on May 21, 1737, we find a notice of its performance in the Queen Street theater. The same theater advertises in the*Gazette* of February 21, 1735-36, that there "will be acted on Monday next A Tragedy, called the Orphan. " Thus there are four notices of *The Orphan* within a year.

The lines in the second prologue to the *Orphan,*

No carking Miser of his Teeth afraid,

His shilling sinks to see the Miser play'd,

suggest the familiarity with Moliere which we know by the advertisements of books existed; and there would seem to be some probability that entertainments ultimately of French origin were popular in a colony where numbers of the inhabitants were of French parentage. The pantomime actors of the Commedia dell'Arte, however, who played the grotesque adventures of Harlequin and Scaramouch in the public court room, probably brought their show directly from London, since these characters had become common there.30

The notice of the pantomime entertainment in Charleston shows that it was given at the conclusion of an English opera, much as a farce like *The Devil to Pay* would be rendered after *The London Merchant;* and the entire advertisement is worth quoting. It occurs in the *Gazette* of February 15,1734-35.

"On Tuesday the 18th Inst. will be presented at the Court-room, the Opera of Flora, or Hob in the Well,31 with the Dance of the two Pierrots, and a new Pantomime Entertainment in Grotesque Characters, called The Adventures of Harlequin and Scaramouch, with the Burgo- Master trick'd. Tickets to be had at Mr. Shepheard's in Broad-Street at 40 *a.* each. To begin at 6 o'Clock precisely."

80 See Genest's *Some Account of the English Stage, from 1660 to 1830,* Vols. II and III, for frequent mention of Harlequin and Scaramouch as popular characters.

u Ibid., Vol. Ill, p. 351.

How indispensable a knowledge of the Italian farces was considered by French wits may be inferred from a quotation in the *Gazette* of July 16, 1750,32 describing a man "of Wit and Merit, . . . who has Boileau at his Fingers' End, who knows something of Moliere, and some Jests taken from the Italian Farces of Arlequin, and is acquainted with every pretty Story." The interest in French literature and French ideals could hardly be plainer. In another instance,33 we find satiric French verses on the heroism of Louis XV copied into the *Gazette,* along with a translation into English doggerel. Examples of this sort could be multiplied.

But the advertisements of books for sale "by the printer hereof" and other local booksellers would establish the French influence beyond a doubt, if we had no other references to do so. Moliere's plays are advertised over and over again, French books of travel are common, French religious manuals and even French critical works like Bossu's *Epic Poetry* are well known. In fact a bookseller's general summary of his literary merchandise was likely to take the form of "a curious collection of the most modern books in English and French."34 Fortunately for us, many of these "curious collections" are described in detail in the *Gazette,* so that insome instances we know the very edition that the bookseller was offering for sale. And, in general, the book advertisements in the South Carolina weekly afford important evidence of the love of literature in the colony.

From *Memoirs of Literature,* VoL III, p. 392.

"No. 703, October 5, 1747.

"See *The South Carolina Gazette,* No. 138, September 18, 1736.

They begin with the first issue of the paper, January 8, 1731-32, but contain nothing of literary value for several months, unless the seventh edition of Watts's version of the Psalms be included in that category. In the fifteenth number, however, on April 15,1732, one Edward Wigg advertises a fairly long list of books for sale, many of which are either literary or historical. There is even a mention of one or two scientific dictionaries; and a list of secular books for sale in 1732 is noteworthy in any case. Then, too, it must be remembered that Wigg was not attempting to give an inventory of his entire stock, but only of his new books, "lately imported from Great Britain," as he tells us in his advertisement. If his list fails to include Shakespere, Milton, Swift and Addison, it is probably because his public would assume that he had them. He was not publishing an account of his library to enhance his literary reputation, as was the *Courant,* ten years before.

We shall give Wigg's list with spelling and arrangement of titles unaltered.

Gay's Fables.
System of Magicks
Boyle's Voyages.9
Lindsey's *History of Scotland.*
"Probably Defoe's.
"A novel by Chetwood.
Millar's *History,* 2 Voll.
Bishop Aylmer's Life.
Peeling against Whiston.
Abelard's *Letters.*
Musical Miscellany, 6 voll.
Select Novels, 6 v.
Cambray's *Tales and Fables.*
Hales *Contemplations,* 3 v.
Halyburton's *Great Concern.*
Art of fallowing Land.
Reading's *Life of Christ.*
Ditto in 2 v.
Droits des Soverains 2 v.
Ramsey's *Poems and Songs.*
Pitcarn *Poemata.*
Needier's *Works.*
King Henry's Life.
Edwards's *Justification.*
Memoirs of Queen Anne.
Bradley's *Botanical Dictionary,* 2 v.
Treatise of the Art of Thinking.
Kitchen Gardner.
Stone's *Mathematical Directory.*
Bossu's *Epick Poetry,* 2 v.
Law concerning Masters and Servants.
Petit's *Diseases of the Bones.*
Deffeis *Geography.*
Paschon'd *Translation of the Abbots.*
Finder's *Spanish Grammer.*
With Variety of Plays and Pamplets.

A "variety of plays" or a "great variety of plays" is regularly added to every advertisement of books in Charleston, and "Select novels" also occurs frequently. On the whole, an examination of Wigg'sstrange assortment of theology, gardening, botany and literature shows that Charleston had a reading class of remarkably varied interests.

Before the close of 1732, Whitemarsh had added to his own stock of religious treatises a few operas and a tragedy, and on November 4 he advertised the whole incongruous collection for sale. His notice reads:

To be Sold by the Printer hereof,

Barclay's *Apology* /or *the Quakers.*

Watts's *Psalms.*

The Honour of the Gout.

Bowman's *Sermon.*

Beggar's Opera.

Village Opera.

Robinhood's Opera.

The fatal Extravagant, a Tragedy.

A short plain Help for Parents, and Heads of

Families, to feed their Babes with the sincere

Milk of God's Word.

The Nature of Riches.

A few months later37 he had added to these "a curious Collection of Books," the titles of which he gives as follows:

Tillotson's *Works,* in 3 Vol. fol.

Burchet 's *Naval History.*

Whitby on Isaiah.

Dr. Sam. Clarke's *Sermons,* 10 vol.

Dan. De Foe's *Works, 2* vol.

History of Tryals, 2 vol.

Ogilby's *History of America.*

Memoirs of Kerr of Kersland, 2 Vol.

" March 10, 1732-33.

Spectators.

Guardians.

Mist's Letters, 2 vol.88

Plays, etc.

He repeats this advertisement on March 24,1732-33, with the addition of Moliere's plays, and a few tin- important memoirs and sermons. Thenceforth Moliere's plays regularly appear in Whitemarsh's advertisement, which gradually extends to a long list of histories, memoirs, essays and Latin classics. /- The bookselling thus developing in the same way /that it had developed in Benjamin Franklin's Phila- jdelphia office was interrupted by Whitemarsh's death in the summer of 1733. When Louis Timothee took over the *Gazette* on February 2, 1733-34, he seems to have taken none of Whitemarsh's books. At least he does not advertise them, and, as a rule, the book notices of the Timothys show an interesting tendency toward colonial publications – especially Franklin's publications and reprints. Franklin was supplying the capital for the Charleston papers. Naturally he would send down books and pamphlets from his own press, on the chance of increasing their circulation. Never was a more indefatigable advertiser than Franklin. Thus we find *Poor Richard's Almanac* elaborately described every year in *The South Carolina Gazette.* The six numbers of

Franklin's *General Magazine,* also, had all reached Charleston by August, 1741, and are advertised for sale "by The Printer hereof" on

" There were two series of two volumes each. Defoe probably edited the earlier series of 1721-22, which may be the one referred to here.

August 15, 1741. In 1746, Elizabeth Timothy, the widow who carried on the business for several years, has an advertisement of books for sale at her house "next the Printing Office." This advertisement is repeated at intervals throughout the year, and includes the following books:

Testaments.

Confessions of Faith with Notes at large.

Pamela or Virtue Rewarded.

Spelling Books.

Cato on Old Age.

Familiar Instructor."9

Watts's *Divine Songs.*

"Watts's *Psalms and Hymns.*

Allen's *Alarm.*

Dr. Armstrong's *Poems on Health.*

Reflections on Courtship and Marriage.

Now by 1746 Franklin had published *Pamela, Cato on Old Age,* and *The Family Instructor.* It is altogether probable that the appearance of just these books on Mrs. Timothy's list indicates the cir- i culation of Franklin's Philadelphia reprints in [Charleston. Only one list of books from England for sale by the Timothys deserves quoting. That we find in an advertisement running through 1744.

Burnet's *History of his own Times,* 6 vol.

Milton's *Paradise Lost, with Addison's Notes.*

Addison's *Miscellaneous Works,* 2 vol.

Prior's *Poems.*

Lord Shaftesbury's *Characteristicks,* 2 vol.

And *Night Thoughts,* a Poem by the famous Dr.

Young.

"Probably a misprint for *The Family Instructor of* Defoe.

But other booksellers in Charleston were active in advertising, though here, as in Philadelphia, probably none of them kept a shop for the exclusive sale of books. In fact they seem to have sold whatever happened to be shipped over. For instance, it would be hard to put Peter Harry into any narrow classification. His advertisement runs through February, 1733-34, and the most characteristic items in it are as follows: "Lately Imported and Sold by Peter Harry in his Store at Mrs. Romsey's on the Bay, fine Bohea tea, . . . Head Flowers in Boxes, Laces and Edgings, *Psalm-books, Play-books,* the *Guardians* in 2 vol., Women's Short Cloaks, Men's Scarlet Great Coats ..." and so on through long descriptions of gorgeous apparel.

Likewise Crokatt and Seaman must have kept something like a department store. We read in the *Gazette* of September 18, 1736: "Just imported in the Billander King George, and to be sold by Crokatt and Seaman, . . . great variety of men's and boys' ready made cloaths, a curious collection of the most modern books in English and

French, most sorts of English and India silks, laces and edgings," besides millinery and grocer's supplies. Addison's *Evidences of Christianity* and "sundry other books" come over in the Charming Betty, and are for sale, as we read in the advertisement of September 5, 1741. The ship Samuel, from London, brings over " sundry goods, particularly a very choice collection of printed Books, Pictures, Maps and Pickles, to be Sold very reasonable by Robert Pringle.' '40 And it

" See *The South Carolina Gazette,* No. 511, January 9, 1744.

is not until October 24, 1748, that we find anything like an advertisement of a collection worthy the name. John Sinclair at length has "Several Hundred Volumes in Religion, Law, Physicks, Mathe- maticks, History, Poetry, Voyages, Travels, Plays, Novels, Romances and Musick, a Catalogue of which may be seen with the lowest Prices affixed thereto."

The advertisements for books lost or lent show that Carolinians read and valued good literature as keenly as did Philadelphians. The volumes of Milton, Addison, and *Cato's Letters* were all cherished possessions in Charleston households, and the loss of them was felt as a calamity. Plays of all sorts were undoubtedly more popular in South Carolina than in any other colony. The man who owned the *Spectator* and the *Tatler* always had a volume of plays on the same shelf, – Lee, Otway, Phillips, Steele, as the case might be. Not infrequently he would own the plays of all of them,41 so that the drama was much read, as well as acted. Moliere and Congreve were always popular.

Nothing could be more dramatic than the entrance of George Whitefield about 1740 into the life and thought of such a society as that of Charleston. The ; closing couplet of the epilogue to the *Orphan* might well stand as a fairly adequate indication of the spirit of the place:

Wise, innocent, serene, she smiles at Ease

Nor hanging Witches, nor abjuring Plays.

According to most modern standards this is the nat-

"See for example the advertisement in the *Gazette,* No. 203, December 15, 1737.

ural, sane attitude of cultivated intelligence. But although Whitefield took no part in witchcraft trials, his zealous preaching constantly dwelt on the total depravity of all purely natural living. Hence the storm of conflicting opinion when he preached in any pulpit that he could find in Charleston. Nominally he was of the Church of England, but nowhere did the Church offer him such vigorous resistance as in Charleston. St. Philip's firmly closed its doors against his uncanonical services and his "en- thusiastick fits." The Rector, Alexander Garden, Commissary or Bishop of South Carolina, was the chief means of bringing Whitefield to ecclesiastical trial. On the other hand, nowhere in the colonies did his new-found friends in other religious folds flock so enthusiastically to hear him or to defend him. Charleston was divided for several years into two sharply contrasted religious parties.

The literary influence of all this has hitherto escaped attention. What more natural than that leading exponents of each side should send their views to the weekly paper? What more natural than that these views should be colored by all the denunciatory literature they knew? So we have bitter controversial essays and satiric poems almost weekly through 1740, and less often from 1741 to 1745. Addison was completely forgotten during these years of intense feeling. The excited combatants were in no mood for polished urbanity, and they hurled the bitterest passages from the *Dunciad* and *Hudibras* at one another, with the change of a wordnow and then to make the meaning plain. Soon they were writing Hudibrastic couplets themselves.

A long paper from "Arminius" begins the holy war for the Church on January 26, 1740, and continues through three numbers of the *Gazette* before a friend of Whitefield replies in an essay ending with Pope's line "Dulness is sacred in a sound Divine." Who Arminius was, we do not know. He was certainly a member of St. Philip's parish, however, if not the Reverend Alexander Garden himself. The other numerous controversialists signed themselves C, Z, or T, or were entirely anonymous. At first they all preserved at least a semblance of fair play in the argument, which centred about total depravity and other doctrines of Whitefield. But before many weeks it became a mere contest in abuse and ridicule, – a mere question as to which side should hurl the worst insults from the *Dunciad* first. Once an adherent of Whitefield is alluded to as "this Yahoo."42 And Whitefield himself is openly compared to Ralpho.43 Often lines from *Hudibras* are directly quoted to point the comparison, or to make any other contemptuous . reference plainer.

One disputant opens his essay in the *Gazette* of August 8, 1740, with an elaborate appreciation of *Hudibras*. "The Characters in Hudibras," writes he, "will, I see, forever be new and fashionable in spite of Time and Ridicule; like old Gold, they be-

"In *The South Carolina Gazette,* No. 395. Postscript, September 19, 1741. "Ibid., No. 337, August 8, 1740, and No. 397, October 3, 1741.

come more valuable for being tried by Use and Experience, they have stood the Test of Nature, Time and Truth. . . . And how Prophetically is the

Learning and Religion of Mr. W d described in

the Person of Ralpho." He then quotes the famous lines on the New Light, by way of ridiculing White- field's claim to special inspiration. *r* Naturally the original poems are the most inter- / esting to us. They form an odd collection of adula- j tory couplets, on the one hand, and bitingly satirical ones on the other. Prior's verses to Sherlock are slightly changed to apply to Whitefield, and of course his enemies promptly insist that the lines are misapplied! A churchman, over the signature " C.," sends an original *Epilogue on the late Polemical Writings on Religion,* – an epilogue which proves to be no epilogue but rather a fresh prologue. It is written in excellent Hudibrastic couplets, making mock of Whitefield's religion, and insinuating that he was all too eager for contributions in support of his Orphan House in Savannah.

"His Zeal prefers our Penny down."

"Z" replies to "C" two weeks later45 with some original verses against the lax believers and preachers of the Church. These lines in spite of their absurdity represent an attempt at bold, vigorous satire that is well worthy of notice. "Z" introduces his verses by saying that "C's" poem of two weeks before was " a very Rhapsody of Inconsistencies, huddled together in a confus'd senceless Stile,"and reminds Mr. Timothy that "as this World is a Stage, and one Man in his Turn plays many Parts; and as Mr. T. made no doubt that . . . Mr. C's late elaborate Piece would be acceptable to most of your Readers, so I doubt not, but what is here offer'd, will be accepted by the wiser few that are left." Z's chance quotation from the speech of the melancholy

Jaques can hardly be taken as evidence of any close acquaintance with *As You Like it,* though such acquaintance would be interesting coupled with his theology. Of this theology we get a fair view in the poem, which follows immediately upon his brief introduction. There is something particularly cheerful in his treatment of a naturally depressing subject. We quote the most characteristic lines:

41 See No. 326 of *The South Carolina Gazette,* May 24, 1740. "Ibid., No. 328, June 7, 1740.

But I am afraid it will be worse
With him when he shall hear the Curse
Pronounc'd against the Unbelievers,
Then it will be Known who are Deceivers,
Those who preach Original Sin
And the lost State that we are in,
And do maintain that one and all,
Are void of Grace by Adam's Fall,
Or those that love to lol in Chaise,
And freely think that Heaven's Ways
Are wide enough that they in Sin,
May whip their Horse and so ride in!
But oh that such wou'd once be wise,
And learn Eternal Happiness to prize,
And escape the Terrors of the Burning Lake
For Christ our only Saviour's Sake.

Whitefield took large contributions from all the colonies for his orphanage at Savannah. Churchmen looked askance at this project, hinting broadly that it took a great deal of money to support a few stray orphans in a wilderness. Even Benjamin Franklin, a warm friend of Whitefield, thought the orphanage should have been more centrally located.48 Whitefield's orphans, and, indeed, the people of Savannah in general, were standing jokes in *The South Carolina Gazette.* And they were often the subject of satiric verse. For instance, in the *Gazette* of November 12, 1744, we find one of these little poems on Whitefield's "Orphan-House,"

Whose tuneful Orphans suit the gilded Scheme
Seated at Georgia in a silken Dream.

From all that we have been able to learn of this excellent orphanage, which still exists at Bethesda, just outside of Savannah, its orphans would never at any time feel themselves to be seated in a silken dream.

The profound impression that Whitefield made in Charleston could be inferred from the marked change in the book advertisements of the *Gazette* after 1740. Instead of comedies and tragedies we find "Mr. Garden's Sermons and Letters, Dr. Stebbing's Sermon against religious Delusion, . . . Mr. Whitefield's Sermons, Letters, and Journals, Mr. Smith's Sermons, Mr. Wesley's Sermon on Free- Grace, . . . Wesley's Hymns,"47 and again "To be sold by the Printer hereof, Two *Letters* from the

Rev. Mr. W d to one of his Friends in London,

One of which vindicating his having asserted, thatArchbishop Tillotson knew no more of Christianity than Mahomet, the other shewing the Fundamental Error of the

Book entituled *The Whole Duty of Man,* ... A Sermon preach'd by the Rev. Mr. W
d entituled *The heinous Sin of profane Cursing and Swearing."8* Dancing and balls
in the face of calamity were also severely condemned under Whitefield's influence.
Laicus writes an essay on the evils of this frivolity, prefaced by the quotation from
Virgil, "Monstrum Horrendum! "49 To note all the quotations from Pope, Swift, and
Gay, individually, or the numerous extracts from *Cato's Letters* and from English
magazines, would extend the present chapter unduly. The Charleston paper was
somewhat isolated, and kept its purely ! literary ideals longer than the Northern
weeklies, some of which had become newspapers by 1740. Even in 1750 *The South
Carolina Gazette* was preserving its early tradition, and at the close of the year, on
December 31, we find a number of Samuel Johnson's *Rambler50* taken entire into the
Gazette. Correspondents of the Charleston weekly, throughout this early period, refer
in the most familiar way to the characters of the *Tale of a Tub* and *Gulliver's Travels.*
"Your Piece of Wit, . . . makes me imagine you are either a Houyhnhnm yourself,
(as described by Capt. Gulliver) or understand their language," remarks a writer in a
facetious dispute about an old racehorse,51 while his adversary rejoins:

l. e., in Philadelphia,

" See *The South Carolina Gazette,* No. 407, December 12, 1741.

Ibid., No. 341, September 6, 1740.

" Ibid., No. 308, January 19, 1740.

The Bambler of October 2, 1750, on *Frugality.*

" See *Tim South Carolina Gazette,* No. 530, May 21, 1744.

One Fool endeavours to describe another

Yahoo proves Houyhnhnm is his Brother.52

"Twickenham's bard" is the most familiar English author of all, not excepting even
Addison. Hardly a number of the *Gazette* is without a quotation or an allusion, and
poems definitely imitative abound. In fact, Pope is invoked as one invokes a muse,
especially when a noteworthy character or event is to be celebrated. Philanthropos
sends a *Poem to the Reverend and Learned Doct. Neal, on his excellent Sermon
preached at Charleston on Sunday the 26th of May, 1734.* In glowing verses53 he
exclaims:

Had I a Genius, and poetick fire,

Equal to that which did bright Pope inspire

My chearful Muse, nay rather, all the Nine

Should in one loud Chorus of Applauses joyn,

To sing thy praise, 0 eloquent Divine!

When Oglethorpe returned from Georgia, a poem celebrating his exploit appeared
in the *Gazette,* in which Pope is thus invoked:

Let Twickenham's Bard in his immortal Lays

Give thee the humble Tribute of our Praise.

No brighter Scene his Homer could display

Than that in thy Adventures we survey.5

On June 17, 1745, just after Pope's death, we find in the Charleston paper, "Verses
sent by Philagathus, written extempore by a Native of this Place on the Death of the

great and celebrated Alexander Pope, Esq." These verses though stilted and halting reveal an extravagant admiration for the dead poet.

" See *The South Carolina Gazette,* No. 531, May 28, 1744.

"Ibid., No. 19, June 8, 1734.

Ibid., No. 47, December 21, 1734.

To examine in detail the frequent extracts from English magazines and periodicals, would mean, in large part, a repetition of the facts noted in other chapters. *The Universal Spectator* with its combination of serious essay and dialogue appears very often in *The South Carolina Gazette. Cato's Letters* were inculcating ideals of representative government that would eventually bind the colonies together. But if our chief emphasis has been laid on the original essays and poems of the *Gazette,* it is because they, more than all mere extracts, prove that this little paper, unmentioned in many bibliographies of colonial publications, was attempting literature.

9

SECTION 9

BIBLIOGRAPHY

The following publications have been found useful for
general reference.

Chables Feancis: *Milton's Impress on the Provincial Literature of New England.* In *Proceedings
of the Massachusetts Historical . Society,* Vol. XLII,
- pp. 154-170. Boston, 1909.

Aveb, M. F.: *Check-list of Boston Newspapers, 1704-1780,
with bibliographical notes by Albert Matthews.* In
Publications of the Colonial Society of Massachusetts,
Vol. IX. Boston, 1907.

Buckingham, Joseph T.; . *Personal Memoirs and Recol-
lections of editorial Life.* 2 vols. Boston, 1852.

r Buckingham, Joseph T.: *Specimens of Newspaper Literature.* Boston, 1850.

Catalogue of Ante-Revolutionary Publications: In *Transactions and Collections of the American Antiquarian
Society,* Vol. VI, pp. 309-666. Albany, 1874.

Dalcho, Fredebick: *An Historical Account of the Protestant Episcopal Church in South Carolina.* , Charleston, 1820.

Fobd, Paul Leicesteb: *Franklin Bibliography.* Brooklyn, 1889.

Franklin, Benjamin: *Writings.* Ed. Albert Henry Smyth. 10 vols. New York, 1907.

/ Goddard, Delano : *The Press and Literature of the Promn-*
/ *i cial Period.* Article in *Memorial History of Boston,*
/ Vol. II, Chap. XV, pp. 387-436. Ed. Justin Winsor,
A/ Boston, 1881.

Green, S. A.: *Early History of Printing-in New England.*
In *Proceedings' of the Massachusetts Historical Society.*
Second Series, Vol. XI, pp. 240-254. Boston, 1897.

/green, S. A.: *Ten Foe-Simile Reproductions relating to*
I r New England. Boston, 1902.

/green, S. A.: *Ten Foe-Simile Reproductions, relating to*
Old Boston and. Neighborhood. Boston, 1901.

Gbeen, S. A.: *Ten Fac-Simile Reproductions, relating to*
Various Subjects. " Boston, 1903.

I. hildebubn, Charles R.: *Issues of the Pennsylvania Press,*
1685 to 1784. Philadelphia, 1885.

Hudson, Frederic : *Journalism in the United States from*
1690-1872. New York, 1873.

King, William L.: *The Newspaper Press of Charleston,*
South Carolina. Charleston, 1872.

Mabtin, C. M. and B. B.: *The New York Press and its*
Makers in the eighteenth Century. In *Historic New*
York, Vol. II, pp. 119-162. New York, 1899.

.. matthews, Albebt: *Bibliographical Notes* to a *Check-list*
of Boston Newspapers, 1704-1780. In *Publications of*
the Colonial Society of Massachusetts, Vol. IX. Boston,. 1907.

Nelson, William : History of American Newspapers. In
New Jersey Archives, Vols. XI, XII, and XIX.
Paterson, 1894. This valuable history is incomplete,
owing to loss of manuscripts by fire. The treatment
of the press of various states is alphabetical, and, in the
present condition of the work, extends only from Alabama to New Hampshire, inclusive. Thus the colonial
newspapers of New York, Virginia and South Carolina
have not as yet been treated by Mr. Nelson.

Ruthebfubd, Livingston: *John Peter Zenger, His Press,*
His Trial, and A Bibliography of Zenger Imprints.
New York, 1904.

Smyth, Albebt Henry : *Philadelphia Magazines and their Contributors, 1741-1850.* Philadelphia, 1892.

Thomas, Isaiah : *The History of Printing in America.* In *Transactions and Collections of the American Antiquarian Society,* Vols. V and VI. Albany, 1874.

Tuttle, Julius Hebbert: *The Libraries of the Mathers.* In *Proceedings of the American Antiquarian Society,* New Series, Vol. XX, pp. 269-356, April, 1910. Worcester, 1911.

Two Centuries of the First Baptist Church of South Carolina. Ed. H. A. Tupper. Baltimore, 1889.

Tyler, Lyon Gabdineb: *Williamsburg, the old Colonial Capital.* Richmond, 1907.

Winsor, Justin : *Libraries in Boston.* Article in *Memorial History of Boston,* Vol. IV, Chap. II, Part II, pp. 279-294. Ed. Justin Winsor, Boston, 1881.

NEWSPAPERS IN THE AMERICAN COLONIES, 1704-1750

The following list is not a complete bibliography. Only those newspapers mentioned in the text, or of special importance from the literary point of view, will be noted. The authoritative bibliography of all colonial newspapers will be published by the American Antiquarian Society. Meanwhile the following list may be useful in indicating where files of the original papers may conveniently be found. Mr. Nelson's bibliography, in his *History of American Newspapers* (in *New Jersey Archives,* Vols. XI, XII, and XIX) has not as yet included the rare files of Southern papers, nor the New York papers which will be noted below.

Chbonological List

Publick Occurrences, both Foreign and Domestick: Small quarto sheet, one page blank. Suppressed by the government of Massachusetts, for containing "Reflexions of a very high nature." Ed. Benjamin Harris, Boston, 1690. The only extant copy is in the State Paper Office, in London. But reprints may be found in Hudson's *History of Journalism in the United States,* p. 44, in *The New England Historical and Genealogical Register,* April, 1876, and in *The National Intelligencer,* Washington, 1857. A Fac-Simile is given in S. A. Green's *Ten Fac-simile Reproductions relating to old Boston and Neighborhood.* This pamphlet can hardly be considered a newspaper.

The Boston News-Letter: Established April 24, 1704. Files in the possession of the American Antiquarian Society, the New York Historical Society, and the Boston Public Library. Partial file in the possession of the Massachusetts Historical Society.

The Boston Gazette: Established December 21, 1719. Files in the possession of the American Antiquarian Society, the Massachusetts Historical Society, and the Wisconsin Historical Society.

The American Weekly Mercury: Established December 22, 1719. Files in the possession of the Pennsylvania Historical Society, the Ridgeway Library of Philadelphia, the Library Company of Philadelphia. The New York Public Library has a fairly complete file from 1733 to 1738, and a scattering file from 1738 to 1741. The Colonial Society of Pennsylvania has issued reprints of the *Mercury* from 1719 through 1723. 4 vols. Philadelphia, 1898-1907.

The New England Courant: Established August 7, 1721. The only extant file is in the possession of the Massachusetts Historical Society.

The New York Gazette: Established October 16, 1725. Incomplete files from 1725 to 1733 are in the possession of the New York Public Library, the New York Historical Society, and the New York Society Library. From 1733 to 1744, the New York Public Library has a fairly complete file, the British Museum and the Pennsylvania Historical Society have the best files for certain years, and the New York Historical Society has scattering files. For full details, see the excellent bibliography prepared by Mr. Wilberforce Eames of the New York Public Library, and prefixed to the volumes of *The New York Gazette* in the New York Public Library.

,-' *The New England Weekly Journal:* Established March 20, 1727. Files in the possession of the Massachusetts Historical Society, and the Boston Athenaeum. The Boston Public Library and the New York Historical Society have files for 1738. The American Antiquarian Society has a file for 1739 and 1740.

The Maryland Gazette: Established 1727. The first
extant number is dated December 10, 1728.

Since the files of this paper are scattered and
imperfect, and since full information as to where they may be found, has never
been published, a brief summary of the facts may be useful. The Maryland Historical
Society has a file from December 10, 1728, to July 22, 1729, inclusive. The New
York Public Library has two numbers of 1729, ten numbers of 1730, five numbers
of 1733, and nine numbers of 1734. Of the new series, begun April 26, 1745, the
Maryland Historical Society has an incomplete file from 1745 to 1760. The Library
of Congress has one number of 1746, a few scattering numbers of 1752, and a file,
nearly complete from 1753 to 1755. The Massachusetts Historical Society has a few
scattering numbers, ten in all, from 1748 to 1770.

The Universal Instructor in all Arts and Sciences, and Pennsylvania Gazette:
Established December 24, 1728. Files in the possession of the Pennsylvania Historical
Society, and the Library Company of Philadelphia.

The Pennsylvania Gazette: Established October 2, 1729. Complete files in the possession of the Pennsylvania Historical Society, and the Library Company of Philadelphia. A file, nearly complete from 1735 to 1795, is in the New York Public Library,
which also has all the numbers of 1729 after October 2, the date of Franklin's first
issue.

The Weekly Rehearsal: Established September 27, 1731. Files in the possession
of the AmericanAntiquarian Society and the Massachusetts Historical Society. This
newspaper was published in Boston, by Jeremiah Gridley, afterwards attorney general
of the province of Massachusetts Bay. For the first six months, somewhat ponderous
original essays appeared weekly in its pages. But before a year had passed, the essays
were discontinued, and the paper became a news-sheet only.

The South Carolina Gazette: Established January 8, 1732. Complete file, from
1732 to 1801, in the possession of the Charleston Library Society. Two numbers of
1736 are in the New York Public Library.

The New York Weekly Journal: Established November 5, 1733. Best file in the
possession of the New York Public Library. The New York Historical Society and the
Pennsylvania Historical Society have scattering files.

The Virginia Gazette: Established August 6, 1736. First extant number is dated
September 10, 1736. File from 1736 to 1740 in the possession of the Virginia
Historical Society. No extant files from 1740 to 1750. From 1750 to 1752 the New
York Public Library has a file. After this date, scattering numbers are to be found in
various libraries of Virginia.

Lightning Source UK Ltd.
Milton Keynes UK
20 July 2010

157259UK00001B/434/P